Second Language Teaching and Learning in the Net Generation

NFLRC Monographs is a refereed series sponsored by the National Foreign Language Resource Center at the University of Hawai'i under the supervision of the series editor, Richard Schmidt. NFLRC Monographs present the findings of recent work in applied linguistics that is of relevance to language teaching and learning, with a focus on the less commonly-taught languages of Asia and the Pacific.

Case studies in foreign language placement: Practices and possibilities
Thom Hudson & Martyn Clark (Editors), 2008
ISBN 0–9800459–0–8

Chinese as a heritage language: Fostering rooted world citizenry
Agnes Weiyun He & Yun Xiao (Editors), 2008
ISBN 978–0–8248–3286–5

Perspectives on teaching connected speech to second language speakers
James Dean Brown & Kimi Kondo-Brown (Editors), 2006
ISBN(10) 0–8248–3136–5, ISBN(13) 978–0–8248–3136–3

ordering information at nflrc.hawaii.edu

Second Language Teaching and Learning in the Net Generation

edited by

Raquel Oxford
Jeffrey Oxford

National Foreign Language Resource Center
University of Hawai'i at Mānoa

Manufactured in the United States of America.

The contents of this publication were developed in part under a grant from the U.S. Department of Education (CFDA 84.229, P229A060002). However, the contents do not necessarily represent the policy of the Department of Education, and one should not assume endorsement by the Federal Government.

ISBN: 978–0–9800459–2–5

Library of Congress Control Number: 2009927885

The paper used in this publication meets the minimum requirements of the American National Standard for Information Sciences–Permanence of Paper for Printed Library Materials.
ANSI Z39.48–1984

book design by Deborah Masterson

distributed by

National Foreign Language Resource Center
University of Hawai'i
1859 East-West Road #106
Honolulu HI 96822–2322
nflrc.hawaii.edu

About the National Foreign Language Resource Center

THE NATIONAL FOREIGN LANGUAGE RESOURCE CENTER, located in the College of Languages, Linguistics, & Literature at the University of Hawai'i at Mānoa, has conducted research, developed materials, and trained language professionals since 1990 under a series of grants from the U.S. Department of Education (Language Resource Centers Program). A national advisory board sets the general direction of the resource center. With the goal of improving foreign language instruction in the United States, the center publishes research reports and teaching materials that focus primarily on the languages of Asia and the Pacific. The center also sponsors summer intensive teacher training institutes and other professional development opportunities. For additional information about center programs, contact us.

Richard Schmidt, Director
National Foreign Language Resource Center
University of Hawai'i at Mānoa
1859 East-West Road #106
Honolulu, HI 96822–2322

email: nflrc@hawaii.edu
website: nflrc.hawaii.edu

NFLRC Advisory Board

Contents

Abbreviations used in this book

ACMC	Asynchronous Computer-Mediated Communication
CAI	Computer-Assisted Instruction
CALL	Computer-Assisted Language Learning
CLP	Collaborative Language Program
CMC	Computer-mediated Communication
CVC	Classroom-based VideoConferencing
D2L	Desire2Learn
EFL	English as a Foreign Language
ESL	English as a Second Language
FOMT	Free Online Machine Translation
IM	Instant Messaging
L2	Second Language
MOO	Multiuser Object-Oriented
MUD	MUltiuser Dimension
MUVE	MUltiuser Virtual Environment
NS	Native Speaker
OAB	Oral Assessment Builder
OECD	Organisation for Economic Co-operation and Development
RSS	Really Simple Syndication
S1	Student 1
S2	Student 2
SCMC	Synchronous Computer-Mediated Communication
SFLL	Standards for Foreign Language Learning
SLA	Second-Language Acquisition
TELL	Technology-Enhanced Language Learning
TLC	Target-Language Culture
UW	University of Wisconsin
ZPD	Zone of Proximal Development

Introduction

Raquel Oxford
Jeffrey Oxford
University of Wisconsin-Milwaukee

Never before has the state of American education been under such intense scrutiny and the demands for public accountability so vociferous. Although calls for reform are often directed at implementing programs to improve student achievement or models for reducing the dropout rate, a growing trend is to focus on the disconnect between schools and the students they serve. In spite of instruction being more learner-centered, teachers may not take into account students' linguistic and cultural differences or their learning style preferences, which are influenced by technology use and exposure. Technology and its applications in sociocultural, economic, and political settings made a tremendous impact on the later part of the 20th century and play an essential role in American society today. Many groups, from policy makers to pundits, are beginning to realize fully the multiple implications of the demographic and technological shift that has occurred over the last two decades and how the learning paradigm has evolved into something totally different from that of the educators' generation.

One component of efforts to increase teacher efficacy is to help teachers become more technology literate and to use technology to improve teaching and learning. Yet, we must also know our students. The changing student demographic and learning paradigm and the impact of technology on the study of second languages call for an examination of foreign-language instruction and how it has responded to what Don Tapscott, in his book *Growing Up Digital* (1998), first called the Net Generation. The Net Generation, those born from 1977 to 1997, has grown up immersed in a digital- and Internet-driven world. These children of the Baby Boomers, also referred to as Generation Y or the Millennials, are what Prensky (2001) described as digital natives, in a designation that connects to our world of language learning: "Our students today are all 'native speakers' of the digital language of computers, video games and the Internet" (p. 1). It is readily apparent that to reach and teach these individuals, traditional pedagogical techniques need to be revisited and new techniques developed and/or perfected using media that they understand. Yet, instruction

Oxford, R. & Oxford, J. (2009). Introduction. In R. Oxford & J. Oxford, (Eds.), *Second language teaching and learning in the Net Generation* (pp. 1–8). Honolulu: University of Hawai'i, National Foreign Language Resource Center.

is the responsibility of digital immigrants (i.e., those who have had to "become fluent" in later life with technology), a fact that leads many researchers increasingly to ask questions about how technology is best integrated into educational settings and how most effectively to match technological capacities with students' learning needs. Caution must be exercised to avoid overestimating the actual skills of digital natives (Bennett, Maton, & Kervin, 2008). Researchers and practitioners alike agree that successful integration of technology into the classroom in a pedagogically sound manner involves more than simply introducing a software program or other innovation to the students in a classroom. Technology integration must be thoughtfully planned out based on curricular goals and instructional models—implying the use of new teaching strategies that actively engage students and rely on collaboration among teachers. In fact, Bennett et al. (2008) specifically called for

> a considered and disinterested examination of the assumptions underpinning claims about digital natives such that researchable issues can be identified and dispassionately investigated... It is [a] call for considered and rigorous investigation that includes the perspectives of young people and their teachers, and genuinely seeks to understand the situation before proclaiming the need for widespread change. (p. 784)

Even before the publication of the essay by Bennet et al. (2008), the editors of the current volume, *Second Language Teaching and Learning in the Net Generation*, had come to question the "common wisdom" concerning the Net Generation and issued a call for papers to specialists, primarily university faculty, focusing on how the integration of technology within the curriculum affects the teaching and learning of second languages. The manuscripts received included data-based research studies, policy essays, revised/new methodologies, curriculum studies, and qualitative analyses of technological implementations within the second-language classroom and addressed issues such as the use of the Internet, podcasting, video streaming, e-mail, instant messaging (IM) language, real-time chat rooms, blogs, wikis, e-tutoring, Second Life, online and hybrid courses, and electronic portfolios and how these are used in and/or affect world-language teaching and learning. From the essays received, the editors selected the ones deemed most pertinent, informative, and practical for inclusion in the volume. Thus, the collection is a combination of research and practical explanations of how technology is both being used and can be used to improve second-language acquisition (SLA).

Second-Language Teaching and Learning in the Net Generation is not a textbook in and of itself, although we imagine that it could be useful as a volume within teacher preparation or methodology courses and professional development opportunities (e.g., school district or inservice training, relicensure). It provides an overview of technologies and perspectives for new teachers, in particular, although it is also appropriate for a range of audiences including language lab directors, experienced teachers new to technology, experienced (or inexperienced) teachers wanting to learn how to apply additional or new technologies in their second-language classroom, teaching assistants, or others reflecting on what is being done with technology in the second-language classroom and how to get teachers to think about how to use it.

One of the points that stands out in all the essays is the importance of implementing available technology in a pedagogically sound fashion. Today's youths (i.e., the Net Generation) have grown up with technology all around them; electronic games/toys have been designed for the youngest children, and this generation is not attracted to technological gadgets and programs simply because of hype. At the same time, teachers cannot assume that students' familiarity with technology in general will, *de facto*, make all technology appropriate for a pedagogical setting. As Fenn (1995) has noted, as part of the hype cycle, the newest and latest technology is generally of the highest popular appeal, but the passage of time is required for that emerging technology to achieve and settle into a "plateau of productivity," that is, pedagogical functionality. This volume, then, examines various technologies and offers concrete advice on how they can be successfully implemented in the second-language curriculum.

Chapter 1, "(Re)situating the Role(s) of New Technologies in World-Language Teaching and Learning," by Van Compernolle and Williams, offers an overview of the evolution of computer-assisted language learning (CALL) from computer-as-tutor (right/wrong answers) through the computer-as-pupil (students interact with computers) stage, to finally, the computer-as-tool or computer-mediated communication (CMC) stage, when students interact with other humans and authentic realia via the computer. A review of the extant research reveals three major trends within the approach to CALL research that treats technology as a tool for communication. First, various forms of online social networking, publishing, and communication can help foster intercultural understanding, providing learners with virtually limitless possibilities for publishing and communicating online. Second, CMC provides opportunities for language learners to engage in regular, prolonged communication with native speakers of the target language, during which their sociolinguistic and sociopragmatic competence can develop. Third, computer-based focus-on-form tasks can help learners notice and analyze their own discourse, which can lead to improvements in overall formal linguistic accuracy.

Van Campernolle and Williams believe that the New London Group's (1996) framework of a pedagogy of multiliteracies offers the most flexibility for the integration of new technologies into world-language curricula. This theory of pedagogy emphasizes the symbiotic relationship between *teaching*, *learning*, and *doing* in particular sociocultural contexts, recognizing learning not as an individual psychological process but as a social phenomenon. Thus, for language learners and teachers, the task becomes one of reshaping the classroom as a place that fosters the co-construction of knowledge, understanding, and practice with technology serving as a fully integrated tool used to achieve these pedagogical objectives. In other words, teachers cannot simply use technology for technology's sake; they must take advantage of specific age- and content-appropriate tools to accomplish specific pedagogical objectives.

Chapter 2, "Internet and Language Teaching/Learning: Reflections on Online Emerging Technologies and Their Impact on Foreign-Language Instruction," by Niño, explores some of the most prominent online emerging technologies for language teaching/learning, paying particular attention to these technologies' functionalities, their potential use in language classes, and the advantages and disadvantages of using them in foreign-language instruction. Some of the technologies examined include Google, wikis and blogs, Skype and videoconferencing, YouTube, podcasting, automatic speech recognition and speech processing/synthesizing software, online dictionaries and free online machine translation, and social networking sites. Obviously, few, if any, of these technologies were created with an educational aim in mind, but given that students are becoming very familiar and literate in the use of the Internet and its multiple online tools, educators must face the challenge of adapting these emerging technologies for educational purposes to increase perceived content relevancy. At the same time, students can be taught how to use the vast collection of resources that the Internet provides in a constructive way via problem-based collaborative tasks in which they can develop their critical thinking by justifying the selection of certain resources for a particular purpose. In this manner, the learner acquires greater control of the learning process. For language tutors, the challenge remains to find new ways in which technology can be used to enhance the foreign-language learning experience.

Chapter 3, "'Digital Natives' and Their Self-Rated Electronic Literary Skills: Empirical Findings From a Survey Study in German Secondary Schools," by Fuchs, reports on a survey study at five German secondary schools in the high-tech industrial area of Baden-Württemberg that explored students' self-rated electronic literacy skills and its implications for the foreign-language classroom. Fuchs' findings support previous studies in that they show a gap between theory and praxis—the importance of students' media competence and electronic literacy skills—and the lack of actual training and computer use that students experience in schools. In fact, the integration of technology into teaching does not appear to be systemic but implemented by individual teachers only; whether the results can be generalized remains to be seen in other studies, but anecdotal evidence indicates that such is the case in many schools. In Fuchs' study, 50% of the English as a foreign language (EFL) teachers used technology, but none of the EFL teachers used a form of CMC. This indicates that technology—when used—has been used without making connections to concepts such as writing for an authentic audience, meaningful communication, or intercultural learning. In light of the growing body of research on CMC and telecollaboration and the potential benefits for language study and intercultural learning, this demonstrates an urgent need to connect theory and practice in teacher-education programs. More specifically, teacher educators should support online or blended learning formats and model the implementation of technology in their seminar formats. Hence, teachers need to be encouraged, and perhaps trained, to integrate blogs, wikis, IM/chats, CMC, and Internet-based collaboration to foster authentic language fluency.

Chapter 4, "Hybridizing the Curriculum: Needs, Benefits, Challenges, and Attitudes," by Goertler, reviews research regarding hybrid foreign-language instruction and discusses the results from a survey-based study on students' readiness for hybrid instruction. The author quotes Kraemer's 2008 study in which 26% of the surveyed university-level language programs offered hybrid (21%) or online courses (5%), with the majority of those courses in German or Spanish and a generally negative attitude toward hybrid instruction on the part of the students. Of those students who answered the question, 422 answered that they would like to take a language course in a hybrid format, 784 would consider it, and 850 would not take a hybrid foreign-language course. Although the differences were small, the overall perception of hybrid instruction seemed negative, which would typically not be expected of students classified as digital natives based on their computer literacy and age. An implication of the research is, then, that simply because someone is a digital native, that person does not necessarily want to learn a subject matter in a digital format. The qualitative comments, in fact, clarify that there are still many misconceptions about technology use in world-language teaching. More education on hybrid instruction has to be provided for instructors and students to buy in. Furthermore, for successful implementation and improvement of attitudes, more training has to be offered to both students and teachers, and better access has to be provided to the technology.

Chapter 5, "Reaching Students: A Hybrid Approach to Language Learning," by Rosen, discusses the University of Wisconsin's development of a hybrid model for teaching languages to students on numerous university campuses via classroom-based videoconferencing (CVC). This model combines a course management system with online voice tools, wiki projects, Wimba voice chat, discussion boards, and learncasts to offer students access to languages currently deemed critical to national and state interests. Now, 10 years since the program's inception, it is reaching over 300 students in 15

Arabic, Chinese, Japanese, and Russian courses each semester, and data gathered through summative assessments indicate that the students are doing as well in acquiring productive and receptive skills as students learning in nondistance settings with equivalent contact hours. When CVC students at the origination site (i.e., with a teacher physically present) were compared to those at distance sites (i.e., no teacher physically present in the room), the students at a distance do as well as or better than those at the origination site.

Chapter 6, "The Influence of Technology on Second-Language Writing," by Oxford, reports on a study involving two intermediate-level university Spanish classes and the effects of technology-enhanced grammar and vocabulary practice on students' essay-writing abilities. Both groups used the same text, workbook, and composition exercises and had the same instructor, but the "experimental" class was composed of a minimum of 30 minutes in a lab setting per week with a grammar-practice program, *Spanish Partner.* The treatment of grammar practice with *Spanish Partner* showed a small to moderate effect in several areas of measurement although without statistically significant differences overall between the experimental and control groups. In spite of this, the composition subscale score gains for grammar/language use and vocabulary for those who had experienced the computer grammar and vocabulary practice were higher than those of the control group. Therefore, although there was no statistically significant difference overall, the data do suggest that integrating specific technology tools and activities may be important for teachers and curriculum planners to better nurture specific abilities in SLA; using the writing program *Atajo*, for example, facilitated the writing experience by allowing time for reflection, rereading, and cut-and-paste editing techniques. In light of the study's findings of a generally positive student reaction to the use of technology in the foreign-language classroom, this could be an important pedagogical—as well as public relations—move. Finally, although this study did not focus exclusively on mechanics, it is clear that the Net Generation students did not effectively use the available technology tools, such as spell checkers, and that in spite of repeated practice, some students will continue to "misuse" technology. The implication is, then, that in some cases, students require more guidance to use technology than might be expected. Providing more explicit directions and monitoring of students is critical if they are to reap the benefits of the activity.

Chapter 7, "Podcasting and the Intermediate-Level Spanish Classroom," by Bird-Soto and Rengel, briefly reviews the technology of podcasts in general and their place in academia before expanding on the authors' experiences with implementing podcasts in their Spanish classrooms. Their initial project, *Personalidades de la Cultura Hispánica*, involved authentic interviews and conversations with authors, artists, and other outstanding "personalities" and eventually resulted in a collection of 25 podcasts. Bird-Soto and Rengel argue that students responded positively to the podcasts in both the intermediate- and advanced-level Spanish courses and that the students readily embraced the technology as an enjoyable pedagogical tool. In fact, later projects that the students produced in other classes included topics ranging from music (merengue, salsa, bachata, Tex-Mex), to artists (Pablo Picasso, Jennifer López) and politics (human rights violations during Argentina's *Guerra Sucia* and Chile's Augusto Pinochet regime), composed of 7- to 10-minute podcasts created outside of the classroom. These podcasts allowed students to research, write, and produce oral presentations on topics that interested them, thereby targeting both oral and listening skills in an environment in which the students readily participated.

Ducate and Lomicka report that 87% of the students responded that they enjoyed podcasting and that many responded that they would enjoy doing a similar project in a future language class in Chapter 8, "Podcasting in the Language Classroom: Inherently

Mobile or Not?" This essay looks at uses of podcasting in language learning and its potential for promoting mobile language learning both in and out of the classroom. Ducate and Lomicka's first two studies involved students in 4th- and 5th-semester French and German classes who produced their own podcasts three to four times during the semester and then listened to and commented on their classmates' podcasts. In a third study, 5th-semester French students listened weekly to a French news podcast, and in a fourth study, students from a foreign-language teaching-methods class selected a podcast in the target language to listen to and report on weekly. The results from these four podcasting projects illustrate that according to student feedback, podcasting can be an effective way to increase competence in foreign-language speaking, listening, and pronunciation. One surprising finding is that several of the students involved in these projects chose not to download the podcasts because they did not know how, suggesting again that foreign-language teachers cannot assume that digital-native students are totally technologically "literate."

Chapter 9, "The Coalescence of Spanish Language and Culture Through Blogs and Films," by Lazo-Wilson and Lozano Espejo, highlights curricular and instructional innovations in a small Spanish-language program with a large population of first-generation university students. The two instructors for this course used traditional face-to-face meetings with students to highlight aspects of popular everyday culture in Spanish-speaking countries by using contemporary films viewed in class to heighten the language and culture learning experience for students. The students also used the classroom blog to underscore topics not covered in class, to express themselves in light of the topics covered, and to exercise their linguistic forms in the more informal setting of the blog. Interaction with Spanish speakers from multiple countries aided in the development of intercultural competence and motivated the students to write more and to self-correct their texts. The students felt that there was more of a purpose surrounding their writing, more "real" communication, topics that tapped into their interests, expansion of vocabulary, and furthermore, they *enjoyed* the feedback received from their native-speaker peers in Colombia. The students' interest levels increased to the extent that they no longer were concerned with the task to receive a grade; they simply wanted to communicate with their peers. The blogs, alongside teacher and student reflections, served as catalysts that changed the "normal" environment of the classroom to make it more interactive, in keeping with the sociocultural perspective of language learning.

Chapter 10, "Pragmatic Variation Among Learners of French in Real-Time Chat Communication," by McCourt, explores variation in learners' uses of the French second-person pronouns *tu* (T) and *vous* (V) in a series of 1-hour WebCT chat tasks over 12 weeks as part of their normal coursework. Each task involved discussing a particular topic in French with other group members, and the topics were related to themes covered in the first- and second-semester course textbook, *Horizons*. The results of this study clearly show a great degree of variation in the use of T and V among the learners, suggesting that the configuration of learners in a CMC environment did not provide one in which the inappropriate use of T or V had any social consequences. This shortcoming perhaps impeded the learners' development of sociopragmatic competence because experiencing negative social consequences following the inappropriate use of T/V appears to be a key factor in developing learner awareness of the social implications of second-person address. A major finding of the study, then, is that normal in-class coursework alone is not sufficient to instill within the students a culturally responsive sense of sociolinguistic variations; the promotion of language socialization in the foreign-language classroom should be supplemented by exposure to a variety of discourse options within authentic cultural contexts, such as electronic discourse (e.g., chat, e-mail, forums), transcripts of scenes from films, newspaper and magazine articles, excerpts from literary texts, and advertisements.

Chapter 11, "These Horses Can Fly! and Other Lessons From Second Life: The View From a Virtual *Hacienda*," by Clark, offers a brief history of Second Life before detailing a hybrid course that the author developed under this model. By developing a Spanish *hacienda* in Second Life, Clark has been able to simulate an immersion experience for students that provides some of the culture and language that is needed outside of the classroom. On a survey in the 1st year of a 3-year study, 67% of the respondents mentioned interaction with classmates on the computer as the feature of the use of Second Life in the Spanish classroom that contributed most to their learning. Clark goes on to argue that almost any lesson in a traditional Spanish 1 text can be adapted in some way in Second Life and that professors can teach entire courses in Second Life, with the students always meeting in-world, completing activities and gathering for discussion.

Chapter 12, "A New Language for the Net Generation: Why Second Life Works for the Net Generation," by Cooke-Plagwitz, examines characteristics of Linden Lab's Second Life interface and outlines how and why these properties make Second Life an ideal foreign-language instructional tool for the Net Generation. Because learners in Second Life are typically represented by avatars that they have personally designed, their online experience may be more lifelike in the sense that it mimics a face-to-face experience in which learners synchronously interact with others' avatars, and thus, it enhances their sense of being a part of a group. More introverted students may even be more comfortable in the virtual environment and better able to participate and learn there than in the face-to-face classroom because "disguises" afforded by an avatar often impart a newfound sense of confidence to a timid student. That is, multiuser virtual environments such as Second Life have much to offer the field of foreign-language education and Net Generation students. They have the potential to change the way students learn and the way teachers teach by enabling classes to meet in a 3D virtual environment in which they can collaborate with other students from around the world. This provides countless opportunities for language learners to gain oral, aural, and cultural proficiency through interactions with native speakers in lifelike settings while the realistic nature of the 3D environment provides authentic learning conditions that are difficult to make available in traditional classroom settings.

Chapter 13, "Web-Based Language Portfolios and the Five Cs: Implementation in Foreign-Language College Classrooms," by Warren, examines whether having students create Web-based portfolios based on the Standards for Foreign Language Learning is an effective way to implement the learning of culture and to assess that learning in the foreign-language curriculum. Portfolios have a number of strengths. In terms of validity, portfolios are easily related to current SLA theory and directly tied to the objectives of a typical college-level course. Thus, a portfolio can be a strong, overall assessment tool that can give a teacher a great deal of insight into student learning and the curriculum while allowing students to work independently and take control over their own learning. This particular case study followed the piloting of a portfolio project in two intermediate college-level Japanese-language classes at a large public university and in one advanced 300-level German-language class at a medium-sized public university. The students were asked whether the portfolio project helped them learn about the target-language culture, and the average response on the final survey was very close to "agree somewhat." Many students mentioned that they were able to write more in the target language in a shorter period of time toward the end of the semester than at the beginning, showing improved language skills.

Chapter 14, "Awakening to the Power of Video-Based Web-Conferencing Technology to Promote Change," by Charbonneau-Gowdy, focuses on the findings of a study into the influence of CMC on the identities of two groups of military officers learning English in a 5-month immersion program and for 4 weeks online. The findings indicate that for some learners who felt marginalized in the classroom, the use of this particular technology offered an alternative scenario. When computers were used for transmitting facts about the language—for manipulating words and structures in drill exercises or for supporting testing—they felt that their social, intellectual, and cultural funds of knowledge seemed of little value; they claimed that they quickly forgot or felt that they could not use the knowledge that was presented. However, when computers were used specifically for communication and the exchange of ideas or the acting out of "different types of selves," evidence showed that the conversations offered several of the participants opportunities for constructing more empowered identities and greater investment in language learning and even allowed some participants to use these conversations to read their lives in a critical way. They looked critically at the way that they had been historically governed, the system of education that had deprived them of the opportunities they desired, and the military jobs that ignored their intellectual capital. Using the conversations to dialogically (re)construct their lives, some of the participants were able to envision new possibilities and to connect their lives beyond their national borders to the global community. The author argues, then, that when computers are used to support the kinds of conversations in which this particular group of learners participated, there is a possibility of generating new understandings and providing new possibilities for global communities of learning in a second language.

In sum, the researchers and practitioners writing for this volume all agree that successful integration of technology into the classroom in a pedagogically sound manner involves more than simply introducing a software program or other innovation to the students in a classroom. Technology integration must be thoughtfully planned out based on curricular goals and instructional models—implying the use of new teaching strategies that actively engage students and rely on collaboration among teachers. Only then can instructors most fully assist students in reaching the academic goals of world-language study and in becoming more fully engaged in the diverse, global society in which we all now live.

References

Bennett, S., Maton, K. & Kervin, L. (2008). The "digital natives" debate: A critical review of the evidence. *British Journal of Educational Technology*, 39(5), 775–786.

Fenn, J. (1995). *When to leap on the hype cycle* (Gartner Group report ID Number SPA-ATA-305).

New London Group. (1996). A pedagogy of multiliteracies: Designing social futures. *Harvard Educational Review*, 66, 60–92.

Prensky, M. (2001). Digital natives, digital immigrants: A new way to look at ourselves and our kids. *On the Horizon*, 9(5). Retrieved March 10, 2009, from http://www.marcprensky.com/writing/

Tapscott, D. (1998). *Growing up digital: The rise of the Net Generation*. New York: McGraw-Hill.

(Re)situating the Role(s) of New Technologies in World-Language Teaching and Learning

Rémi A. van Compernolle
The Pennsylvania State University

Lawrence Williams
University of North Texas

This chapter aims to (re)examine the role(s) of new technologies in world-language teaching and learning at a time when the digital natives (Prensky, 2001) of the Net Generation (Tapscott, 1998) are being taught by Baby Boomers and members of Generation X, so-called "digital immigrants" (Prensky, 2001), who have not always lived in a world where access to computers was commonplace or one in which digital and networked technologies were a central part of the educational and social dimensions of life. Although teachers are usually from a different generation than their students and necessarily have different worldviews and life histories, the Net Generation has grown up with technologies that have allowed them to access, integrate, and use information and shape social spaces in fundamentally different ways. The same cannot be said for previous technologies when they were invented, such as chalk, the phonograph, and the videotape, which were used in the classroom primarily by the teacher and normally only for tasks with a whole-class participation structure. The phonograph and the videotape in particular may have given learners of world languages more access to authentic discourse; however, such media are not as accessible, malleable, and portable as today's digital technologies.

Instead of focusing on the differences between yesteryear's new technologies and those that have been developed quite recently, world-language teachers should keep pedagogy as the principal guide for implementing the goals of any curriculum. We still need to be reminded that the newest and greatest software or network-based tool is not necessarily better suited to the expected educational outcomes of our students (see Adolph & LeBlanc, 1998; Scott, 1998). Thus, the present chapter provides an overview of the evolution of computer-assisted language learning (CALL), a summary of research on using new technologies as tools for

van Compernolle, R. A., & Williams, L. (2009). (Re)situating the role(s) of new technologies in world-language teaching and learning. In R. Oxford & J. Oxford, (Eds.), *Second language teaching and learning in the Net Generation* (pp. 9–21). Honolulu: University of Hawai'i, National Foreign Language Resource Center.

communication, and a review of the New London Group's (1996) pedagogy of multiliteracies, a framework into which the use of both old and new technologies can be integrated.

Approaches to CALL research and practice

The use of computers and networked technologies in world-language teaching and learning has expanded rapidly since the 1960s. From phonographs and audiolingual language labs, to multimedia centers and computer-mediated communication (CMC) in the classroom, new technologies have always played a central role in reshaping approaches to language pedagogy (Salaberry, 2001). Crook (1994) described this evolution in terms of three principle metaphors: "computer-as-tutor," "computer-as-pupil," and "computer-as-tool." Each of these three metaphors can be associated with shifting trends in approaches to language pedagogy, namely, structuralist, cognitive, and sociocognitive approaches, respectively (Kern & Warschauer, 2000, pp. 7–13).

The computer-as-tutor metaphor has its origins in the structuralist approach to foreign-language learning. Language, viewed as a concrete, monolithic system, needed to be memorized to approximate—or "master"—a prescriptive norm. This was principally achieved through drills and the imitation of "model" discourse, with minimal errors in formal (phonetic, lexical, grammatical, syntactic) accuracy on the part of the learner. This approach is perhaps epitomized by the language labs of the 1950s and 1960s (the "audiolingual" era), which provided learners with model sentences to listen to and repeat. With the development of computer technology, this drill-and-memorization approach took the form of computer applications that prompted learners to provide "correct" responses. For instance, early computer applications[1] would display a sentence with the verb missing for the learner to conjugate. If the learner entered the appropriate form (e.g., person or tense), he or she was provided with immediate positive feedback. If the response was wrong, the computer would provide negative feedback. These applications received much praise from language educators, mostly because of their capacity to provide automated and immediate feedback. However, the emphasis on rote memorization and drill did not lend itself to capturing how learners *learned* a language or what they could *do* with that language.

The second wave of CALL—the computer-as-pupil model—refocused attention toward what learners actually did with the language they were learning. This approach was theoretically grounded in cognitive frameworks of language learning, which emphasized the individual psycholinguistic processes underlying language acquisition. Once technological advances had made it possible for computer users to control computer programs, the computer-as-tutor model of CALL gave agency to the learner. Instead of the computer controlling what the learner could do, which had been the case in earlier CALL models, the learner controlled the computer. Thus, in the computer-as-pupil model, "the computer provides tools and resources, but it is up to the learner to *do* something with these in a simulated environment" (Kern & Warschauer, 2000, p. 9).[2] Such computer applications generally include a type of virtual reality environment, in which the learner interacts with programmed characters. Although this type of CALL offers learners the opportunity to do something with the language they are learning, it potentially distances the teacher from the student, and "thus compromise[s] the collaborative nature of classroom learning" (Kern & Warschauer, 2000, p. 10; paraphrasing Crook, 1994).

---

1 Although the computer-as-tutor model is generally regarded as the first wave of CALL, these applications continue to persist in various forms, such as online workbooks and other computer programs aimed at the general public and available for purchase in many bookstores.

2 This type of CALL remains an extremely popular area of research and practice, especially among those researchers and materials developers wishing to design autodidactic materials.

The combination of technological developments (e.g., computer networking) and theoretical developments in approaches to language pedagogy (e.g., emphasis on meaningful communication in authentic discourse contexts) since the 1990s has led to a third wave of CALL within the sociocognitive (or sociocultural) framework of language learning. This framework focuses not on using the computer to replace the teacher (i.e., computer-as-tutor or computer-as-pupil), but using the computer (and other technologies) to enhance language teaching within the broader context of the collaborative classroom by expanding the opportunities students have to communicate with other people. "Sociocognitive approaches to CALL shift the dynamic from learners' interaction *with* computers to interaction with other humans *via* the computer" (Kern & Warschauer, 2000, p. 11). Thus, the computer is viewed as a tool to facilitate human interaction and collaborative language learning. New ways of using information and communication technologies have led to an expansion of hypertext and CMC since the 1990s. Learners can now access authentic texts, audio and video, and other learners or native speakers of the language they are learning from the classroom, home, or any other place with a connection to the World Wide Web. Instead of self-contained, autodidactic computer applications designed specifically for language learning, networked technologies give learners access to existing discourse communities, and they make it possible for learners (and other people) to create new ones via CMC, hypertext, and various forms of social networking applications. Given the widespread nature of CMC and hypertext in today's society, language teaching professionals must rethink the use of existing technologies in language education, "examining not only the role of information technology in language learning but also the role of language learning in an information technology society" (Kern & Warschauer, 2000, pp. 12–13).

The evolution of CALL research and practice can thus be summed up as follows. In the first wave, computer applications were seen as the source of instruction. Most of them followed the traditional initiation-response-feedback model of language instruction. In the second wave, computers were seen as things to be controlled by learners. This meant offering students the opportunity to do something with what they knew, although these applications were, for the most part, self-contained and autodidactic. The third wave of CALL represents a dramatic shift in the way technology is thought to enhance language learning because it refocuses the emphasis on human interaction in authentic discourse communities. Within this third wave of CALL research is where we see the greatest potential for technology-enhanced language learning and teaching, yet we do not wish to minimize the demonstrated or potential advantages of tools and tasks that were promoted and implemented during the first two waves of CALL research and practice. In the following selective review, we highlight three promising areas of current CALL research centered on the use of technology as a tool for communication: intercultural communication, sociolinguistic and pragmatic development, and online communication and linguistic accuracy. We review representative studies to illustrate these three areas, and we describe and enumerate what we see as the main advantages of and challenges facing each one.

Technology as a tool for communication

Intercultural communication

The cornerstone of sociocultural/sociocognitive approaches to CALL research and practice is technology's capacity to serve as a means of facilitating *human interaction* and *communication* (Kern & Warschauer, 2000, p. 11). Ever since networked technologies (e.g., the Internet) became increasingly popularized in the 1990s, they have helped link *people to information*; by extension, therefore, the new generation of Internet technologies (e.g.,

O'Reilly, 2005; "Web 2.0") emphasizes linking *people to people*. As Warschauer and Grimes (2008, pp. 1–2) pointed out, although earlier Web technologies allowed people to publish content online, few were actually able to do so because this typically required specialized software and/or skills. The result was widespread access to information controlled by small numbers of tech-savvy Internet users. Web 2.0 technologies, on the other hand, have expanded the potential for interactive participation through various forms of social networking, tagging, (co)authoring, and (co)editing enabled by user-friendly Web-based software. In turn, the number of possibilities for human interaction, information sharing, and online publishing made possible by Web 2.0 technologies is virtually limitless. This shift represents a sort of democratization of publishing, which has great implications for the co-construction of knowledge and the sharing of this knowledge.

> Blogging is creating tens of millions of authors and connecting them to audiences in ways previously unseen. Wikis are empowering collaborative multiauthored writing to better harness collective knowledge. Social networking sites are enabling both the many-to-many distribution from authors to audiences of multimodal artifacts and the automated presentation of user-selected content. (Warschauer & Grimes, 2008, p. 16)

However exciting Web 2.0 applications are for the language-teaching profession, and whatever their potential for mediating intercultural communication may be, navigating this ever-expanding universe of online communication spaces can present many difficulties for language teachers and learners. Not only do users need to be familiar with the technology itself, but perhaps more importantly, online communication requires an understanding of the complex sociocultural context in which it takes place (Kern, 2006, p. 200; Warschauer & Grimes, 2008, p. 16). Thus, some recent research on intercultural telecollaboration has focused on the tensions between learners from two (or more) cultural backgrounds that occur in such contexts (e.g., Belz, 2001, 2003; Kramsch & Thorne, 2002; Thorne, 2003; Ware, 2005).

Thorne (2003) argued that although available technologies may be the same across cultures, one of the challenges facing Internet-mediated intercultural communication is differing "cultures-of-use" affecting the specific way(s) in which the same tools are used to mediate communication by people from different cultural backgrounds. Thorne pointed out that these differences in how technology is perceived and used by people in different social contexts often leads to difficulties in fostering intercultural communication.

> When cultures-of-use do not minimally align, derived as they are from social-material conditions, the ideational worlds of intersubjectivity and phatic communion become a challenge to envision and difficult to achieve. This raises a profoundly important issue as to whether cross-cultural communication also needs to explicitly take into account cross-class and cross-social material condition differences. If CMC use expands beyond the privileged communities within privileged nation states that currently have full access to the Internet…and if telecollaborative language teaching continues to expand as a method of foreign language teaching and learning, we will "need to prepare students to deal with global communicative practices that require far more than local communicative competence" (Kramsch & Thorne, [2002], p. 100). (Thorne, 2003, pp. 47–48)

Ware (2005), summarizing work by Belz (2003), noted three factors contributing to intercultural misunderstandings in telecollaboration: "a) differences in how each culture values the study of foreign languages; b) diversity of prior experiences with electronic communication; and c) institutional differences in how foreign languages are taught at each participating site" (p. 65). Ware found in her study of U.S. students of German who participated in asynchronous telecollaboration with German learners of English that "missed communication" occurred primarily because of differing motivations for communication among the U.S. and German learners. Although the German learners of English showed interest in constructing interpersonal relationships even within the structured, pedagogical setting, the U.S. students saw the online tasks as an extension of previous coursework and thus, treated the exchanges as a means of completing the tasks assigned. The Americans' orientation to the task at hand, their preference for brevity in online communication, and their recalcitrance to engage in interpersonal communication with the German students led to many missed opportunities for meaningful interaction. Ware argued that future research would benefit from analyses of how learners not only co-construct discourse but also how they "co-construe" their participation in telecollaboration.

Hanna and de Nooy (2003) have shown that learners of French engaged in public, asynchronous French-language discussion fora benefited more from topic-appropriate discussion in English with speakers of French than attempting to "practice their French" without relating to the topic of the discussion thread because the latter did not conform to forum members' expectations for interaction. In fact, the two American learners who did not even attempt to speak French, but were concerned with having meaningful exchanges about social issues in France and around the world (i.e., the discussion thread topics), were warmly welcomed by forum participants. The two other learners who set out to practice their French and sought little more than electronic penpals were virtually shunned by the forum community because the online fora they had chosen to participate in were not designed for language learning per se or the establishment of language-learning "e-pal" connections. Thus, sending learners off into cyberspace for so-called "language practice" may not necessarily be beneficial given the expectation of many online communities to communicate in accordance with established criteria (e.g., topic of discussion, participation framework). As a result, Hanna and de Nooy argued for "recasting 'practicing French,' in our instructions to students, as practicing Frenchness: performing it through participation in a cultural practice" (p. 81). Of course, the same is also certainly true for languages other than French.

Sociolinguistic and pragmatic development

In addition to its potential to foster intercultural understanding (e.g., Kern, 2006; Kramsch & Thorne, 2002; Levy, 2007; Thorne, 2003), some scholars have advocated the use of technology-mediated communication for fostering greater awareness of sociolinguistic and sociopragmatic features of discourse. Kinginger (1998) noted in her study of learners of French engaged in telecommunication with *extra muros* partners in France that perhaps the most beneficial part of the telecollaborative experience took place not actually during the event itself, but later, during "separate sessions devoted to examining the qualities of the spoken language" (p. 511). Thus, learners' access to "real data," as opposed to textbook French, helped them become more aware of different (informal) varieties and registers of language traditionally absent from learner texts. Thus, the number of discourse options (Kramsch, 1985) available to the learners was greatly expanded. In addition, such an emphasis on learning and evaluating "real language" received an overwhelmingly positive reaction from students (p. 510). Likewise, van Compernolle (2008) argued for using excerpts of synchronous chat communication as a means of sensitizing learners to sociolinguistic variation and appropriate patterns of participation. He highlighted the need for giving learners greater access to online communication spaces through in-class analyses of electronic discourse that serve to prepare learners for their eventual participation in public, nonpedagogical online communication.

Other researchers have used CMC to explore second-language pragmatic development (see Belz, 2007). Belz and Kinginger (2002), for instance, explored the use of informal (T) and formal (V) address pronouns among learners of German and French engaged in Internet-mediated intercultural collaboration (*du/Sie* in German and *tu/vous* in French). This type of exchange gave students great and prolonged access to native speaker (NS) peers who provided much-needed peer assistance (Tharp & Gallimore, 1988) with regard to T/V use. The researchers' analysis of the data revealed a decrease in (inappropriate) variation in the use of address pronouns following explicit requests to be called T on the part of the NSs (see also Belz & Kinginger, 2003; Kinginger & Belz, 2005). In a related study, Belz and Kinginger (2003) noted that learner-NS exchanges provide a context in which the social consequences of the inappropriate use of T and V can lead learners to understand the social meanings of these terms of address: "awareness of the social meaning of address forms is greatly enhanced by experiences in which learners participate in the use of those forms within contexts motivating them to maintain positive face" (p. 641).

Online communication and linguistic accuracy

In addition to its place in fostering intercultural communication and the development of sociolinguistic and sociopragmatic competence, CMC can be used to promote linguistic accuracy. This is an important part of much CALL research because of the need to strike a balance between social and communicative functions of language and linguistic accuracy (Lee, 2004; Levy & Kennedy, 2004), which is often perceived by students as the underlying goal of language education (Chavez, 2002; Ware, 2005). Our own interviews[3] with learners of French have revealed a similar trend, although more socially oriented language tasks have also been nearly universally appreciated (see also Kinginger, 1998).

The focus-on-form approach to language learning (Long, 1991), which emphasizes drawing learners' attention to their own language, has gained popularity in CALL research. Within the sociocultural framework, this has come to mean, for the most part, language learners' engagement in e-partnering exchanges, where they comment on each other's language use or where nonnative speakers are paired with NSs who provide peer assistance (Brammerts, 1996; O'Rourke, 2005; Ware & O'Dowd, 2008). In addition, some recent research (e.g., Belz, 2006) has encouraged the use of learner corpus analysis to focus students' attention on their own errors and language development.

Ware and O'Dowd's (2008) study, for example, examined the effect of peer feedback on language development among postsecondary U.S. learners of Spanish and Spanish learners of English within two contexts: e-tutoring and e-partnering. The students involved in e-tutoring were explicitly instructed to provide corrective feedback on any form perceived as incorrect, while those involved in e-partnering did so on their own initiative. Ware and O'Dowd found that both e-tutoring and e-partnering students appreciated corrective feedback; however, such feedback was provided only when students were explicitly instructed to do so (i.e., e-tutoring). This research has broad implications for the development of linguistic accuracy in telecollaboration, including, for example, teaching learners how to provide corrective feedback on specific language forms.

Although much of the focus-on-form literature is centered on grammar development, other researchers have expanded the approach to include more socially oriented language tasks. In

3 These interviews with 2nd-year learners of French are part of ongoing research on socially oriented approaches to foreign-language education, including the analysis of authentic spoken and electronic discourse. Many learners have expressed their preference for focusing on particular linguistic structures, grammatical forms, and vocabulary, even within the context of using and analyzing discourse in specific sociocultural contexts.

such studies (Belz, 2003; Kern, 1996; Thorne, 2003, 2006; Ware & Kramsch, 2005), students are asked "to see language and culture as two sides of the same coin" (Ware & O'Dowd, 2008, p. 45). Thus, students focused on specific language forms used in CMC environments to formulate their own hypotheses about the relationship between language and culture or social context. This type of task has the potential to draw learners' attention to the specific forms and structures characteristic of particular sociocultural contexts.

Summary

The selective review provided above has illustrated three major trends within the approach to CALL research that focuses on technology as a tool for communication. First, various forms of online social networking, publishing, and communication can help foster intercultural understanding, and they provide learners with virtually limitless possibilities for publishing and communicating online. However, learners also appear to need some background knowledge of the other culture and its values of technology for the potential benefits of such international communication opportunities to be fully realized. Second, CMC provides opportunities for language learners to engage in regular, prolonged communication with NSs of the target language, during which their sociolinguistic and sociopragmatic competence can develop. Importantly, however, this seems to require the explicit questioning of socially inappropriate language use on the part of NSs, or, as shown by Kinginger (1998), during separate teacher-led discussions of language use in transcripts of events. Third, computer-based focus-on-form tasks can help learners notice and analyze their own discourse, which can lead to improvements in overall formal linguistic accuracy. Nonetheless, as Ware and O'Dowd (2008) showed, this is most effective in conditions where learners are explicitly instructed to provide corrective feedback.

Using technology as a tool for communication thus provides a number of exciting possibilities for the language classroom, but it also presents a number of challenges. These challenges are making us rethink the role of the computer and other communication technologies in language education. The pedagogical implications described in the following section illustrate what we consider technology's place to be in the broader context of formal, structured educational settings. We see technology not as a means for language learning in and of itself but rather, another pedagogical tool whose value is determined by its use for specific pedagogical objectives in the classroom. As such, we do not believe that technology can be separated from the rest of the classroom. In other words, our view is that technology forms only one part of a larger, cohesive, multifaceted approach to world-language teaching and learning.

Pedagogical implications

Despite the body of research that has been generated on CALL and other technology-enhanced approaches to language learning and teaching, it remains unclear how new communication technologies best serve language learners and teachers for the specific activity of *language learning*. The question of whether using technologies improves language learning does not have a straightforward answer. In fact, empirical evidence is notably lacking that technology-enhanced tasks facilitate language learning in ways that non-technology-enhanced tasks cannot. Rather, the use of technology is not what makes a task worthwhile so much as the *specific uses* of technology (Kern & Warschauer, 2000, p. 2) and perhaps even more importantly, teachers' roles in fostering learners' critical reflection about their own participation and language use in online communication.

There is consensus in CALL research that it is not technology per se that affects the learning of language and culture but the particular uses of technology. This emphasis

> on use highlights the central importance of pedagogy and the teacher. Success in CMC, multimedia authoring, and distance-learning projects has been repeatedly shown to depend largely on teachers' efforts in coordinating learners' activities…, structuring language and content learning…, and helping learners to reflect critically on language, culture, and context.… Belz and Müller-Hartmann (2003) emphasize the need to move beyond reductive accounts of the teacher as a guide on the side and stress the importance of the teacher in identifying and explaining culturally contingent patterns of interaction in electronic discourse. (Kern, 2006, p. 200)

Our view of technology's role in world-language teaching and learning is that technology cannot be used in isolation, that is, as a separate event largely independent on other tasks and pedagogical practices typically associated with world-language teaching (e.g., listening tasks, compositions, oral practice). Technology-enhanced language teaching is not a method of instruction, nor should it be its own theoretical framework (Kern, 2006, p. 200). Instead, we need to rethink the *particular uses* of technology within existing theoretical frameworks for world-language teaching and learning (Chapelle, 2003; Kern, 2006; Salaberry, 2001). Thus, the question is, how does technology enhance, shape, and change how we approach the teaching and learning of language within current pedagogical frameworks?

For our part, we believe that the New London Group's (1996) framework of a pedagogy of multiliteracies offers the most flexibility for the integration of new technologies into foreign-language curricula. This theory of pedagogy emphasizes the symbiotic relationship between *teaching, learning,* and *doing* in particular sociocultural contexts, recognizing learning not as an individual psychological process but as a social phenomenon. Thus, for language learners and teachers, the task becomes one of reshaping the classroom as a place that fosters the co-construction of knowledge, understanding, and practice (Hall, 2001) with technology serving as a fully integrated tool used to achieve these pedagogical objectives. In other words, a technology-centered task does not always have to be the focus or climax of a lesson; rather, technology can be used during the course of any type of task, even one that is not necessarily designed *around* technology.

The New London Group's (1996) pedagogy of multiliteracies encourages teachers to conceptualize tasks to include one or more of the following types of learning opportunities: situated practice (e.g., reading and/or repeating printed or recorded dialogues), transformed practice (i.e., creating or reshaping discourse to personalize and/or recontextualize it), overt instruction (i.e., direct explanations of content and concepts), and critical framing (i.e., taking a reflective step back to consider how and why a particular word, sentence, text, or object was designed and developed). These types of learning opportunities do not fall into a particular order or hierarchy, and no single one has any lesser or greater intrinsic value. Instead, these different spheres of learning opportunities provide multiple approaches to pedagogical tasks, which lends to the flexibility of integrating technology into any part of this framework.

Perhaps the most promising aspect of an integrated approach to technology-enhanced language teaching is that it minimizes the use of technology as a "special" type of task, all too often associated with "fun" activities that learners like to do because they break up the monotony of the traditional textbook-based curriculum. In our view, a "fun" activity appreciated by learners does not necessarily entail meaningful language learning. Instead, we believe that any technology-enhanced task—as any other task—must be theoretically grounded and pedagogically motivated. Therefore, teachers cannot simply use technology for technology's sake, but they must take advantage of these relatively modern tools to accomplish specific pedagogical objectives. Thus, information and communication technologies are akin to other tools used for pedagogical purposes, such as textbooks, audio CDs, overhead projectors, blackboards, and so forth. In other words, language educators should use technology when it is the most appropriate tool available to accomplish a specific task.

This approach has several implications for classroom interaction and culture, not the least of which is the role of the teacher. Although earlier models for CALL relegated the teacher to a backseat position in the classroom, we believe that a multiliteracies pedagogy that includes a fully integrated view of technology's place in the curriculum assigns a central role to language educators. Their role becomes one of assisting learner performance, providing opportunities for learners to engage in meaning-making tasks, and fostering critical analysis of their own and others' discourse and interaction in specific sociocultural contexts. This is important because such an approach has the potential to prepare learners for the various types of interactions they may participate in and observe in a wide range of sociocultural contexts (Kern, 2006, p. 203).

Another implication of this integrated approach to technology-enhanced language teaching is the role of student peers. Because networked technologies allow people to engage in synchronous and asynchronous forms of CMC, learners can communicate with other learners or native speakers of the language they are learning via the Internet. Although teachers have a central role in designing, implementing, and guiding students to critical reflection on their interactions, new configurations for student-student and student-NS interaction made possible by these new technologies offer much potential for peer-assisted performance, whereby "peers themselves become the primary sources of learning for one another in the interactions over tasks of independent learning centers" (Tharp & Gallimore, 1988, p. 176). Thus, telecollaboration with NSs of the target language or interlearner CMC provide valuable resources for language-learning opportunities. However, as the literature shows, this may be most effective when participants are explicitly instructed to provide corrective feedback on language form (see Ware & O'Dowd, 2008, and its references).

Technology's role does not end at the culmination of a particular technology-based task. Instead, within an integrated approach, tasks created around technology should serve as a launching pad for other types of tasks. For instance, corpus analysis of learner-produced (Belz, 2006) and NS-produced (Kerr, 2003, pp. 268–270; van Compernolle, 2008) CMC followed by critical reflection can draw learners' attention to the various interactional, sociolinguistic, pragmatic, discursive, and sociocultural aspects of electronic discourse and how these aspects of language and social interaction are similar to or different from those found in other forms of communication in different contexts (see also Kinginger, 1998). This critical reflection on technology-based tasks has the potential "to make the familiar unfamiliar, to reframe and rethink our conceptions of language, communication, and society" (Kern, 2006, p. 203). In our view, what happens *after* the technology-based task (i.e., how teachers and learners integrate it as part of a broader, cohesive curriculum) is perhaps even more important than the event itself. Put another way, the technology event has little meaning or value if it is not revisited and expanded upon later, in separate sessions devoted to the critical framing of the event.

This integrated approach to technology-enhanced language teaching also entails challenges, specifically in relation to teachers' attitudes toward technology. Departments of applied linguistics and foreign languages at many universities around the US and in other countries often offer such courses as "Teaching with technology" or "Technology-enhanced foreign-language teaching," as if the use of technology in language pedagogy requires special courses or extra training isolated from more mainstream or traditional teaching-methods or second-language acquisition courses. We believe that this separation of teaching-methods/ second-language acquisition courses from those dealing with technology-enhanced language teaching further perpetuates the idea that the use of technology exists in isolation from existing theoretical frameworks for the teaching and learning of languages. Thus, the full integration of technology into the world-language curriculum is difficult to envision as long as technology and teaching methods remain independent from one another.

Another challenge facing this integrated approach involves student attitudes toward the use of technology in the classroom. Although the vast majority of our current and future students are no doubt proficient—if not expert—users of the various technologies we use in the classroom, it remains unclear whether they realize the full potential of these technologies for language-learning purposes. For instance, many of our students have expressed the view that creating a collaborative learning environment is difficult despite the use of networked technologies and opportunities for telecollaboration with NSs simply because they are used to the professor being the primary source of instruction in the classroom. Thus, the question shifts to whether learners need to be explicitly taught *how* to provide peer assistance for this to occur (see Ware & O'Dowd, 2008). We believe that within a sociocultural approach to language learning and teaching, learners do in fact need some training in pedagogy, if only to make them aware that they themselves have the potential to (re)shape the culture and outcomes of classroom-based learning.

Conclusion

Our discussion of the role of technology in world-language teaching and learning has focused on the evolution of CALL research and practice, the various ways of using technology as a tool for communication, and the pedagogical implications of fully integrating the use of communication technologies into a world-language curriculum. Although the advantages of technology appear to be clear, we have also described and enumerated a number of challenges facing language educators in today's information technology society. We believe that the full potential of information and communication technologies in the world-language classroom remains to be realized. For this to occur, technology can no longer be treated in isolation from other aspects of language pedagogy; rather, its use must be integrated into existing approaches to language learning, such that tasks involving technology are theoretically grounded and motivated by specific pedagogical objectives (Salaberry, 2001, pp. 51–52). Thus, "What are learners supposed to do/learn?", "How is this going to help them in their future interactions in specific sociocultural contexts?", and "How can this task be integrated into the broader context of language learning?" should become central questions that language educators ask themselves when deciding how technology can and should be used for world-language teaching and learning.

References

Adolph, W., & LeBlanc, L. (1998). A revolution from above: The race for technology in foreign languages. In J. A. Muyskens (Ed.), *New ways of learning and teaching: Focus on technology and foreign language education* (pp. 19–35). Boston: Heinle & Heinle.

Belz, J. (2001). Institutional and individual dimensions of transatlantic group work in network-based language teaching. *ReCALL, 13*, 213–231.

Belz, J. (2003). Linguistic perspectives on the development of intercultural competence in telecollaboration. *Language Learning & Technology, 7*(2), 68–117. Retrieved April 28, 2008, from http://llt.msu.edu/vol7num2/belz/default.html

Belz, J. (2006). At the intersection of telecollaboration, learner corpus analysis, and L2 pragmatics: Considerations for language program direction. In J. Belz & S. Thorne (Eds.), *Internet-mediated intercultural foreign language education* (pp. 207–246). Boston: Heinle & Heinle.

Belz, J. A. (2007). The role of computer mediation in the instruction and development of L2 pragmatic competence. *Annual Review of Applied Linguistics, 27*, 45–75.

Belz, J., & Kinginger, C. (2002). The cross-linguistic development of address form use in telecollaborative language learning: Two case studies. *Canadian Modern Language Review, 59*, 189–214.

Belz, J., & Kinginger, C. (2003). Discourse options and the development of pragmatic competence by classroom learners of German: The case of address forms. *Language Learning, 53*, 591–647.

Brammerts, H. (1996). Language learning in tandem using the Internet. In M. Warschauer (Ed.), *Telecollaboration in foreign language learning. Proceedings of the Hawai'i Symposium* (pp. 121–130). Honolulu: University of Hawai'i Press.

Chapelle, C. (2003). *English language learning and technology: Lectures on applied linguistics in the age of information and communication technology*. Amsterdam: John Benjamins.

Chavez, M. (2002). We say "culture" and students ask "What?": University students' definitions of foreign language culture. *Die Unterrichtspraxis, 35*(2), 129–140.

Crook, C. (1994). *Computers and the collaborative experience of learning*. London: Routledge.

Hall, J. K. (2001). *Methods for teaching foreign languages: Creating a community of learners in the classroom*. Upper Saddle River, NJ: Prentice Hall.

Hanna, B., & de Nooy, J. (2003). A funny thing happened on the way to the forum: Electronic discussion and foreign language learning. *Language Learning & Technology, 7*(1), 71–85. Retrieved March 25, 2007, from http://llt.msu.edu/vol7num1/hanna/default.html

Kern, R. (1996). Computer-mediated communication: Using e-mail exchanges to explore personal histories in two cultures. In M. Warschauer (Ed.), *Telecollaboration in foreign language learning* (pp. 105–120). Honolulu: University of Hawai'i Press.

Kern, R. (2006). Perspectives on technology in learning and teaching languages. *TESOL Quarterly, 40*, 183–210.

Kern, R., & Warschauer, M. (2000). Introduction: Theory and practice of network-based language teaching. In M. Warschauer & R. Kern (Eds.), *Network-based language teaching: Concepts and practice* (pp. 1–19). Cambridge, England: Cambridge University Press.

Kerr, B. (2003). Prescriptivism, linguistic variation, and the so-called privilege of the non-native speaker. In C. Blyth (Ed.), *The sociolinguistics of foreign-language classrooms: Contributions of the native, the near-native, and the non-native speaker* (pp. 267–272). Boston: Heinle.

Kinginger, C. (1998). Videoconferencing as access to spoken French. *Modern Language Journal, 82*, 502–513.

Kinginger, C., & Belz, J. (2005). Sociocultural perspectives on pragmatic development in foreign language learning: Microgenetic case studies from telecollaboration and residence abroad. *Intercultural Pragmatics, 2*(4), 369–422.

Kramsch, C. (1985). Classroom interaction and discourse options. *Studies in Second Language Acquisition, 7*, 169–183.

Kramsch, C., & Thorne, S. (2002). Foreign language learning as global communicative practice. In D. Block & D. Cameron (Eds.), *Globalization and language teaching* (pp. 83–100). London: Routledge.

Lee, L. (2004). Learners' perspectives on networked collaborative interaction with native speakers of Spanish in the U.S. *Language Learning & Technology*, 8(1), 83–100. Retrieved April 21, 2008, from http://llt.msu.edu/vol8num1/lee/default.html

Levy, M. (2007). Culture, culture learning and new technologies: Toward a pedagogical framework. *Language Learning & Technology, 11*(2), 104–127. Retrieved March 20, 2008, from http://llt.msu.edu/vol11num2/levy/default.html

Levy, M., & Kennedy, C. (2004). A task-cycling pedagogy using stimulated reflection and audio-conferencing in foreign language learning. *Language Learning & Technology*, 8(2), 50–69. Retrieved February 8, 2008, from http://llt.msu.edu/vol8num2/default.html

Long, M. (1991). Focus on form: A design feature in language teaching methodology. In K. de Bot, R. Ginsberg, & C. Kramsch (Eds.), *Foreign language research in cross-cultural perspective* (pp. 39–52). Amsterdam: John Benjamins.

New London Group. (1996). A pedagogy of multiliteracies: Designing social futures. *Harvard Educational Review, 66*, 60–92.

O'Reilly, T. (2005, September 30). What is Web 2.0: Design patterns and business models for the Next Generation software. Retrieved February 24, 2009, from http://oreilly.com/pub/a/oreilly/tim/news/2005/09/30/what-is-web–20.htm

O'Rourke, B. (2005). Form-focused interaction in online tandem learning. *CALICO Journal, 22*(3), 433–466.

Prensky, M. (2001). Digital natives, digital immigrants: A new way to look at ourselves and our kids. *On the Horizon*, 9(5), 1–6. Retrieved March 5, 2008, from http://www.marcprensky.com/writing/

Salaberry, R. (2001). The use of technology for second language learning and teaching. *Modern Language Journal, 85*, 39–56.

Scott, V. M. (1998). Exploring the link between teaching and technology: An approach to TA development. In J. A. Muyskens (Ed.), *New ways of learning and teaching: Focus on technology and foreign language education* (pp. 3–17). Boston: Heinle & Heinle.

Tapscott, D. (1998). *Growing up digital: The rise of the Net Generation*. New York: McGraw-Hill.

Tharp, R., & Gallimore, R. (1988). *Rousing minds to life: Teaching, learning, and schooling in social context*. Cambridge, England: Cambridge University Press.

Thorne, S. (2003). Artifacts and cultures-of-use in intercultural communication. *Language Learning & Technology*, 7(2), 38–67. Retrieved April 4, 2008, from http://llt.msu.edu/vol7num2/thorne/default.html

Thorne, S. (2006). Pedagogical and praxiological lessons from Internet-mediated intercultural foreign language education research. In J. Belz & S. Thorne (Eds.), *Internet-mediated intercultural foreign language education* (pp. 2–30). Boston: Heinle & Heinle.

van Compernolle, R. A. (2008, April). *Sociolinguistic norms and variation in French-language on-line chat communities and implications for foreign language pedagogy*. Paper presented at the meeting of the American Association for Applied Linguistics, Washington DC. Retrieved May 2, 2008, from http://docs.google.com/Present?docid=dd5gmkw2_13hqmhfrfg&skipauth=true

Ware, P. (2005). "Missed communication" in online communication: Tensions in fostering successful online interactions. *Language Learning & Technology*, 9(2), 64–89. Retrieved April 15, 2008, from http://llt.msu.edu/vol9num2/default.html

Ware, P., & Kramsch, C. (2005). Toward an intercultural stance: Teaching German and English through telecollaboration. *Modern Language Journal*, 89, 190–205.

Ware, P., & O'Dowd, R. (2008). Peer feedback on language form in telecollaboration. *Language Learning & Technology*, *12*(1), 43–63. Retrieved March 2, 2008, from http://llt.msu.edu/vol12num1/wareodowd/default.html

Warschauer, M., & Grimes, D. (2008). Audience, authorship, and artifact: The emergent semiotics of Web 2.0. *Annual Review of Applied Linguistics 2007*, *27*, 1–23.

Internet and Language Teaching/Learning: Reflections on Online Emerging Technologies and Their Impact on Foreign-Language Instruction

Ana Niño
The University of Manchester

The Internet is widely used nowadays as a source of multimedia resources that serve many different purposes, including foreign-language instruction. Both language tutors and students use Google, iTunes, YouTube, and e-mail, among many other online applications, on an everyday basis and have started exploring the potential of these tools for practicing listening, reading, speaking, and writing skills in a foreign language. Nonetheless, a great challenge is finding the most appropriate tools for various teaching/learning needs. Language tutors aim to provide relevant online materials (i.e., those linked to students' levels and course requirements) to enhance their teaching practice. This also involves being aware of emerging technologies and of their advantages and drawbacks for language instruction. Although language students are exposed to a vast number of online resources, they may not be able to distinguish the ones that are most and least appropriate for their learning. Regardless of their levels of proficiency, students either want to make good use of the resources available online to do their assignments or find an easy way out and use the resources illicitly. Consequently, students should be made aware of how they can use their linguistic and strategic knowledge as a basis to progress in their learning.

In this chapter, some of the most prominent emerging online technologies for language teaching/learning are explored, with particular attention paid to their functionality, their potential use in the language class, and the advantages and disadvantages of using them in foreign-language instruction.

CALL, the Internet, and foreign-language instruction

Using Internet tools can be considered a form of computer-assisted language instruction because, as do other computer-assisted language learning (CALL) tools, Internet tools provide a means for interactive and individualized learning. Whereas the use of CALL software has been reported to provide significant gains only in receptive language skills

Niño, A. (2009). Internet and language teaching/learning: Reflections on online emerging technologies and their impact on foreign-language instruction. In R. Oxford & J. Oxford, (Eds.), *Second language teaching and learning in the Net Generation* (pp. 23–30). Honolulu: University of Hawai'i, National Foreign Language Resource Center.

(reading and listening), computer-mediated communication (CMC) has aided in improving the development of listening and speaking abilities. CMC in its two forms, asynchronous (e.g., e-mail and forums) and synchronous (e.g., text chat, voice chat, and audio and video conferencing), is a common and practical way of communicating with other Internet users in a foreign language.

Thus, the question arises: What are the advantages, if any, of using the Internet for foreign-language instruction? From a pedagogical point of view, Sayers (1993) stated that network-based technology can contribute significantly to the following:

- Experiential learning. Students are enabled to learn by doing, thus becoming the creators in addition to the receivers of knowledge.
- Motivation. Computers are usually associated with fun, games, and a wide spectrum of activities, which make students feel more independent.
- Enhanced student achievement. The technology positively affects students' attitudes toward learning, helps them build self-instruction strategies, and promotes their self-confidence.
- Authentic materials for study. Students can access authentic reading resources from anywhere at any time.
- Greater interaction. Students can send e-mails, join social networking sites or virtual worlds, and receive immediate feedback on their online exercises.
- Individualization. Both shy and less inhibited students can become engaged in student-centered collaborative learning.
- Independence from a single source of information. Students are presented with opportunities to escape from "canned" knowledge and discover multiple information sources, thus promoting interdisciplinary learning in a multicultural world.
- Global understanding. Multicultural communication can be practiced on a comprehensive level via the Internet.

In the next section, we will provide practical examples of the aforementioned pedagogical principles by means of presenting various online emerging technologies and exploring their potential for enhancing foreign-language teaching/learning.

Online emerging technologies

Google

Chinnery (2008) distinguished five main uses of the preeminent search engine Google as a pedagogical tool:

1. **Informative tool.** It corrects spelling errors, defines words, looks for common collocations, searches for authentic texts, finds synonyms and antonyms, displays images that can help disambiguate cultural references, and searches in multiple languages with the option of having entire Websites translated using free online machine translation.
2. **Productive tool.** It allows learners to instantly author, publish, and share their own textual and audiovisual productions for a global audience via sites such as Google's Blogger (http://www.blogger.com) and Google Docs (http://docs.google.com) for Web-based word processing.

3. **Collaborative tool.** It has tools for group activities and updates such as Google Calendar (http://www.google.com/calendar) for scheduling and sending out reminders and Google Groups (http://groups.google.com) for sending out announcements and facilitating asynchronous class discussions.
4. **Communicative tool.** It provides opportunities for interaction and negotiation in the target language via sites such as Gmail (http://mail.google.com); Google Talk (http://www.google.com/talk/), an instant messenger-cum-Internet telephony service; and GOOG–411 (http://www.google.com/goog411/), an automated telephone directory that integrates speech recognition and text messaging.
5. **Aggregative tool.** It integrates multiple functions via sites such as iGoogle (http://www.google.com/ig/); Google Page Creator (http://www.pages.google.com/); and Google Reader (http://www.google.com/reader), a Web-feed aggregator that can integrate news feeds, blogs, podcasts, and video podcasts.

With regard to Google as a language-learning tool, Robb (2003) and Hubbard (2004) emphasized its value as an authentic text mine and valuable reference for written production/communication. Robb identified the use of Google as a quick and dirty corpus that is more accessible than any other corpus, with a huge database and including blogs and discussions that come very close to spoken language. Hubbard pinpointed four main uses of Google for writing instruction: checking grammar and usage when responding to writing, checking grammar and usage during tutorial conferences, checking definitions and uses of technical terminology, and helping students learn to write and edit on their own. Hubbard also reiterated the importance of Google in enhancing reading comprehension: It is a rich source of authentic and sometimes genre- and topic-specific language. The disadvantages of Google for educational purposes include copyright, censorship, and privacy concerns that students should be aware of before exposing themselves to any Google content.

Wikis and blogs

The word *wiki* is Hawaiian for "quick" and refers to a type of Website with pages that any user can easily contribute to and edit, including text, photos, and videos. Some examples are Wetpaint (http://www.wetpaint.com) and the widely known Wikipedia (http://www.wikipedia.org/). These sites are especially suited to collaborative online projects and comprise a structured set of pages linked to each other and an open editing system in which anyone can edit any page. Their main objective is sharing knowledge, and their contributions are serious and meant to be permanent. One of the disadvantages is that although wiki sites can be secured with passwords to prevent malicious use, the security and privacy of their use causes general concerns. Moreover, their anonymous contributions challenge their potential to become trusted sources of information.

Blogs are Websites that allow the posting of interactive entries on particular subjects suggested by the author/s. They may contain descriptions, images, videos, and links to other sites or blogs. An example of a blog that can be used for educational purposes is one created by BBC Mundo for speakers of Spanish (http://www.bbc.co.uk/blogs/spanish/hablas_espanol/); people can subscribe to it and post their comments on news about the Spanish-speaking world. In pedagogy, blogs constitute a creative form of keeping track of what is happening in the language class, of reflecting on class discussions, of posting homework, and of linking to Internet resources that are relevant and useful to students. Blogs are usually run by the class teacher, but each student can have his/her own blog and be part of a wide language-learning community. For educational purposes, the blog site must remain accessible for the duration of the course, and it should allow restricting the audience that can access and comment on it to prevent malicious behavior. The blog maintenance for a class (especially if every student has a separate blog) can be time consuming and may require incentives for participation.

Skype and videoconferencing

Skype (http://www.skype.com) is an online tool that provides telephone service through Voice-over-Internet Protocol, allowing personal computers to act like telephones. Skype Video (http://www.skype.com/videocalling) provides video calls and video conferencing. To use it requires only a microphone, earphones, and a Webcam. It is widely used nowadays because it is free when the calls are made from computer to computer. It allows linking up to five people for conference calls, where one of the users acts as a host, inviting the other participants. Soziety (http://www.soziety.com) is an example of a language-exchange social network based on Skype. For language learning, it is useful for instant free conversational practice with distant users or for class-to-class exchanges, although because it concentrates mostly on oral skills, it is more suited to one-to-one sessions.

Videoconferencing allows audio and video interactions between individuals. It provides immediate communication via visual cues, such as facial expressions, that make communication more authentic. It is commonly used in distance learning for collaborative work and class projects and in this way, its use can integrate the four skills for language practice. Some examples of videoconferencing software used for language-learning purposes are Lyceum (http://lyceum.open.ac.uk/) and Adobe Acrobat Connect Pro (formerly Macromedia Breeze, http://www.adobe.com/products/acrobatconnectpro/). In a study of student perceptions about videoconferencing between students of German and native speakers in Germany (Coverdale-Jones, 2000), the students mentioned two advantages of using the technology: the immediacy of communication with a real person from their own age group and interactivity. However, these students also viewed videoconferencing as a reduced form of communication in comparison to face-to-face interaction. From the tutor perspective, software such as Adobe Acrobat Connect Pro requires valuable time for class preparation and good technical support.

YouTube

YouTube (http://www.youtube.com) is a video-sharing site where users can upload, view, and share video clips. Its main advantages for language learning are that it is fun and visual and it shows authentic culture-related materials such as trailers, TV ads, films, show extracts, news, music, documentaries, and cartoons. Students can practice listening, reading, pronunciation, and intonation skills and pause and repeat the video clips as many times as they want. They can also respond to other users' opinions about the videos via the integrated forum. An example of the potential of YouTube for foreign-language instruction is the following link, which presents a tutorial on the pronunciation of the Spanish alphabet: http://www.youtube.com/watch?v=Kc02Ohhnuxs&eurl=http://www.europa-pages.com/lessons/spanish-pronunciation.html. Some disadvantages from the language-instruction point of view are the poor audio or video quality of some of the clips and the lack of language-specific searches (e.g., for a specific language variety or genre). From the student perspective, the ability to make language-specific comments on the level of difficulty of a particular video clip would be helpful.

Podcasting

Podcasts can be understood as audio blogs that users create and upload to Websites or servers and that can then be downloaded and played on portable audio devices or on computers.

One example of a language-learning podcast is at the Notes in Spanish site (http://www.notesinspanish.com/), which makes available audio files of authentic conversations in Spanish about real-life topics for learners of all levels (from beginners to advanced). For foreign-language learning, podcasts are resources for listening and publishing oral output such as presentations created both by language tutors and students. Language tutors can create their own podcasts adapted to students' levels and capabilities or to the course content. Podcasts, therefore, constitute authentic relevant speech in the form of monologues or dialogues, but also may include such disparate realia as answering-machine messages, public transport announcements, news, minilectures, or narratives. This flexibility of usage allows for a wide range of activities and materials, and it can be motivating for students to be involved in a language-learning community that can act as a real audience and with whom they can interact via their podcasts. They can listen to the podcasts as many times as they like. For lower levels, tutors can incorporate transcripts so that students become accustomed to listening to authentic speech from early stages of learning. Among the advantages of podcasts for foreign-language instruction are their portability, ease of use, attractiveness, motivating effect on students (due to their ease of accessibility via computers and software, such as iTunes, http://www.apple.com/itunes, and QuickTime, http://www.apple.com/quicktime, which can be downloaded from the Internet free of charge), and their ability to facilitate self-paced learning. Thorne and Payne (2005) suggested that podcasts could be used to provide learners with samples of real speech and other authentic materials. Stanley (2006) suggested that podcasts could be used as supplements to textbook materials, sources for authentic listening materials, ways for students to gain information on specific aspects of the language such as idiomatic expressions or grammatical constructions, and with student-produced podcasts, as a way for students to communicate with each other in other countries. Like wikis and blogs, podcasts are sometimes vandalized, and this can affect the quality and accuracy of their content. Podcasts may also cause accessibility problems for hearing-impaired students and staff.

Automatic speech recognition and speech synthesizers

Automatic speech recognition (ASR) or speech processing describes the use of computers to recognize spoken words. The EyeSpeak Website (http://www.eyespeakenglish.com), for example, provides information about software for helping students improve their English pronunciation. ASR has proved to be useful for pronunciation and intonation training, where learners read sentences on the screen, and the computer provides feedback as to the accuracy of the utterance (Neri, Cucchiarini, & Strik, 2003). In many cases, though, packages such as Tell Me More (http://itunes.stanford.edu/) provide mere scores against a native-speaker model instead of more specific corrective feedback that could provide the students with clues as to how to improve their oral proficiency.

Speech synthesizers are computer systems that aim to artificially produce human speech. Some speech synthesizers such as eSpeak (http://espeak.sourceforge.net/) are available online. Handley and Hamel (2005) suggested the following applications for using text-to-speech synthesis systems that generate speech from text input for CALL purposes: talking dictionaries (electronic dictionaries that integrate digital recordings of human speakers or speech synthesis for the oral presentation of dictionary entries), talking texts (tools that read aloud any inputted text), dictations, pronunciation training at segmental and suprasegmental levels, and dialogue partners. Goodwin-Jones (2003, p. 6) stated that "voice recognition and text-to-speech, combined with natural writing input, could add a powerful dimension to interactive multimedia or Web-based applications." One drawback of these systems is that language tutors may reject spoken language that sounds artificial.

Online dictionaries and free online machine translation

Many search engines and Websites present online dictionaries and free online machine translation (FOMT) sites as common lexical reference resources. Online dictionaries can be monolingual, bilingual, or multilingual. Sites such as WordReference (http://www.wordreference.com) provide synonyms, antonyms, verb conjugators, and forums to discuss the translation of challenging words or phrases into the target language. Dictionaries such as YourDictionary (http://www.yourdictionary.com) include spelling, pronunciation, and etymology results, and sites such as Dictionary (http://www.dictionary.com) incorporate a style guide. To access examples of terminology, phraseology, idiomatic sentences, and words in context, a subscription is required.

Some argue that FOMT is not a good example of machine translation technology, but it is the most widely available form and can be accessed via search engines such as Google (http://www.google.com/language_tools) and Altavista (http://babelfish.yahoo.com/). FOMT provides translations of words, phrases, sentences, and entire Websites at the click of a mouse and is available in a wide variety of languages. Its ability to provide an immediate translation from and into many languages, including minority languages, makes it a rather good reading comprehension aid when a person only wants to get the gist of what a particular text is about. This is why FOMT is mainly used for assimilation (Gaspari, 2007) rather than dissemination. This does not prevent some language learners from using these sites as "phrase dictionaries," unaware of the kinds of errors these systems make. Other illicit ways language learners use FOMT sites is for writing or translation assignments; they copy and paste whole sentences or texts of FOMT output and pass them off as their own writing in the target language, something obviously counterproductive for language learning and unfair to classmates who make the intellectual effort to do the homework on their own or with reference to other language resources. Language tutors may be challenged to distinguish FOMT output from students' genuine output; this has proven to be a very difficult task because many foreign-language student and machine errors overlap. Language instructors should be aware of this new form of cheating and of the typical errors that FOMT systems make. From the perspective of language tutors, we recommend finding ways to use FOMT systems in class to make students aware of what these systems can and cannot yet do; this will allow students to realize the different factors that may affect their output, such as source and target languages, source text type, and word order. Finally, finding ways of punishing wrong uses of FOMT would be useful for language teachers. McCarthy (2004) made some suggestions to minimize the risk of students taking advantage of FOMT sites such as Babel Fish (http://uk.babelfish.yahoo.com/translate) as a shortcut to language-learning and translation assignments and made a proposal of how to deal with cheating students.

Social networking sites

Social networking sites build online social networks of people who share interests or activities. Popular sites are Facebook (http://www.facebook.com), MySpace (http://www.myspace.com), and Bebo (http://www.bebo.com), which are mainly associated with colleges and universities. Similar sites are Fotolog (http://www.fotolog.com), for sharing pictures and comments with family and friends, and Del.icio.us (http://del.icio.us), a site where you can save, bookmark, access, and share your favorite sites. These sites are useful for keeping in touch with others, collaborating, joining groups, and posting or storing information such as photos, videos, and notes. These sites are multilingual, easy to use, and free of charge;

they are open to all upon registration, which involves the creation of an account or digital identity, and messages can be shared among members of a group by posting to the group's wall. Although these sites have much potential for collaborative language practice, their advantages and disadvantages for this particular purpose are yet to be explored.

More specific is the use of e-portfolios for language instruction. An e-portfolio is a collection of documents and other objects for educational purposes. An example e-portfolio tool is Pebblepad (http://www.pebblepad.com), where users can create, store, and review multiple assets to provide rich stories of learning or achievement for multiple purposes including formal and informal assessment, appraisal, and accreditation. From a pedagogical point of view, these sites promote informal interaction of students around topics that are relevant or of interest to them and therefore, encourage participation and the development of problem-solving skills through discussion and reflection on topics via collaborative writing. E-portfolios are an alternative method of presenting work to fellow students and contribute to community building. On the other hand, e-portfolios require tutor training, good planning, and may involve curriculum redesign.

A new and more advanced form of online social networking is Internet-based virtual worlds such as Second Life (http://www.secondlife.com), an interactive virtual-world environment where people can build, watch, and present sound and video and possibly teach. Digital residents of these worlds have their own identities and can make digital creations that they can buy, sell, and trade with other residents. Residents can communicate via text-based local chat and global instant messaging. An example of the application of an online virtual world for educational purposes is the island in Second Life created by the Cervantes Institute (http://secondlife.cervantes.es/) for the promotion of the language and culture of Spanish-speaking countries. On this island, users from different countries—most of whom are students studying Spanish, language instructors, or people interested in the Spanish-speaking world—can attend exhibitions; listen to interviews, lectures, concerts, and documentaries; and even walk around replicas of some of the most attractive places on the globe. This adds fun and a new dimension to the way languages can be learned. This software may not be welcomed by mature learners, though, and requires a sufficient level of familiarity with the software, which can be slow at times.

Summary and conclusions

This chapter outlines some of the advantages and disadvantages of various online technologies and their impact on language instruction.

Many of the online tools presented are meant for informative and communicative purposes and can foster a sense of community. Through blogs, wikis, podcasts, bookmarking, or social networking sites, students can keep in touch and updated on shared interests and expand their knowledge of and negotiate/discuss topics that are relevant within the community. This sense of belonging applied to the language-learning context can foster peer learning and communicative sociocultural learning via negotiation of meaning and interaction with people of different cultures or with interest in a particular culture.

Not all the online technologies mentioned above were created with an educational aim in mind. However, given that students are becoming very familiar with and literate in the use of the Internet and the tools available there, the challenge for the tutor is to explore innovative approaches to the effective use of emerging online technologies and to be ready to troubleshoot and overcome any technical and pedagogical challenges. At the same time, students can be taught how to use the vast collection of resources that the Internet provides in a constructive way using problem-based collaborative tasks in which they can develop their critical thinking by justifying the selection of certain resources for a particular purpose. Thus, the learner acquires greater control of the learning process. Future generations of students will also surely provide us with many clues as to how to ensure effective implementation of an ever-growing range of online communication technologies for face-to-face, blended, and distance language learning.

References

Chinnery, G. M. (2008). You've got some GALL: Google-assisted language learning. *Language Learning and Technology, 12*(1), 3–11. Retrieved August 1, 2008, from http://llt.msu.edu/vol12num1/net/default.html

Coverdale-Jones, T. (2000). The use of videoconferencing as a communication tool for language learning: Issues and considerations. *IALL Journal, 32*(1), 27–40.

Gaspari, F. (2007). *The role of online MT in Webpage translation.* Unpublished doctoral dissertation, The University of Manchester, Manchester, England.

Goodwin-Jones, R. (2003). E-books and the tablet PC. *Language Learning and Technology, 7*(1), 4–8. Retrieved August 1, 2008, from http://llt.msu.edu/vol7num1/pdf/emerging.pdf

Handley, Z., & Hamel, M. J. (2005). Establishing a methodology for benchmarking speech synthesis for CALL. *Language Learning and Technology,* 9(3), 99–120. Retrieved August 1, 2008, from http://llt.msu.edu/vol9num3/handley

Hubbard, Paul. (2004, September). Using Google as a tool for writing instruction. Presentation at EuroCALL Conference, Vienna, Austria. Retrieved August 1, 2008, from http://www.stanford.edu/~efs/eurocall04/Eurocall04-Hubbard_files/frame.htm

McCarthy, B. N. (2004). Does online machine translation spell the end of take-home translation assignments? CALL-EJ Online, 6(1). Retrieved August 1, 2008, from http://www.tell.is.ritsumei.ac.jp/callejonline/journal/6–1/mccarthy.html

Neri, A., Cucchiarini, C., & Strik, H. (2003). Automatic speech recognition for second language learning: How and why it actually works. In M. J. Solé, D. Recasens, & J. Romero (Eds.), *Proceedings of the 15th International Congress of Phonetic Sciences* (pp. 1157–1160). Barcelona, Spain: Universitat Autònoma de Barcelona.

Robb, Tom. (2003). Google as a quick n' dirty corpus tool. *TESL Electronic Journal Online.* Retrieved August 1, 2008, from http://www-writing.berkeley.edu/TESL-EJ/ej26/int.html

Sayers, D. (1993). Distance team teaching and computer learning networks. *TESOL Journal* 3(1), 19–23.

Stanley, G. (2006). Podcasting: Audio on the Internet comes of age. *TESL Electronic Journal Online* 9(4). Retrieved August 1, 2008, from http://www-writing.berkeley.edu/TESL-EJ/ej36/int.html

Thorne, S., & Payne, J. (2005). Evolutionary trajectories, Internet-mediated expression, and language education. *CALICO Journal, 22*(3), 371–397.

Digital Natives and Their Self-Rated Electronic Literacy Skills: Empirical Findings From a Survey Study in German Secondary Schools

Carolin Fuchs
Teachers College, Columbia University

Large-scale studies in German secondary schools have provided mixed results regarding the use of technology. On the one hand, the use of technology for teaching foreign languages in German schools is said to have become increasingly widespread. A recent large-scale study by the German Federal Ministry for Education and Research reported that 65% of German secondary schools use the Internet for foreign-language teaching (Krützer & Probst, 2005). On the other hand, only one third of schools in Germany used computers in 2006, compared to an average of 56% of schools in Organisation for Economic Co-operation and Development (OECD) countries (Vereinigung der Bayrischen Wirtschaft e.V., 2008). Additionally, little is known about participants' perspectives on using technology, for example, how students learn how to use technology (see Kern, 2006) and how they rate their proficiency.

This survey study at five German secondary schools explored students' self-rated electronic literacy skills. The findings support previous studies in that there appears to be a gap between theory and praxis (e.g., Fuchs, 2006a; Meskill, Anthony, Hilliker-Vanstrander, Tseng, & You, 2006), that is, a gap between the importance of students' media competence and electronic literacy skills—especially with regard to their professional lives—and the lack of training that students receive in schools. This chapter outlines implications for language-teacher education programs and future research directions.

Background and prior research

Key skills for the Net Generation

Media competence and electronic literacy have long been labeled key skills for today's students (Hamm, 2001) and teachers (Willis, 2001). For instance, it has been well established that the use of technology can promote students' computer and information literacy skills, which may then enhance efficiency and necessary professional skills.

Fuchs, C. (2009). Digital natives and their self-rated electronic literacy skills: Empirical findings from a survey study in German secondary schools. In R. Oxford & J. Oxford, (Eds.), *Second language teaching and learning in the Net Generation* (pp. 31–51). Honolulu: University of Hawai'i, National Foreign Language Resource Center.

In particular, computer-assisted language learning (CALL) educators and researchers have stressed the potential of computer-mediated communication (CMC) and Internet-mediated communication such as telecollaboration for foreign-language learning due to an emphasis on genuine communication, student-centered learning, and the learning of language forms for communicative purposes (Egbert & Hanson-Smith, 2007). Not only can CMC provide unlimited sources of authentic language use and native-speaker and nonnative speaker interaction (Herring, 1996), but CMC can also promote learning contexts for meaningful social interaction among teachers and peers (see Vygotsky, 1978). These learning environments may result in increased motivation (Fuchs, 2001; Lee, 2004; LeLoup & Ponterio, 2003), language fluency (Kern, 1995), pragmatic knowledge (Belz, 2007), and intercultural learning (Belz, 2002; Müller-Hartmann, 1999; Kramsch & Thorne, 2002; O'Dowd, 2003, 2007). Learners can also develop their own voices and agency when interacting with a range of people, and how this can result in a "sense of empowerment" has been demonstrated within the context of a language-learner chat on the Internet (Kramsch, A'Ness, & Lam, 2000, p. 96). Moreover, focus discipline research has shown that CMC can be more beneficial for developing multiliteracies than other content-based instruction, and students need such literacies to succeed beyond the ESL classroom—namely, in academic, social, and professional contexts (Kasper, 2000).

As a result, various initiatives in Germany and in Europe have promoted electronic and media literacy. In 1996, the registered association Schulen ans Netz was founded, and it was the joint goal of the German Federal Ministry for Education and Research and the Deutsche Telekom AG to hook up every school in Germany to the Internet (Schulen ans Netz, n.d.). By 2001, 34,000 schools were connected; however, the association quickly realized that although the technology was now available, the pedagogical competence to use it was not. Consequently, since 2006, a new initiative called "Lifelong learning" has focused on the meaningful use of digital media, not limited to use in schools but transferable to other areas.

Another recent initiative, the European Charter for Media Literacy (2006), has aimed at "rais[ing] public understanding and awareness of media literacy," "advocat[ing] the importance of media literacy in the development of educational, cultural, political, social and economic policy," and "support[ing] the principle that every European citizen of any age should have opportunities, in both formal and informal education."

Nevertheless, a literature review revealed a wide range of views on what electronic and media literacy should encompass. For instance, Shetzer and Warschauer supported the notion of electronic literacy as a framework for interpreting and expressing meaning and the ability to find, organize, and use information (i.e., "information literacy," 2000, p. 173). According to the European Centre for Media Competence (Europäisches Zentrum für Medienkompetenz), media literacy refers primarily to digital media (cf. Aufderheide, n.d.; Considine, 1995) and includes competencies such as reflecting on and evaluating the content of offers and services, dealing with such materials in an effective, creative, and critical way, and actively, responsibly, and consciously dealing with challenges posed by information society (as cited in Hillebrand & Lange, 1996, pp. 35–36). Richards (2000), on the other hand, has argued that electronic literacy is a "*dialogical* process" regardless of the mode and medium of communication between author and audience (p. 73, italics in original). Aside from how differently these key skills have been defined, the next section underlines the urgent need for schools to train students in such key skills.

Classroom reality or the absence of key skills

A recent study attests that schools in Germany use computers less frequently as a tool for learning compared to any other country in the OECD: Roughly one third (31%) of the schools in Germany used computers in 2006, compared to an average of 56% in OECD countries (Vereinigung der Bayrischen Wirtschaft e. V., 2008, pp. 73–74).

Other large-scale survey studies stressed that even though 87% of students considered computer skills important or very important for their professional lives, two thirds of students in German schools rarely worked with computers in class. Computer use was lacking in schools and across the curriculum; that is, computers were primarily used in information technology science as the subject matter for teaching, not as a means for learning or as a cultural tool (IT-Fitness-Studie, 2007). Moreover, another 2007 survey study by the German media competence initiative "Internet-ABC" included 1,248 students, teachers, and parents in Germany and looked at how well learning and teaching with the Internet is put into practice. The authors concluded that the infrastructure at German schools, teacher education, and parent training in information technology had much room for improvement. Additionally, students believed that teachers' media competence could be improved: Only one third of the teachers received the grades "good" (28%) or "very good" (4%) for using computers or the Internet. On average, the teachers' media competence was ranked "satisfactory" from their students (IT-Fitness-Studie, 2007). Moreover, the teaching of "online competence" in schools could also be optimized (Internet-ABC, 2007).

According to the results of a recent study on the future of media-based teaching and learning materials, most teachers expected learning software, the Internet, intranets (in schools), computer-supported projections, CD-ROMs and DVDs, and e-mail to gain increasing importance by the year 2010. They also thought highly of these technologies and media and were hoping for more developed teaching and learning materials and increasing support. However, the study also found that even though teachers were in agreement with these results, this did not necessarily correlate with teachers' willingness to use such technologies. The teachers were primarily concerned with identifying students' individual learning problems, goal-oriented selection and use of the media, checking the reliability and trustworthiness of information, efficient search and research using the computer, competent use of standard software, and critical selection of information (Vollstädt, 2003). None of the teachers' foci appeared to contrast with how electronic literacy has been defined. Yet, there was a gap between theory and practice, that is, between the importance that the teachers assigned to the students' media competence and the teachers' actual implementation of technology in the classroom.

Research in the US has also pointed to a mismatch between theory and praxis. Meskill, Mossop, DiAngelo, and Pasquale (2002) have called for developing and maintaining a particular conceptual frame for the potential role of technologies for language and literacy development. Novice teachers should be educated in thoughtful uses of technologies through a complex process of implementing and reflecting, supported by experienced practitioners. Accordingly, Murray (2000) has urged educators to discuss and adopt technologies into their classrooms only after scrutinizing such technologies critically and from a historic point of view because the outcomes of computer-based literacy are neither unavoidable nor ideologically neutral. She deemed it essential for educators to help shape and create the ideological climate surrounding technology use to avoid others telling them how to use technology.

In light of the key skills expected of the Net Generation and the need for schools to prepare students for their professional lives, the research questions for this exploratory empirical study were as follows:

1. What does the infrastructure look like with regard to students' access and frequency of use of computer technology?
2. How important are students' electronic literacy skills and media competence? Is technology integrated into teaching?
3. How did students learn to use computer technology?
4. How do students rate their electronic literacy skills?

Research design

Participants and demographic context

The participants in this exploratory survey study were 697 students, 30 teachers (of whom 10 taught English as a foreign language, EFL), and 7 administrators at five secondary schools in the southwest of Germany. The state of Baden-Württemberg ranks third in population (10,738,753 on December 31, 2006) and area (35,751,565 km²). A state with very limited natural resources, Baden-Württemberg is one of the technology leaders and most successful regions in Europe. The state is strong in exports and has a high density of research institutions and a high percentage of employees in high-tech industries (Baden-Württemberg Homepage, n.d.).

A brief summary of Germany's three-tier secondary public school system is shown in Table 1. The education system is regulated by the 16 *Bundesländer* (states); hence, there can be vast differences across the country.

Table 1. Germany's three-tier secondary public school system (grades 5–9/10/13*)

Gymnasium	Realschule	Hauptschule
comprehensive/senior secondary school (equivalent to a grammar school in the UK or a lycée in France)	middle school/practical school	general/junior secondary school
grades 5–13**; one-third of students; have to take one language starting in grade 5; can take other languages later (e.g., English, French, Latin, Spanish); English obligatory for all students; final exam (Abitur) prerequisite for matriculation at university	grades 5–10; less than one third of students; have to take one language, English, in grade 5; have the option of taking additional languages later	grades 5–9; less than half of students; have to take one language, English, in grade 5
final English exam comprehensive written test (4–5 hrs) with focus on a piece of classical literature, text comprehension, and production, translation, vocabulary; oral exam (only mandatory when minimum standards not met)**	final English exam text comprehension, translation, production, vocabulary, representing information through tables, diagrams, mind maps; oral exam (not mandatory):* text comprehension, translating sentences from German into English, short dialogue	final English exam reading and listening comprehension, e.g., true/false, matching exercises (approx. 2 hrs); oral exam (not mandatory)**

* In some states in Germany, Gymnasium has recently been reduced to 12 grades (from previously 13 grades).
** The exam was not mandatory during the study but has since been made mandatory.

The exit mechanism for EFL shows an emphasis on the grammar-translation method and includes oral exams that were not mandatory at the point of the study. This conflicts with the call for a more communicative curriculum and the integration of CMC.

Participant information

The main emphasis of this paper is on the students as a representative sample of digital natives (or the Net Generation) for this particular region in Baden-Württemberg; however, results from the other participants are also mentioned whenever necessary.

Table 2. **Students**

total number of students	age 10–13	age 14+
678	338	340
(originally 697)	(338)	(359)

A total of 697 students over the age of 10 participated, out of which 678 students were divided into two age groups: 10–13 and 14 or older. All students could be categorized as part of the first generation of digital natives. The category of digital natives has been broadly defined as "anyone under 40" (Rüschoff, 2007) or more precisely, as K–college (Prensky, 2001).

Methodology

Data collection

The researcher (and author) did not limit her investigation to language classes because she did not want to exclude volunteering teachers simply because they were not language teachers. Additionally, to obtain information from a representative student sample, she could not include only language teachers and their classes.

The student survey consisted of three parts and 12 items for students (see Appendix), including four-level Likert, multiple-choice, and open-ended questions. The reason for not using a five-level Likert scale was to get a tendency.

The first part of the survey elicited personal and professional background information on the participants' gender, age, country/state of birth, grade, parents' professions, and whether the student had used computers in elementary school and for what purposes. The second part included questions on the students' computer and Internet skills, access, and use, that is, whether they had computer/Internet access at home, how much time they spend at the computer, and how they had learned how to use computers. The students were also asked in which subjects they had used computer technologies and/or the Internet in schools, the areas in which they felt that the computer in class had primarily helped them, and why they did or did not like using computers in class. Finally, the students were asked what Internet sites they consulted to obtain information for their homework (and to write down the URLs or briefly describe the sites and why they liked them). The questionnaires for the teachers and administrators were similar except that they also contained questions on values, challenges, and visions with regard to using technology for teaching.

When translating the original questionnaire into German, the main issue the researcher encountered was the term "electronic literacy" because the term has not been used in the German literature, nor does it translate. Instead, the terms "computer skills," "media competence," and "media literacy" have been used. Hence, the researcher decided to use "media competence" because it appeared to have been the most widely used term in Germany.

Prior to administrating the questionnaires in December 2005, the researcher tested the instrument with a group of language professionals and undergraduate research assistants for content, clarity, and presentation. This testing procedure contributed to face validity and content validity of the study instrument (e.g., Brown, 2001); however, the instrument was not separately tested for reliability. Next, the researcher e-mailed teachers and principals at the different kinds of schools in Germany (Hauptschule, Realschule, Gymnasium), explaining the purpose of the study and asking if they were interested in participating. After all of the participants had completed an informed consent form, the questionnaires were mailed to the contact person at each participating school, who then distributed the questionnaires to the teachers and their respective classes. The researcher chose not to administer the questionnaires online because she anticipated a lower return rate compared to the in-class administration of the paper-and-pencil versions. The researcher also did not want to assume that all of the participants had access to computers to fill out web-based questionnaires. Moreover, if the participants did not have flat-rate Internet service, they would have been charged by the minute for filling out the questionnaire online.

Data analysis

To compare the younger students (338 10- to 13-year-olds) to an equal number of older students (340 14+-year-olds), some participants' data had to be excluded from the analysis (which primarily involved older Gymnasium children). Additionally, the number of participants varied for every question because some students only partially answered the questionnaire. The main focus of this study was on the age groups. All results were controlled for by school type; however, differences between school types turned out to be marginal compared to those between age groups. The familywise error rate could be inflated, but this is not an issue for this study because it is exploratory and does not seek generalizability of the results to a wider population. Separate chi-squares for the 10- to 13-year-olds and the 14+-year-olds were conducted to determine whether there were differences among school types (separately for each age group). The age groups were put together into the same factorial ANOVAs. Full tables, graphs, and statistical analyses are available from the author upon request.

For the teacher and administrator surveys, simple tallies were conducted for the Likert and multiple-choice items. For the open-ended questions, codes and categories were developed as they emerged from the data without trying to force them into categories already outlined in the existing literature to avoid impeding the development of the researcher's own categories. Open coding was done line-by-line or applied to sentences, paragraphs, or entire answers and then categorized by grouping the codes around phenomena in the data that were related to the research questions. Next, these categories were linked to abstract codes either taken from the literature (i.e., constructed codes) or from the participants, that is, *in vivo* codes (Strauss & Corbin, 1998). For instance, "to prepare students for their professional lives" emerged as one category under "other" when teachers were asked how they considered students' media competence to be important.

Results

What does the infrastructure look like with regard to students' access and frequency of use of computer technology?

Students' technology access

All 338 10- to 13-year-olds and 340 14+-year-olds in the three school types answered "yes" to the question of whether they had Internet access with or without computers.

Frequency of use of the computer/Internet

The average hours per day the students estimated they spent at the computer/on the Internet (N=626) is shown in Table 3.

Table 3. **Response to the query, "I spend X hours per day at the computer"**

school type	age group	mean	std deviation	n
Gymnasium	10–13	1.117	1.195	46
	14+	1.526	1.472	65
Hauptschule	10–13	0.932	1.051	132
	14+	1.510	1.306	81
Realschule	10–13	0.932	0.808	146
	14+	1.647	1.495	156

Overall, the students (N=626) indicated that they spent an average of 1.26 hours per day at the computer, with the 10- to 13-year-olds estimating their use at 0.96 hours and the 14+-year-olds, 1.58 hours. Here, we have a main and highly significant effect for age group only: $F(1, 620)=41.2$, $p > .001$, which means that the children older than 14 tended to spend more hours per day on the Internet. This seemed to be independent of the type of school they were attending.

How important are students' electronic literacy skills and media competence? Is technology integrated into teaching?

Importance of students' media competence

Of the 30 all-subject teachers, 64% considered students' media competence "very important," and 10% considered students' media competence "important." In addition, 17% thought that media competence was important "to prepare students for their professional lives," as a "long-lasting means for learning," and to help students decide which media use would be "meaningful" for them.

Use of technology in teaching

Of the 30 all-subject teachers, 60% stated that they were currently using technology for teaching, 6.7% did not use technology, 6.7% rarely used technology, and 26.6% did not provide an answer. Of these teachers, 93% had spent an average of 0.75 hours per week in the computer room (SD=0.84), and 2 teachers did not reply. Of the 10 EFL teachers, 50% had used computers in their teaching, but none had used any form of CMC. Additionally, the integration of technology into teaching did not seem to be consistent across the curriculum but was done by individual teachers only.

Most of the teachers considered technical limitations such as the lack of computers a challenge (i.e., too few computers, computers that were not usable, and a computer room that was too small). Some teachers also mentioned that hardware issues were a challenge. For example, they complained that the small screens only allowed a few students to be at computers at the same time.

Furthermore, the data showed that the EFL teachers primarily used commercial software for English-language teaching, such as English Tutor, Cornelsen G2000, Klett Ensemble, and Alfons. The teachers expressed concerns with regard to Internet use because they thought that students could be overwhelmed by the data and information and that students could easily access violent or pornographic websites.

How did students learn to use computer technology?

The majority of the students in both age groups did not use computers in elementary school, as illustrated in Table 4.

Table 4. Response to the query, "Did you use computers in elementary school?"

10–13-year-olds only

school type	no	yes	err	total
Gymnasium	49	9	0	58
Hauptschule	90	50	1	141
Realschule	108	49	0	157

14+-year-olds only

school type	no	yes	err	total
Gymnasium	61	11	0	72
Hauptschule	62	29	0	91
Realschule	132	44	0	176

When asked how they had learned how to use computers, the majority of the 10- to 13-year-olds (n=354) and the 14+-year-olds (n = 340) indicated "by [themselves]," as shown in Table 5. This result is regardless of the school attended. Students ranked "through friends and/or acquaintances" second and "at school" or "other" third.

Table 5. Response to the query, "I have learned how to use computers through..."

10–13-year-olds only

school type	at school	by myself	other	friends/ acquaintances	total
Gymnasium	4	35	9	10	58
Hauptschule	23	52	20	46	141
Realschule	20	84	25	26	155

14+-year-olds only

school type	at school	by myself	other	friends/ acquaintances	total
Gymnasium	1	56	1	15	73
Hauptschule	12	54	4	21	91
Realschule	14	124	2	36	176

How do students rate their electronic literacy skills?

Students' self-rated abilities in software and desktop applications

Software and desktop applications do not require the use of the Internet (see Table 6). The students (N=689) rated their abilities regarding the following items on a 4-point Likert scale (from 1=insufficient to 4=very good): word processing, spreadsheets, presentation software, databases, graphic design programs, multimedia software, and games.

Table 6. Self-reported ability in software and desktop applications; 1=insufficient, 2=satisfactory, 3=good, 4=very good

school type	age group	mean	standard deviation	n
Gymnasium	10–13	2.568	0.730	58
	14+	2.282	0.585	73
Hauptschule	10–13	2.573	0.569	141
	14+	2.538	0.554	90
Realschule	10–13	2.495	0.609	156
	14+	2.480	0.606	171

The mean score of 2.538 for the 10- to 13-year-olds was slightly higher than the mean score for the 14+-year-olds of 2.452. There was only a marginal interaction between school type and age group, but there was a main significant effect for age group. There was a main effect for age group (with a .05 alpha level): $F(1, 683)=5.12$, $p < .025$, and a marginal interaction between school type and age group: $F(2, 683)=2.51$, $p=.082$. The main effect for age group suggests that the 14+-year olds were less confident in software/desktop applications. However, even though the interaction was only marginal, the main effect for age was actually due to children in the Gymnasium only who were less confident in software/desktop applications.

Students' self-rated abilities in Internet applications

Internet applications require using the Internet (see Table 7). The students (N=685) rated their ability regarding the following: web browsers, search engines, web-design software, information searches, downloading programs, shopping, and online banking.

Table 7. Self-reported ability in internet applications; 1=insufficient, 2=satisfactory, 3=good, 4=very good

school type	age group	mean	standard deviation	n
Gymnasium	10–13	2.471	0.730	56
	14+	2.678	0.615	73
Hauptschule	10–13	2.636	0.728	140
	14+	2.560	0.625	91
Realschule	10–13	2.581	0.724	154
	14+	2.668	0.719	171

The mean score of 2.585 for the 10- to 13-year-olds was slightly lower than the mean score of 2.640 for the 14+-year-olds. There were no main effects or interactions.

Students' self-rated abilities in CMC

CMC encompasses both synchronous and asynchronous means of communication (see Table 8). The reason CMC was included separately and not as one of the Internet applications was because of the special focus on computer- and Internet-mediated communication in this study, given the immense potential of CMC for language teaching and learning (see Fuchs, 2006b). The students (N=680) rated their abilities regarding the following: e-mail, chat, instant messaging (IM), multiuser object-oriented/multiuser dimension (MOO/MUD) environments, text messaging (SMS), Skype, and discussion forums.

Table 8. Self-reported ability in computer-mediated communication; 1=insufficient, 2=satisfactory, 3=good, 4=very good

school type	age group	mean	standard deviation	*n*
Gymnasium	10–13	2.149	0.812	56
	14+	2.379	0.589	73
Hauptschule	10–13	2.249	0.723	138
	14+	2.190	0.695	90
Realschule	10–13	2.227	0.766	153
	14+	2.387	0.725	170

The mean score for the 10- to 13-year-olds of 2.27656 was slightly lower than the mean score for the 14+-year-olds of 2.33221. There was only a marginal main effect for age group: $F(1, 674)=3.36$, $p=.067$. The older children in Gymnasium and Realschule appeared more confident in CMC, whereas age made no difference in the Hauptschule.

Discussion

Students' technology access and frequency of use

With regard to computer and Internet access, all students in both age groups (N=678) indicated that they had Internet access with or without computers. This is in line with a recent study in Germany that found that 95% of 1,204 participants between 12 and 19 years of age had Internet access in their homes (*Medienpädagogischer Forschungsverband Südwest* [*MPFS*], 2007). According to the MPFS study, in the year 2005, 84% of 12- to 19-year-old students in the southwest of Germany indicated that they used the computer or the Internet daily or several times a week. Of 6- to 13-year-olds, 78% used computers, and 52% used the Internet at least sometimes. Furthermore, in 2006, using computers was the favorite pastime for 22% of 1,203 6- to 13-year-olds (*MPFS*, 2007). Another large-scale study by the German media competence initiative Internet-ABC found that the Internet had been used in most German schools. Of the students, 45% indicated that they used the Internet once a week in school, primarily to "search for information for class" (88%). Moreover, almost 43% stated that they liked searching for information online much better than looking up answers in their textbooks (Internet-ABC, 2007).

In the present study, the 10- to 13-year-old students estimated their use at 0.96 hours per day and the 14+-year-old students, at 1.58 hours per day. The children older than 14 tended to spend more hours per day at the computer or on the Internet regardless of the type of school they were attending. This could potentially be due to the increased workload in higher grades, which may require students to spend more time at the computer and/or online. Additionally, almost all of the teachers had access to computers with Internet access at their school, and 83.3% were able to use computers with Internet access for their teaching. These findings support another survey study in which only 18% of interviewees stated that they did not have the technical prerequisites to provide Internet access in class (Internet-ABC, 2007).

Unsurprisingly, given the growing use of the Internet in German schools, almost all of the participants in the present study indicated that they had access to computers and the Internet. Yet, systematic integration of technology into (language) teaching appears to be lacking (cf. Krützer & Probst, 2005). In this study, the integration of technology into teaching did not seem to be consistent across the curriculum but was carried out by individual teachers only. This supports the results of the IT-Fitness-Studie (2007) which also attests a lack of computer use in schools and across the curriculum. The IT-Fitness-Studie also found that two thirds of students in German schools hardly worked with computers in class, 28% did not use computers at all in class, and 36% of students used computers less than two hours per week in class. Computers were primarily used in IT science, that is, as the subject matter for teaching, not as a means for learning or as a cultural tool. Only in the subject "IT science" were computers "frequently" used (68%) compared to other subjects such as economics (20%), physics (19%), or math (18%). In language teaching, computers were used even less frequently (2007). Similar results have been documented in other studies. For example, in the Internet-ABC study, only 37% of parents indicated that their children's schools had a conceptual framework for using media and that there were parent-teacher meetings regarding the use of Internet technology. Roughly 50% of the parents indicated that they did not know how the Internet was used in their children's schools; 42% of the parents assumed that their children conducted online searches, and 44% stated that their children used their computers at home primarily to conduct online searches for school (Internet-ABC, 2007).

Importance of students' media competence and use of technology in teaching

More than half of all of the teachers considered students' media competence "very important" and thought that media competence was important for preparing students for their professional lives and as a "long-lasting means for learning." The teachers' perspectives appear to match those of students in the IT-Fitness-Studie, which found that 87% of students considered computer skills important or very important for their professional lives (2007). Yet, these results do not seem to match with how the teachers actually used technology in their teaching. For instance, two of the goals of media competence were to teach the "ability to use media as a long-lasting means for learning" and "to prepare students for their professional lives"; however, because only a few more than half of the all-subject teachers (60%) and only half of the EFL teachers (50%) used technology in their teaching, whether students are actually taught these skills in school remains questionable. The author agrees with the authors of the IT-Fitness-Studie that the goal should be to teach computer skills in schools systematically across the curriculum and to support teacher education and professional development.

The fact that the teachers expressed concerns that students could be overwhelmed by data and information and that students could easily access violent or pornographic websites confirms the results of the Internet-ABC study (2007), namely, that many websites were considered incomprehensible (30%), not user-friendly (25%), or contained violence or pornography (27%). It would be interesting to investigate how the filtering systems in those schools work, that is, learning what websites can be accessed by whom.

Teachers expressed that technical limitations such as hardware (e.g., small computer screens) and the lack of computers were challenges. Although other large-scale studies in the same geographical area have shown similar findings (*MPFS*, 2007), these results seem surprising given the fact that Baden-Württemberg is one of the wealthiest states in Germany, with unemployment at 4.9%, compared to an overall unemployment rate in Germany of 8.4% at the point of the study (Bundesagentur für Arbeit, 2007).

How students learned to use computer technology

Not even half of the 10- to 13-year-olds or the 14+-year-olds used computers in elementary school. Along the same lines, the majority of the students in both age groups indicated that they had learned how to use computers by themselves, regardless of which school they attended. These results support those of other recent survey studies that found that 58% of students had learned how to use computers by teaching themselves (IT-Fitness-Studie, 2007) and that almost half of the children indicated that they were self-taught with regard to acquiring the essential "online competence," and only one fourth of students stated they were taught in class (self-taught, 44%; taught through teachers, 26%; taught through parents, 25%; taught through others such as friends or magazines, 5%; Internet-ABC, 2007).

Students' self-rated electronic literacy skills

With regard to the students' self-rated abilities in software/desktop applications, there was only a marginal relationship between school type and age group but a main significant effect for age group. The latter suggests that the 14+-year-olds were less confident in software/desktop applications. Yet, this main effect may have been due to a higher-order interaction; that is, even though the interaction was only marginal, the main effect for age was actually caused by children in the Gymnasium only who were less confident in software/desktop applications. Strikingly, the students rated their abilities rather low (2.49641); that is, the mean score was between "satisfactory" and "good." The mean score of the 10- to 13-year-olds was slightly higher than that of the 14+-year-olds. According to the descriptive statistics, the students also self-rated their abilities to use Internet applications rather low (2.61238) and their abilities to use CMC barely above "satisfactory" (2.27656). The older children in Gymnasium and Realschule appeared more confident in CMC, whereas there was no age difference in the Hauptschule. Overall, these results are startling considering that all of the students used the computer/Internet on a regular basis and that they could all be considered digital natives according to Prensky (2001). By the same token, the fact that participants gave themselves low scores for specific applications such as MOO/MUD environments does not necessarily mean that they were not familiar with those applications but might mean that they were unfamiliar with this terminology.

Conclusion and recommendations

Although exploratory in nature, the findings presented here clearly point to a lack of integration of technology into teaching and into language teaching in particular. The gap between the importance of using technology and adequately preparing students for their professional lives seems particularly striking in a region such as Baden-Württemberg, one of the leading high-tech regions in Europe. Follow-up research should include interviews with students, teachers, administrators, and principals to gain further insight into this phenomenon.

In brief, few teachers used technology in (language) teaching, although they highly ranked the importance of media competence. Of the EFL teachers, 50% used technology, and 0% used any form of CMC. This result is surprising against the backdrop of the growing body of research on CMC and telecollaboration and the potential benefits for language study and intercultural learning and points to an urgent need to connect theory and practice in teacher education programs. More specifically, teacher educators should support online or blended-learning formats and model the implementation of technology in their seminar formats. In doing so, teacher educators will model "innovative uses of technology" (Willis, 2001, p. 309; see also Fuchs, 2006b) and provide their student teachers with ample opportunities for experiential learning. It is essential to promote technology-based teaching and learning—and computer-mediated collaboration in particular—by focusing on *communities* as the overarching theme of the National Educational Standards (Magnan, 2007; see also Lave & Wenger, 1991). Conducting longitudinal follow-up case studies can also help us find out if and how student teachers apply their newly acquired knowledge about using technology in their classroom teaching. These insights can then feed back into teacher education programs.

Moreover, based on the findings of this study, the potential of the computer as a *means for communication* has not been acknowledged yet (cf. Egbert & Hanson-Smith, 2007). This indicates that technology has been used without making connections to concepts such as writing for an authentic audience, meaningful communication, or intercultural learning. Yet, the idea that computer technology, and CMC in particular, can benefit language study seems obvious, especially in an EFL context such as in Germany (see Egbert & Hanson-Smith, 2008). The students in this study do not seem to be stereotypical of the digital native category because even though they all have access to computer technology, they do not seem to share a common global culture defined by certain attributes and experiences related to how they interact with information technologies and one another (cf. Digital Natives Project, n.d.); despite this, they likely will be increasingly dealing with computer technology, especially with freely available Web 2.0 tools. Social networking tools (e.g., Facebook, Myspace) have become increasingly popular over the last few years even with digital immigrants, and an end is not yet in sight. Hence, teachers need to be encouraged to integrate blogs, wikis, or IM/chats into their teaching. Finally, CMC and Internet-based collaboration can promote students' key skills such as electronic literacy and media competence, as well as foster language fluency or hone pragmatic skills through subsequent transcript analysis (e.g., Belz, 2007).

Acknowledgements

First and foremost, I thank all of the students, teachers, and administrators for their kind support and participation in this survey. I also thank Pat Bolger and Stefan Fuchs for helping with the quantitative analyses and Rick Kern, John Chipman, Carlton Fong, Chris Skok, and Adam Myers for helping pilot the questionnaires and for assisting with data entry.

References

Aufderheide, P. (n.d.). *General principles in media literacy*. Retrieved April 17, 2008, from http://www.newsreel.org/articles/aufderhe.htm

Baden-Württemberg Homepage. (n.d.). Retrieved April 17, 2008, from http://www.badenwuerttemberg.de/

Belz, J. A. (2002). Social dimensions of telecollaborative foreign language study. *Language Learning & Technology*, 6(1), 60–81.

Belz, J. A. (2007). The role of computer mediation in the instruction and development of L2 pragmatic competence. *Annual Review of Applied Linguistics, 27*, 45–75.

Brown, J. D. (2001). *Using surveys in language programs*. Cambridge, England: Cambridge University Press.

Bundesagenture für Arbeit. *Press release 061 of September 27, 2007*. Retrieved September 28, 2007, from http://www.arbeitsagentur.de/nn_27030/zentraler-Content/Pressemeldungen/2007/Presse–07–061.html

Considine, D. (1995). An introduction to media literacy: The what, why and how to's. *The Journal of Media Literacy, 41*(2). Retrieved April 17, 2008, from http://www.ced.appstate.edu/departments/ci/programs/edmedia/medialit/article.html

Digital Natives Project. (n.d.). Retrieved April 17, 2008, from http://www.digitalnative.org/Main_Page

Egbert, J., & Hanson-Smith, E. (Eds.). (2007). *CALL environments: Research, practice, and critical issues* (2nd ed.). Alexandria, VA: TESOL.

European Charter for Media Literacy. (2006). Retrieved April 17, 2008, from http://www.euromedialiteracy.eu/

Fuchs, C. (2001). Munich - Monterey online: Integrating email and chat to foster reading and writing skills in a distance learning course. In R. D. Y. Saito-Abbott, T. F. Abbott, & P. Kennedy (Eds.), *Digital Stream 2000: Emerging technologies in teaching languages and cultures* (pp. 147–165). San Diego, CA: Language Acquisition Resource Center.

Fuchs, C. (2006a). Exploring German pre-service teachers' electronic and professional literacies. *ReCALL, 18*, 174–192.

Fuchs, C. (2006b). *Computer-mediated negotiation across borders: German-American collaboration in language teacher education.* Frankfurt, Germany: Peter Lang Europäischer Verlag der Wissenschaften.

Hamm, I. (2001). *Medienkompetenz: Wirtschaft, Wissen, Wandel* [Media competence: Research, knowledge, change]. Gütersloh, Germany: Verlag Bertelsmann Stiftung.

Herring, S. C. (1996). *Computer-mediated communication: Linguistic, social and cross-cultural perspectives.* Amsterdam: Benjamins.

Hillebrand, A., & Lange, B. P. (1996). Medienkompetenz als gesellschaftliche Aufgabe der Zukunft [Media competence as the future task for society]. In A. Rein (Ed.), *Medienkompetenz als Schlüsselbegriff* [Media competence as key competence] (pp. 35–36). Bad Heilbrunn, Germany: Klinkhardt.

Internet-ABC c/o Geschäftsstelle Landesanstalt für Medien NRW. *Schule 2.0 noch nicht in Sicht—Ergebnisse des Internet-ABC-Meinungsbarometers zum Thema "Internet in der Schule"* [Internet-ABC c/o Branch office of the Regional Office for Media in the State Northrhine-Westphalia. Schools 2.0 not yet in sight—Results from the Internet-ABC Study on the topic "Internet in schools."]. Press release of November 20, 2007. Retrieved January 10, 2008, from http://bildungsklick.de/pm/56792/schule–20-noch-nicht-in-sicht/

IT-Fitness-Studie: zu wenig Computereinsatz an Schulen [IT Fitness Study: Too little computer use in schools]. [Press release]. (2007, November 20). Retrieved January 10, 2008, from http://www.it-fitness.de/Aktuelles/News/computereinsatz_schulen.aspx

Kasper, L. (2000). New technologies, new literacies: Focus discipline research and ESL learning communities. *Language Learning & Technology, 4*(2), 105–128.

Kern, R. G. (1995). Restructuring classroom interaction with networked computers: Effects on quantity and characteristics of language production. *The Modern Language Journal, 79*, 457–476.

Kern, R. G. (2006). Perspectives on technology in learning and teaching languages. *TESOL Quarterly, 40*, 183–210.

Kramsch, C., A'Ness, F., & Lam, W. S. E. (2000). Authenticity and authorship in the computer-mediated acquisition of L2 literacy. *Language Learning & Technology, 4*(2), 78–104.

Kramsch, C., & Thorne, S. L. (2002). Foreign language learning as global communicative practice. In D. Block & D. Cameron (Eds.), *Globalization and language teaching* (pp. 83–100). London: Routledge.

Krützer, B., & Probst, H. (2005). *IT-Ausstattung der allgemein bildenden und berufsbildenden Schulen in Deutschland* [IT Equipment of the general-education and vocational schools in Germany]. Berlin, Germany: Bundesministerium für Bildung und Forschung.

Lave, J., & Wenger, E. (1991). *Situated learning: Legitimate peripheral participation*. Cambridge, England: Cambridge University Press.

Lee, L. (2004). Learners' perspectives on networked collaborative interaction with native speakers of Spanish in the US. *Language Learning & Technology*, 8(1), 83–100.

LeLoup, J. W., & Ponterio, R. (2003). *Second language acquisition and technology: A review of the research*. Washington, DC: Center for Applied Linguistics. Retrieved February 15, 2008, from http://www.cal.org/resources/digest/0311leloup.html

Magnan, S. (2007, February). *From National Educational Standards to Language Use*. Paper presented at the Berkeley Language Center Spring 2007 Lecture Series, Berkeley, CA.

Medienpädogogischer Forschungsverband Südwest: *Medienbeschäftigung* [Mediapedagogical Research Association Southwest: Media use]. (2007). Retrieved January 29, 2008, from http://www.mpfs.de/index.php?id=11

Meskill, C., Anthony, N., Hilliker-Vanstrander, S., Tseng, C.-H., & You, J. (2006). CALL: A survey of K–12 ESOL teacher uses and preferences. *TESOL Quarterly*, *40*, 439–451.

Meskill, C., Mossop, J., DiAngelo, S., & Pasquale, R. K. (2002). Expert and novice teachers talking technology: Precepts, concepts, and misconcepts. *Language Learning & Technology*, 6(3), 46–57.

Müller-Hartmann, A. (1999). Die Integration der neuen Medien in den schulischen Fremdsprachenunterricht: Interkulturelles Lernen und die Folgen in E-Mail-Projekten [The integration of new media into schools' foreign language teaching: Intercultural learning in and consequences of email projects]. *Fremdsprachen lehren und lernen*, *28*, 58–79.

Murray, D. (2000). Changing technologies, changing literacy communities? *Language Learning & Technology*, 4(2), 43–58.

O'Dowd, R. (2003). Understanding the "other side:" Intercultural learning in a Spanish-English e-mail exchange. *Language Learning & Technology*, 7(2), 118–144.

O'Dowd, R. (Ed.). (2007). *Online intercultural exchange*. Clevedon, England: Multilingual Matters.

Prensky, M. (2001). Digital natives, digital immigrants. Retrieved February 25, 2009, from http://www.marcprensky.com/writing/Prensky%20-%20Digital%20Natives,%20Digital%20Immigrants%20-%20Part1.pdf

Richards, C. (2000). Hypermedia, Internet communication, and the challenge of redefining literacy in the electronic age. *Language Learning & Technology*, 4(2), 59–77.

Rüschoff, B. (2007, September). Keynote presented at EUROCALL, Coleraine, Northern Ireland.

Schulen ans Netz e. V. (n.d.). Schulen ans Netz e. V. Retrieved April 17, 2008, from http://www.schulen-ans-netz.de/

Shetzer, H., & Warschauer, M. (2000). An electronic literacy approach to network-based language teaching. In M. Warschauer & R. Kern (Eds.), *Network-based language teaching: Concepts and practice* (pp. 171–185). Cambridge, England: Cambridge University Press.

Strauss, A., & Corbin, J. (1998). *Basics of qualitative research* (2nd ed.). London: Sage Publications Ltd.

Vereinigung der Bayrischen Wirtschaft e.V. (Eds.). (2008). *Bildungsrisiken und -chancen im Globalisierungsprozess. Jahresgutachten 2008* [Educational risks and opportunities within the process of globalization. Annual Report 2008]. Wiesbaden, Germany: Verlag für Sozialwissenschaften, GWV Fachverlage GmbH. Retrieved March 6, 2008, from http://www.aktionsrat-bildung.de/fileadmin/Dokumente/Aktionsrat_Bildung_Jahresgutachten_2008.pdf

Vollstädt, W. (2003). Ergebnisse einer Delphi-Studie der Cornelsen-Stiftung Lehren und Lernen [Results of a Delphy study by the Cornelsen Foundation Teaching and Learning]. In W. Vollstädt (Ed.), *Zur Zukunft der Lehr- und Lernmedien in der Schule. Eine Delphi-Studie in der Diskussion* [Results of a Delphy study by the Cornelsen Foundation Teaching and Learning] (pp. 39–84). Opladen, Germany: Leske & Budrich.

Vygotsky, L. S. (1978). *Mind in society*. Cambridge, England: Harvard University Press.

Willis, J. (2001). Foundational assumptions for information technology and teacher education. *Contemporary Issues in Technology and Teacher Education, 1*(3), 305–320.

Appendix: Questionnaire for students[1]

The purpose of this questionnaire is to obtain data on computer experience, technology access and use, and electronic literacy in the three types of state schools in Germany (Hauptschule, Realschule, Gymnasium).

Please answer all the questions on pages 1–5 after you have read and signed the permission letter. All data will remain anonymous and will only be used for research purposes. Please contact your teacher or me at the address below in case of any questions. Please use a pen. You may use the reverse side if you need more space.

Thank you very much for your cooperation! ☺ Carolin Fuchs

1. Personal information

Age: ______________________________

Country/state of birth: ______________________________

Grade: ______________________________

My father's profession: ______________________________

My mother's profession: ______________________________

1.1. Where did you go to elementary school, and what is the name of the school?

1.2. Did you use computers in elementary school? Please mark.

___ Yes

___ No

1.3. If you marked "No" in question 1.2., please continue on to the next question. If you marked "Yes," please explain briefly for what you were using the computer in school.

2. Computer skills and usage

2.1. Please mark all that apply.

___ I can type fast.

___ I can type somewhat fast.

___ I type slowly.

___ I prefer writing texts without the computer.

___ I have my own computer (or notebook) at home, but **no Internet** access.

___ I have my own computer (or notebook) **with Internet** access at home.

___ My parents have a computer at home, but **no Internet** access.

___ My parents have a computer **with Internet** access at home.

___ I have access to a computer at my school, but no Internet access.

___ I have access to a computer with Internet access at school.

___ I use my notebook to go on the Internet at my school.

1 This is the English translation of the student questionnaire, which was given to participants in its German original. In my translations, I deliberately avoided idiomatic expressions to reflect the German originals as closely as possible.

___ I have **no access** to computers (or notebooks).

2.2. Please fill a number into each gap.

I spend

___ hours **per day** at the computer.

___ hours **per week** at the computer.

I spend

___ hours **per day** on the Internet.

___ hours **per week** on the Internet.

I pay _____ euros per month for Internet access **at home.**

2.3. How do you rate your skills with regard to the following computer applications and Internet services? Please fill in the appropriate numbers on a scale from 1 (insufficient) to 4 (very good).

1=insufficient 2=satisfactory 3=good 4=very good

___ Word processing (e.g., Word)

___ Spreadsheets (e.g., Excel)

___ E-mail programs (e.g., Outlook)

___ Chat (e.g., ICQ)

___ Instant messengers (e.g., MSN, AIM, Yahoo)

___ MOO/MUD (multiuser object-oriented/multiuser dimension) environments

___ SMS

___ Web browsers (e.g., Internet Explorer)

___ Search engines (e.g., Google)

___ Presentation software (e.g., PowerPoint)

___ Databases (e.g., Access)

___ Graphic design programs (e.g., Photoshop)

___ Multimedia software (e.g., Macromedia Director, Mediator)

___ Web-design software (e.g., Netscape Composer, FrontPage, Dreamweaver)

___ Information search on the Internet

___ Skype

___ Discussion forums

___ Downloading programs

___ Shopping (e.g., Bücher, CDs)

___ Online banking

___ Games

2.4. How do you communicate with your friends? Please mark all that apply.

Talking on the telephone (or cell phone)

___ Several times a day

___ 1x per day

___ 1x per week

___ 1x per month

___ Never

SMS—text messages

___ Several times per day

___ 1x per day

___ 1x per week

___ 1x per month

___ Never

E-mail

___ Several times per day

___ 1x per day

___ 1x per week

___ 1x per month

___ Never

Chat (ICQ)

___ Several times per day

___ 1x per day

___ 1x per week

___ 1x per month

___ Never

Discussion forums

___ Several times per day

___ 1x per day

___ 1x per week

___ 1x per month

___ Never

Instant messengers (e.g., MSN, AIM, Yahoo)

___ Several times per day

___ 1x per day

___ 1x per week

___ 1x per month

___ Never

MOO environments

___ Several times per day

___ 1x per day

___ 1x per week

___ 1x per month

___ Never

MUD environments

___ Several times per day

___ 1x per day

___ 1x per week

___ 1x per month

___ Never

Skype

___ Several times per day

___ 1x per day

___ 1x per week

___ 1x per month

___ Never

2.5. I have learned how to use computers in the following ways. Please mark all that apply.

___ By myself

___ Through friends/acquaintances

___ At school

___ At a job

___ Other: ____

2.6. At school, we have used computer technologies and/or the Internet for the following subjects. Please indicate in key words **what** you have used the computer for if applicable.

____

____

____

2.7. I feel that the computer in class has primarily helped me with my studies in the following areas (see question 2.6.). Please indicate in key words **why you liked** the computer in class or **why** you did **not** like it if applicable.

___

___

___

2.8. When I need information for my homework, I go to the following Internet sites. Please write down the URL if you know it or briefly describe the site and **why** you like it if applicable.

___

___

___

Hybridizing the Curriculum: Needs, Benefits, Challenges, and Attitudes

Senta Goertler
Michigan State University

With increasing college enrollments (National Center for Educational Statistics, 2007) particularly in foreign languages (Furman, Goldberg, & Lusin, 2007) and a predicted additional increase in demand for foreign-language skills due to the National Security Language Initiative, we can expect an increased demand for classes that use both online and face-to-face meetings (hybrid or blended) and fully online foreign-language instruction. As research has found, hybrid courses can increase the number of enrolled students while decreasing class sizes and keeping costs consistent or even lowering them (Sanders, 2005).

However, institutions, teachers, and students may not have the necessary skills (Barette, 2001; Kessler, 2006; Winke & Goertler, 2008), resources (Chambers & Bax, 2006; Goertler & Winke, 2008) and favorable attitudes (Blake, 2001) to make implementation possible. College students today are often assumed to have the necessary skills to be in hybrid courses and to welcome such courses because they are digital natives. Yet, due to the digital divide, they may not be digital natives, and furthermore, even if they are, that does not equal a desire to learn languages in a hybrid format.

This chapter reviews the demands of the educational market today, research on students' computer and information literacy, and research on hybrid foreign-language instruction and then discusses the results from a survey-based study on students' readiness for hybrid instruction.

Demands of the educational market

The National Center for Education Statistics (2007) predicted that university enrollment will rise between 14 and 19% from 2004 to 2016. This will most likely also result in increased demand for foreign-language courses. In the past, language course enrollments increased from 608,740 in 1960 to 1,522,770 in 2006. All languages, except for biblical Hebrew, increased in enrollment numbers (Furman, Goldberg, & Lusin, 2007). The number of students enrolled in any language course is clearly increasing, with many of the courses

Goertler S. (2009). Hybridizing the curriculum: Needs, benefits, challenges, and attitudes. In R. Oxford & J. Oxford, (Eds.), *Second language teaching and learning in the Net Generation* (pp. 53–64). Honolulu: University of Hawai'i, National Foreign Language Resource Center.

filled to capacity (Kraemer, 2008a; Sanders, 2005), and recent investigations into foreign-language class sizes at public institutions in the Midwest found larger-than-ideal class sizes of 20–30 students (Goertler & Winke, 2008; Kraemer, 2008b). Therefore, to be able to adhere to the ideal class-size standards of 15–20 pupils (Association of Departments of Foreign Languages, 1993), we need to consider alternative delivery options.

Students' computer and information literacy

An examination of research into computer-assisted language learning (CALL) reveals that students are often assumed to have good computer skills. Yet, frustrations with technology often is listed as one of the challenges in the implementation of technology-enhanced, hybrid, and online courses (e.g., Chenoweth, Ushida, & Murday, 2006).

In the field of education, there has been much talk about digital natives, digital immigrants, and the digital divide. Many of today's college students are considered "digital natives," a term coined by Prensky (2001), which refers to a "native speaker of technology, fluent in the digital language of computers, video games, and the Internet" (Prensky, 2006, p. 9). In contrast to the digital natives are digital immigrants, that is, people "who were not born into the digital world… [who] have adopted many aspects of the technology, but just like those who learn another language later in life…retain an 'accent'" (Prensky, 2006, p. 9). Prensky argued that because most teachers are digital immigrants, they have a hard time effectively teaching the digital native students. Prensky (2006) also argued that students today are accustomed to different forms of learning (Web surfing for information, video games, creating using Flash, searching using Google, analyzing using SETI, reporting using their camera phones, etc.) and communicating (talking via instant messaging, sharing using blogs, exchanging using peer-to-peer technology, coordinating using wikis, evaluating using reputation systems, programming using modding, and socializing in chat rooms).

McHale (2005) postulated that interactive digital tools should be used to engage digital natives (whom he also refers to as Generation M) in the learning process and to simulate real-world skills in the educational system. However, he cautions that we do not know how to teach these digital natives most effectively based on empirical research and that not all of today's students are digital natives. In spite of the fact that the digital divide in America is closing in some areas, it is not in other areas and thus, not all students who fall into Generation M by measure of their birthdates are actually digital natives. Rural areas are improving, according to Salpeter (2006), but minority, lower-education, and lower-income households still have less computer access. Even with more equitable access in some areas, differences remain in the use of computers, which is yet another element that reinforces a digital divide in terms of computer literacy.

Colleges across the country have recognized a lack of information literacy in their students, and this has sparked the development of the iSkills assessment tool by the Educational Testing Service (ETS). Foster (2006) reported an initial ETS study on information literacy, a term defined as "the ability to analyze and communicate information available online" (p. 1). According to Foster, the ETS study on the information literacy of 3,000 college students and 800 high school students found that only 13% of the participants achieved a score that qualified them as computer/information literate. This finding, in part, spurred the inclusion of information literacy in the No Child Left Behind Act, Part D, "Enhancing Education through Technology," in section 2402. Computer literacy is stated as an additional goal:

> (A) To assist every student in crossing the digital divide by ensuring that every student is technologically literate by the time the student finishes the eighth grade, regardless

of the student's race, ethnicity, gender, family income, geographic location, or disability. (U.S. Department of Education, b2A)

In general pedagogical studies, however, less attention has been paid to overall computer literacy. The studies that have investigated computer literacy have found that although students may have generalized computer skills, they often lack specialized skills (Winke & Goertler, 2008). In addition, private and professional computer uses appear to be different, with private computer literacy being more developed than professional (Messineo & DeOllos, 2005). Furthermore, Barrette (2001) found that computer skills not practiced will be lost, while computer skills used will improve. Related to the issue of the digital divide, Messineo and DeOllos reported that minority students had lower computer literacy.

Hybrid foreign-language instruction

Because, perhaps mistakenly, computer literacy is often assumed of college students, colleges and the educational market in general have dealt with the increased demand for classes through online and hybrid instruction. Thus, courses with online components have steadily increased across the nation. In the fall of 2006, 20% of college students were enrolled in online courses, and more than two thirds of higher-education institutions offered online courses (Babson Survey Research Group, as cited in Kennedy, 2008). Earlier, the Postsecondary Education Quick Information System report on Distance Education at Degree-Granting Postsecondary Institutions 2000–2001 (National Center for Education Statistics, 2003) stated that 56% of institutions offered online courses.

More recently, Kraemer (2008a) summarized a variety of reports that all indicated that online teaching and learning is on the rise, especially in hybrid or blended-learning environments, with humanities being one of the leading fields. No data are available in Kraemer's study about the number of foreign-language courses that are offered in a hybrid or online format. However, in a survey of language-program coordinators, Goertler and Winke (2008) discovered that 26% of the surveyed language programs offered hybrid (21%) or online courses (5%). The majority of those courses were in the "major" languages of German and Spanish.

Although a number of programs offer hybrid or online courses, the research on such courses has been limited. Grgurovi (2007) conducted a meta-analysis of various levels of technology-mediated foreign-language instruction and its effect on grammar, pronunciation, reading, vocabulary, writing, communication, and integrated skills. In the 25 comparative research articles that she summarized, blended instruction is suggested to be as effective, if not more effective, than online and face-to-face courses. Goertler and Winke (2008) summarized six of the most prominent research reports of curriculum hybridization projects and found some institutional benefits, a mostly positive attitude by students, and comparable results in learning outcomes, yet some challenges with logistics and the implementation process. Similar result summaries have been reported by Kraemer (2008b). In the reported hybrid programs, the motivation for moving to a hybrid format can be summarized as responding to institutional demands and utilitarian benefits rather than a drive by/for pedagogical consideration and pedagogical accomplishments. Many of the challenges in hybridization can be summarized as a lack of readiness by the institution, the teachers, and the students. (For more detailed information, see Barrette, 2008, and Goertler, Bollen, Gaff, & Winke, 2008).

Methods

The purpose of this study was to assess digital natives' readiness for hybrid foreign-language instruction from the standpoints of computer access, computer literacy, and attitude. The research questions were as follows:

1. What access do students have to technology?
2. What are students' levels of literacy in technology?
3. What is the relationship between computer literacy and access and students' attitudes toward hybrid instruction?
4. What are students' interests in and opinions of hybrid foreign-language instruction?

Context

This study was conducted at a large public university in the Midwest with no university-wide foreign-language requirement; however, it had a university-wide computer requirement. Students are typically from within the state, Caucasian, and between 17 and 23 years of age. The university offers a large variety of languages, from the major languages, such as French, German, and Spanish, to less-commonly taught languages, such as Swahili. The languages are not all housed in the same department and are geographically separated. The computer lab for foreign-language study is in the same building as the Romance and classical languages but not the rest of the languages.

Participants

A survey was administered to all students enrolled in foreign-language courses during the fall of 2007. This did not include English as a second language courses or noncredit courses; however, it did include language-focused and content-focused courses at the undergraduate level. A total of 2,149 students completed the survey. The average age of the students was 20.33 years, ranging from 17 to 65 years, with only 78 participants over 25 years and only 40 participants over 30 years. The participants included 801 men, 1,294 women, and 54 students who chose not to specify their genders. Almost all of the students were native speakers of English; 472 students were freshman, 589 were sophomores, 522 were juniors, 473 were seniors, 13 were master's students, 26 were doctoral students, 25 did not specify, and 29 had unusual enrollment statuses such as lifelong learner or dually enrolled high school student. The students were learning a variety of foreign languages: 128, Arabic; 171, Chinese; 301, French; 182, German; 54, Hebrew; 51, Italian; 218, Japanese; 28, Korean; 40, Portuguese; 49, Russian; 839, Spanish; and 88, less-commonly taught languages (Farsi, Hindi, Thai, Vietnamese, Turkish, Kazakh, Indonesian, Ojibwe, Hausa, Nepali, Tagalog).

Instruments

This study is part of a larger study that investigated students' technology use, access, and literacy, students' attitudes toward technology, and their self-assessed language proficiencies. The contents of the survey portions were reported by Winke and Goertler (2008) and Ahn, Hsieh, and Sydorenko (2008). For the purposes of this chapter, only some of the background information (age, gender, language course, native language, year in school) and four questions are considered.

The first question asked students about their computer access: "Mark if you personally own or have the items below. If you don't have one, mark if you can get it (by borrowing it or by using it in a lab) easily, with difficulty, or not at all." The participants were asked to report on the following technologies: PC desktop computer, PC laptop, Mac desktop computer,

Mac laptop, computer speakers, headphones, microphone, printer, Internet access, Webcam, digital camera, and video camera. This item was used to answer the first research question.

The second question asked students about their computer literacy: "Mark your level of ability to do the following tasks on your computer." The following tasks were listed: (a) cut, copy, and paste; (b) change font size and color; (c) type non-English language characters; (d) insert pictures and graphs; (e) insert audio and video files; (f) develop and maintain a Website; (g) navigate the Internet; (h) save and download files from the Internet; (i) create tables; (j) play audio files from the Web and from my computer; (k) play a video on a Website, on my computer, or stored on a DVD; (l) download and unzip a ZIP file; (m) post messages on an online bulletin board; (n) e-mail individuals and groups, including using the reply and reply-to-all functions; (o) access e-mail from a computer other than my own; (p) forward e-mails; (q) send e-mails with attachments and open e-mails with attachments; (r) create a new, free e-mail account; (s) start/install a program from a DVD/CD; (t) copy files from my computer hard drive to a CD/DVD or vice versa; (u) copy a track from an audio CD onto my computer hard drive and store it in MP3 format; (v) create an audio CD from a set of MP3 files stored on my computer hard drive; (w) make a sound recoding using audio editing software and save it to a disc or hard drive; and (x) edit video. This item was used to answer the second research question.

The third question asked students to respond to the following question with "yes," "maybe," or "no": "Would you be interested in taking a language class where half the instruction is in class, that is, face-to-face with the teacher and other students, and half is independent study online?" The responses to this item and to the two previous items were used to answer the third research question.

The fourth question that was considered simply asked students to make any additional comments. Many of the comments were about the survey itself and were not considered in the analysis, although it should be mentioned that many students commented that the survey was too long and too repetitive, which perhaps explains a large number of blank answers in the results. Together with student responses to the third question, this item was analyzed to answer the fourth research question.

Findings

What access do students have to technology?

To calculate computer access, the student responses to Question 1 were assigned scores. Ownership of a piece of technology was scored 4, having easy access was scored 3, difficult access was scored 2, and no access was scored 1. Students who left four or more technologies blank were not included in the calculation (97 out of 2149); for all others, the sum of their scores on each item made up their access score. The average computer access score is 39.12, with a standard deviation of 4.32. Students' computer access ranged from 17 to 48, with a maximum possible score of 48.

What are students' levels of literacy in technology?

The calculation for computer literacy in response to Question 2 was similar to that for computer access: Students who answered "not at all" scored 1 for that task, an answer of "with difficulty" scored 2, "with very little difficulty" scored 3, and "easily" scored 4. Students who left four or more tasks blank were not considered in the calculation (64 out of 2149); for all others, the sum of their scores for each item was considered their literacy score. The average computer literacy score was 69.04, with a standard deviation of 9.00. Students' computer access ranged from 19 to 80, with a maximum possible score of 100.

Attitudes toward hybrid instruction

In contrast to Winke and Goertler's (2008) findings based on a subset of these data (basic language students in the major languages), the overall data showed a more negative attitude toward hybrid instruction. Of those students who answered the question, 422 answered that they would like to take a language course in a hybrid format, 784 answered that they would consider it, and 850 answered that they would not take a hybrid foreign-language course.

What is the relationship between computer literacy and access and the students' attitudes toward hybrid instruction?

The students who answered the literacy questions, the access question, and the question about hybrid instruction were divided into three groups (408 hybrid supporters, 757 hybrid undecided, and 827 hybrid opponents), and their access and literacy averages were calculated. The 827 hybrid opponents had an average access score of 38.96 and an average literacy score of 68.70. The 757 students who were undecided about hybrid instruction had an average access score of 39.23 and an average literacy score of 69.25. The 408 hybrid supporters had an average access score of 39.39 and an average literacy score of 69.88. As one can see, computer literacy and computer access slightly increased with more favorable opinions toward technology, which can also be seen in the qualitative comments discussed below.

What are students' interests in and opinions of hybrid foreign-language instruction?

Hybrid supporters

Of the 422 students who favored a hybrid foreign-language course, 30 provided explanatory comments. The comments were analyzed and categorized as follows: approval, challenges, experiences, implementation ideas, and pedagogy.

General approval for increasing the amount of technology used for language instruction was provided by 11 students. The comments ranged from general approvals, such as "I think that the more technology use the better overall," to specific, "I think adding more technology to the language classroom would be very helpful especially for future teachers," and even came in the form of appeals, "please increase technology availability for Portuguese."

Nine students commented on specific technological tools or activities that they would find helpful for foreign-language instruction such as DVDs, online homework (one preferred less, one preferred more), access to native speakers, computer games, and interactive online activities. Two students provided ideas about how to structure a hybrid course: One stressed the importance of not creating additional work, and the other suggested using an independent study format for the hybrid courses.

Six students reported on challenges to the hybridization efforts: access to technology ("we need more technology around campus"), lack of human interaction ("there would need to be plenty of human resources to further understanding of what is done online"), and the plethora of tools available that make the best selection challenging.

Hybrid undecided

Of the 784 students who were undecided about the issue of foreign-language hybridization, 54 provided explanatory comments. Many of the students had weighed the advantages and disadvantages of technology-enhanced instruction and had also drawn from their contexts and experiences. The comments were analyzed and categories as follows: change, choice, challenges, lack of preparation, pedagogy, pressure, possibilities, and status quo.

Most comments (32) were thought-out reflections on how and what technology could advance language instruction: "Technology is only useful for communication and discussion purposes" and "a quantified look at technology isn't as productive as a qualitative view. If a class uses minimum technology effectively, this will be more useful than much technology used just for the sake of being up to date or hip." Some of the technologies suggested to be used were course management systems, online games, and audio and video materials. Five students provided specific ideas of additional tools to purchase or activities to implement such as telecollaboration and online games.

Challenges to hybridization in language education were reported by 15 students. These challenges can be summarized as follows: desire to have face-to-face and speaking time ("some things are best learned face-to-face"), the importance of the teacher ("technology is important but not to replace the instructor"), and personal challenges ("the computer hurts my eyes"). Three students also reported lack of preparation: access ("we don't even have internet access" or "I live off campus and I hate having to come to the language learning lab") and literacy ("I don't like technology because I was never taught to use it efficiently").

One student thought that the choice of delivery format should be left up to the instructor. Another student thought that the university was pressuring teachers into using technology for language teaching, which he did not approve of.

Two students reported liking the way things were in their hybrid courses (one Spanish and one German). Two students also provided encouraging words to hybridize the curriculum: "I hope all language classes upgrade," and "I think this is a great idea depending on how the technology is used and integrated. Good luck."

Hybrid opponents

Of the 850 students who would not want to take a hybrid course, 92 provided explanatory comments. The comments were analyzed and categorized as follows: benefits of some technology, community, face-to-face, general dislike, lack of experience, pedagogical consideration, teacher better than computer, teacher preparation, short-changing students, spoken language, and status quo.

Although these students did not want to be in hybrid courses, 11 reported liking specific tools for independent study or in a technology-enhanced course such as course Websites, textbook Websites, audio recordings, videos/DVDs, and online problem solving. A total of 17 students explained that an online environment is not conducive to being a community. As an example, one student wrote: "I would strongly discourage changing language classes to online courses. I think it would be more difficult to learn and less interesting. I love coming to my language class and if it where [*sic*] to be changed to an online course I don't think I would take the language anymore." Another student wrote: "I think the best way to learn a language is face to face with a teacher and other students." The importance of face-to-face communication for language learning was mentioned by 14 additional students, and 7 students stressed that they thought that language learning had as its goal and as its means spoken conversations. "Learning a language should be about learning how to speak it. How else will it be useful if you can't think in the language?" One of those 7 students qualified his statement by saying, "I prefer to never use technology with learning Ojibwe. It's a spoken language."

A general dislike of technology was expressed by 11 students, which explains their disinterest in a hybrid language course. For some of these students, past ineffective technology use played an important role in their dislike of technology: as one student commented, "in high school I took two years of German in a distance learning classroom. It was all video cameras, microphones, internet and phone. No teacher. I learned nothing and it has turned me off from using technology in my future classroom." A lack of experience with CALL made it hard for 4 students to answer the question, for example, "Tricky question when you do not know what using technology in a language class could look like."

On the other hand, 17 students appeared to have thought in more detail about the pedagogical considerations in implementing technology for language teaching and learning. One student wrote, "Language is best learned through conversation and trying to compose sentences and thoughts without preparation. This cannot be simulated digitally. Angel [the course management system at the institution] is useful in course organization and Wikipedia and youtube can be useful but are not enough to base a class on." Several students felt that technology-enhanced classes could be a great asset, but that a hybrid or an online course would not.

Twenty-two students explained that they preferred learning from a teacher rather than a computer. Most of them explained that learning from a teacher would be easier or necessary. "Learning from a professor is much easier than learning from a computer." Others said that technology was not necessary: "You don't need technology to learn a language faster. You need a good instructor."

One student expressed concern that teachers are not properly trained to teach with technology, and therefore, having a hybrid course would not be a good idea. Four students felt that moving instruction into a hybrid format was shortchanging students by saving costs where costs should not be saved: "I paid to learn with a human teacher," and "technology is not a substitute for learning in a classroom. While you probably want to cut down classes to pay TAs less money, it is in my opinion that student learning will suffer." Another student thought that hybrid instruction was for lazy professors: "I think that many professors would use technology as a way to avoid teaching a subject in a classroom." One student was appealing to us to stop the hybridization process: "This is a horrible idea. We had a language lab in my high school and it was the biggest waste of money in the world. Everyone dreaded going to it and it made people very self-conscious and less likely to participate. I will drop this language if you screw it up like this." Four students reported that things should stay the same; that is, not hybrid: "I'd hate to see things get changed as I'm happy with how things are now," and "Keep with tradition."

Interestingly, the status quo was important: that is, the students wanted to stay in the course format in which they were in originally. This was also found as a common answer by Spanish students enrolled in a hybrid course in Goertler, et al. (2008). Along the same lines, bad experiences with hybrid instruction were a good predictor of negative attitudes toward hybrid instruction.

As Blake (2001) has noted, there is a myth that technology is all the same and that people tend to fall into two extreme categories: those who think that technology is all great and those who think that technology is all bad. This myth manifested in the results of this study. The technology lovers saw technology's potential and the need for computer literacy skills. The opponents feared that it would replace the teacher and take away from the community feel and personal interactions. Therefore, another myth described by Blake, that technology will replace the teachers, was also evident in the data. Furthermore, many participants implicitly viewed technology as a method, just as in the third myth that Blake addressed. They were not able to see that technology in itself is neither good nor bad, but that rather, how you use technology can make it a successful or a devastating experience.

Yet, especially in the undecided category were participants who acknowledged that how technology is used is more important than whether to use it. Some students even conceived of the idea that the computer can be used for interaction. As computer-mediated communication research has shown, using the computer for interactive activities actually has advantages over face-to-face communication (see, e.g., Fischer, 2007). Furthermore, the students recognized that technology offers the opportunity to listen to a variety of speakers of a target language and the opportunity for telecollaboration. On the other hand, several students feared that the focus on speaking would be lost in a technology-driven curriculum, either ignoring or not knowing about the opportunities to engage in spoken discourse using computers.

Hardly any students acknowledged that in an online course, the teacher will play a role; it will simply be different from that in a face-to-face course (see, e.g., Wildner-Bassett, 2008). The participants appeared to be under the impression that a hybrid course would be less work, when in fact, hybrid and online instruction has been shown to involve an increase in the time commitment of the teacher of up to 500% (Web-based Education Commission, 2000).

Conclusion

To summarize the results, the computer access scores were high; however, considering the large number of younger participants, they could have been expected to be even higher. Furthermore, as Winke and Goertler (2008) reported on a subset of this data, students had general technology access but were limited in their access to tools that would be necessary for hybrid foreign-language courses such as Webcams and microphones. Additionally, Goertler et al. (2008) reported that such ownership was not better among students in a hybrid Spanish course.

Computer literacy was slightly more problematic than computer access. Literacy was decent, but not high enough to allow completely changing over the curriculum to a hybrid format as some other universities have done (cf. Sanders, 2005). Again, as Winke and Goertler (2008) and Goertler et al. (2008) noted, general computer literacy was good, but specialized technology skills for participating in CALL were problematic even in the Spanish hybrid courses.

Although the differences were small, a trend showed that increased computer literacy and computer access paralleled more favorable attitudes toward hybrid foreign-language instruction. However, the overall perception of hybrid instruction was negative, which is typically not expected of students who would be described as digital natives based on their computer literacy and their age. It can therefore not be assumed that because someone is a digital native that that person wants to learn any particular subject matter in a digital format.

In looking at the qualitative comments, there are clearly still many misconceptions about technology use in foreign-language teaching (see also Blake, 2001; Chambers & Bax, 2006). More education on hybrid instruction has to be provided to be able to obtain buy-in from instructors and students. Furthermore, for successful implementation and improved attitudes, more training has to be offered to both students and teachers, and better access has to be provided.

Although only four students commented on their perceived motivation for hybrid instruction as cost and time saving, they are noteworthy. The original motivation for the college to consider hybrid instruction was to update the curriculum, to increase quality, and to decrease class sizes that were much larger than at comparison universities. These potential positive outcomes had been identified in the research on hybrid instruction. The possibility of saving money was seen as a positive by-product if it occurred after considering the high start-up costs. These positive motivations and potential positive outcomes of hybrid instruction were clearly not effectively communicated to the student population, despite the fact that several campus publications had, at the time of the survey administration, published articles highlighting these positive aspects of hybrid language instruction.

Limitations and further research

Due to the length of the survey, the students became impatient. In the future, a shorter survey is recommended. This survey should be repeated to look for a change over time. Further questions about past experience with hybrid and online instruction would be helpful to identify the relationship between past experiences and current opinions. Seeing the relationship between self-reported computer literacy and actual computer literacy would be interesting.

Although college students today are commonly misperceived to be computer literate, to have computer access, and to be appreciative of a technology-mediated environment, such a generalization cannot be made. More research is needed to better prepare for a hybridization of the curriculum so that educating all stakeholders early in the process can ensure buy-in from all. Hybridizing the curriculum is a long road, not only in designing the curriculum and securing funding for the high start-up costs, but also in getting all stakeholders ready and excited about the opportunities that a hybrid curriculum offers.

To return to the theme of this chapter, are Net Generation students ready for a hybridized curriculum? Based on this study and other research on computer literacy in college-aged students, the answer is "maybe." As has been discussed in this chapter, the answer varies and depends on the individual student and on the format of the hybrid course. As Garfinkel (2003) pointed out in his report on the myths about the Net Generation, some people may never embrace online technologies, and "we need to figure out how we will avoid making life unbearable for them." Adapting this to foreign-language education, we need to make sure that while we embrace the advantages of technology and hybrid education for those students that are ready, we also offer foreign-language education that works for atypical Net Generation students.

References

Ahn, S., Hsieh, C.-N., & Sydorenko, T. (2008, March). *Foreign language learner beliefs about the use of technology in language learning.* Paper presented at the Computer Assisted Language Instruction Consortium, San Francisco, CA.

Association of Departments of Foreign Languages. (1993). ADFL guidelines and policy statements. Retrieved January 15, 2008, from http://www.adfl.org/resources/resources_guidelines.htm#class

Barrette, C. M. (2001). Students' preparedness and training for CALL. *CALICO Journal, 19*(1), 5–36.

Barrette, C. M. (2008). Program administration issues in distance learning. In S. Goertler & P. Winke (Eds.), *Opening doors through distance language education: Principles, perspectives, and practices* (pp. 129–152). San Marcos, TX: Computer Assisted Language Instruction Consortium.

Blake, R. (2001). What language professionals need to know about technology. *ADFL Bulletin, 32*(3), 93–99.

Chambers, A., & Bax, S. (2006). Making CALL work: Towards normalisation. *System, 34*(4), 465–479.

Chenoweth, N. A., Ushida, E., & Murday, K. (2006). Student learning in hybrid French and Spanish courses: An overview of Language Online. *CALICO Journal, 24*(1), 115–145.

Fischer, R. (2007). How do we know what students are actually doing? Monitoring students' behavior in CALL. *Computer Assisted Language Learning, 20*, 409–442.

Foster, A. L. (2006). Students fall short on "information literacy," Educational Testing Service's study finds. *The Chronicle of Higher Education, 53*(10): A36.

Furman, N., Goldberg, D., & Lusin, N. (2007). *Enrollments in languages other than English in United States institutions of higher education, fall 2006*. Retrieved November 26, 2007, from http://www.mla.org/pdf/enrollmentsurvey_final.pdf

Garfinkel, S. (2003, August 8). The myth of Generation N. *Technology Review*. Retrieved March 1, 2009, from http://www.technologyreview.com/communications/13263/page1

Goertler, S., Bollen, M., Gaff, J., & Winke, P. (2008). Students' readiness for, attitudes towards and learning outcomes in hybrid instruction: Multiple perspectives. Manuscript submitted for publication.

Goertler, S., & Winke, P. (2008). The effectiveness of technology-enhanced foreign language teaching. In S. Goertler & P. Winke (Eds.), *Opening doors through distance language education: Principles, perspectives, and practices* (pp. 233–260). San Marcos, TX: Computer Assisted Language Instruction Consortium.

Grgurović, M. (2007). *Research synthesis: CALL comparison studies by language skills/knowledge*. Retrieved November 1, 2007, from http://tesl.engl.iastate.edu:591/comparison/synthesis.htm

Kennedy, M. (2008). Outlook 2008. *American School and University, 80*(5), 14–26.

Kessler, G. (2006). Assessing CALL teacher training: What are we doing and what could we do better? In P. Hubbard & M. Levy (Eds.), *Teacher Education in CALL* (pp. 23–44). Philadelphia: John Benjamins.

Kraemer, A. (2008a). Formats of distance learning. In S. Goertler & P. Winke (Eds.), *Opening doors through distance language education: Principles, perspectives, and practices* (pp. 11–42). San Marcos, TX: Computer Assisted Language Instruction Consortium.

Kraemer, A. (2008b). Happily ever after: Integrating language and literature through technology. *Die Unterrichtspraxis, 41*(1), 61–71.

McHale, T. (2005). Portrait of digital native: Are digital-age students fundamentally different from the rest of us? *Technology & Learning 26*(2), 33–34.

Messineo, M., & DeOllos, I. (2005). Are we assuming too much? Exploring students' perceptions of their computer competence. *College Teaching, 53*, 50–55.

National Center for Education Statistics. (2003). *Distance education at degree-granting institutions: 2000–2001*. Retrieved March 1, 2009, from http://necs.ed.gov/pubs2003/2003017.pdf

National Center for Education Statistics. (2007). *Fast facts about postsecondary enrollment*. Retrieved December 5, 2007, from http://nces.ed.gov/fastfacts/display.asp?id=98

Prensky, M. (2001). Digital natives, digital immigrants. *On the Horizon*, 9(5), 1–6.

Prensky, M. (2006). Listen to the natives. *Educational Leadership, 63*, 8–13.

Salpeter, J. (2006). Inside the divide. *Technology & Learning, 26*(8), 22–28.

Sanders, R. F. (2005). Redesigning introductory Spanish: Increased enrollment, online management, cost reduction, and effects on student learning. *Foreign Language Annals, 38*, 523–532.

U.S. Department of Education. (2001). *No Child Left Behind Act—Part D, Section 2402*. Retrieved March 1, 2009, from http://www.ed.gov/policy/elsec/leg/esea02/pg34.html

Web-based Education Commission. (2000). *The power of the Internet for learning: Moving from promise to practice*. Washington, DC: U.S. Department of Education. Retrieved October 5, 2007, from http://www.ed.gov/offices/AC/WBEC/FinalReport/WBECReport.pdf

Wildner-Bassett, M. (2008). Teacher's role in computer-mediated communication and distance learning. In S. Goertler & P. Winke (Eds.), *Opening doors through distance language education: Principles, perspectives, and practices* (pp. 67–84). San Marcos, TX: Computer Assisted Language Instruction Consortium.

Winke, P., & Goertler, S. (2008). Did we forget someone? Students' computer access and literacy for CALL. *CALICO Journal, 25(3), 482–509.*

Reaching Students: A Hybrid Approach to Language Learning

Lauren Rosen
University of Wisconsin System

In the 1990s, numerous institutions began offering online courses with the expectation of saving money and reaching a broader audience. This trend worried many language educators. Becoming fluent in a language is not something that happens alone in one's living room. It takes interaction with others; a connection not only to the spoken word but also to the culture, gestures, and context in which a language is spoken. Having a conversation takes more than one person. A positive interaction is required to close a business deal with overseas clients. As the world is flattening, it becomes increasingly important that today's graduates can communicate linguistically and with cultural sensitivity when working with a diverse community in their homelands and overseas. Preparing students in a traditional classroom is difficult enough, and doing so in a completely online course seemed nearly impossible, especially with the technology of the 1990s.

Realizing the limitations of learning a language completely online, in 1998, the University of Wisconsin (UW) Collaborative Language Program (CLP) developed a hybrid model for teaching languages to students on numerous university campuses. Although technology continues to improve, with greater bandwidth and faster connections through Internet2, classroom-based videoconferencing (CVC) remains at the heart of all CLP courses. CVC combined with a course management system, online voice tools, wiki projects, and learncasts[1] offers more students access to languages currently deemed critical to national and state interests. Now, 10 years since its inception, the program is reaching over 300 students via 15 courses in Arabic, Chinese, Japanese, and Russian each semester. Data gathered through summative assessments indicate that CLP students are doing as well in acquiring productive and receptive skills[2] as students learning in nondistance settings with equivalent contact hours.

1 These tools are described in detail later in this chapter.
2 The productive skills are writing and speaking; the receptive skills are listening and reading.

Rosen, L. (2009). Reaching students: A hybrid approach to language learning. In R. Oxford & J. Oxford, (Eds.), *Second language teaching and learning in the Net Generation* (pp. 65–84). Honolulu: University of Hawai'i, National Foreign Language Resource Center.

What makes the "impossible" possible? From the beginning, the collaborative language program approached distance learning with the intent to simulate as closely as possible a face-to-face language-learning environment. However, success even in this setting has been shown to depend on the pedagogical framework used. We, that is, the CLP, chose to implement a proficiency-oriented approach that focuses on communication in a learner-centered environment. Working in our favor is the fact that the students have grown up with technology. Their willingness to experiment, combined with faculty who are open to change and technology that is becoming increasingly stable, more feasible, and flexible, is what helped us build a strong learning model. Current technology makes possible a communicative classroom environment that enables us to do this.

Using CVC for our face-to-face instruction facilitates reaching a larger audience of students who otherwise would not have the opportunity to learn these languages. In fact, this technology allows for group settings and extensive oral practice both at the local site, similar to a single classroom setting, and with peers over the interactive two-way videoconferencing network. These communicative activities are an essential element throughout language study and in particular, at the novice level, when the development of oral skills may precede reading and writing in the target language. Note that the languages chosen for our program must begin orally because students are not familiar with the character sets or alphabets required for literacy in these languages. Typing in the target language is also delayed because students accustomed to the U.S. keyboard must learn to use special fonts and keyboard layouts. In addition to regular CVC meetings, students use both synchronous and asynchronous[3] Internet-based tools that support the development of productive and receptive skills. In the process, students explore aspects of the target culture as it relates to themes being studied and their interests.

This article discusses the evolution of the technologies, the technological components used, and the approaches chosen to guarantee sound pedagogy, high student achievement, and low attrition in hybrid language courses. Additionally, the necessity of integrating a variety of technologies to achieve proficiency in a distance language-learning environment is described. In particular, courses for those languages that require extensive oral/aural interactions prior to reading and writing will be addressed. The technologies presented, however, can be used for any hybrid course, regardless of discipline. In addition, students' reactions to the courses and technologies used are presented.

Defining a hybrid course

Hybrid courses, often referred to as *blended courses*, have been defined in a variety of ways, but most meet the following criteria:

- A significant amount (30–79%) of learning has been moved online, making it possible to reduce the amount of time spent in a traditional classroom.
- An attempt has been made to combine the best elements of traditional face-to-face instruction with the best aspects of distance education.

To further clarify these criteria, online elements do replace a significant amount of classroom time, so it is not a *Web-facilitated* course, defined by the Sloan Consortium[4] as 1–29% online (Allen & Seaman, 2008). In the case of CLP courses, face-to-face class time takes place over the classroom-based interactive two-way videoconferencing system. These sessions occur four

3 Synchronous tools, such as chat clients, require same-time communication among participants, whereas asynchronous tools, such as e-mail, allow communication at any time.

4 This is an organization that focuses on the support of and research in areas of online learning and encourages the sharing of knowledge and effective practices related to online education.

times each week, much like any other face-to-face language class. With Arabic, Chinese, Japanese, and Russian courses, many universities' courses meet five to seven times per week because more time is needed to reach advanced levels of proficiency in these category III and IV languages.[5] Unlike many hybrid courses, our goal was not to reduce the amount of time in class but rather to reach more students at dispersed locations who otherwise would not have the opportunity to learn the languages offered by our program. Many institutions do not have sufficient student interest to support full faculty positions for all of the languages that they would like to offer. By sharing instructional resources, more campuses are able to diversify their language offerings to students.

A national survey looking at preferences for course delivery modes published jointly by Babson Survey Research Group and Eduventures reported that 81% of consumers interested in postsecondary education expressed a preference for courses with some face-to-face component, whereas 19% indicated a preference for primarily online courses (Allen, Seaman, & Garrett, 2007). Although this survey was not specific to language learning, our students consistently, and not surprisingly, indicate in their midsemester surveys that their preference is for having the instructor local to their campus. However, they prefer to learn these languages in a hybrid environment over not having this opportunity at all.

In addition to CVC, the instructors use a course management system to build a framework for students to access online course content and their grades. It should be noted that when the CLP first began, the only technology tools readily available and supported were the interactive two-way videoconferencing network, e-mail lists, and the World Wide Web in its more static form. During the 1999–2000 academic year, the UW System adopted its first course management system. Collaborative language program faculty reported in 2006 that the course management system (CMS) options available to and supported by University of Wisconsin System were difficult to use because input and proper display of content in the target language was not consistent or dependable in all areas of the CMS. Furthermore, the tools for collaboration that are part of Desire2Learn (D2L), our currently supported course management system, are not nearly as well developed as standalone applications. Standalone Web-based applications are specifically designed for a single purpose, and they can be linked to a page in the course management system instance for each course. For that reason, instructors link to additional tools such as online voice tools and wiki course sites within the course management system framework rather than using the built-in components. These standalone applications add to student experiences as their proper integration into course content helps develop student language proficiency while building cultural identity and a sense of community across campuses. Clementi (2007) suggested that "content" should be the sixth "C" defining the National Standards for Foreign Language Education: "Content represents important topics and ideas that help students understand the world in which they live and who they are. It allows them to explore and respond to questions about their own culture and other cultures" (Clementi). With this in mind, the integration of various Web-based tools into CLP courses has proven instrumental in the success of our hybrid model; without them, our hybrid courses would have failed. Details of these various Web-based tools are discussed later in this article.

Program structure

For numerous reasons, hybrid instruction, in whatever form it is implemented, is believed to be more effective than a completely online course. One of the primary reasons is the guidance that students receive during class sessions. Regular class meetings keep students

5 Languages are categorized from I (easiest) to IV (hardest) based on the difficulty native speakers of American English may have in learning the language (Omaggio, 2001).

focused on their learning and require them to maintain the pace of the course without relying entirely on their own motivation (Chenowith, Ushida, & Murday, 2006). With a proficiency-oriented learner-centered approach at the forefront, three needs were identified as critical to the success of the program: (a) building a program structure that guarantees a manageable class size, (b) a sufficient cohort of students on all participating campuses, and (c) adequate support for students to remain focused while learning at a distance. Because novice-level language classes are open to a maximum of 25 students per section on UW campuses to allow for ample student interaction, it was decided that the CLP courses would also limit enrollment to 25 students per section, including all connected sites. Some students find Arabic, Chinese, Japanese, and Russian to be more difficult to learn than initially expected, so some attrition occurs in the first few weeks of class. Therefore, instructors often allow up to 32 students to enroll per course. These larger numbers guarantee a sufficient student body at each connected site for learners to participate in small group and pair work even after initial attrition. Obviously, starting with a larger class size also contributes to the sustainability of a four- to five-semester course sequence because more students have the potential to continue studying the language in later semesters. Because interaction is essential to language learning, the number of classrooms connected to any one section of a course is limited to an origination site and a maximum of two receiving locations. This allows students to have ample opportunity to interact orally, not only with the instructor, but also with their peers at all locations. Finally, distance locations hire a facilitator who attends all class sessions to assist students. Their responsibilities are described in detail in the next section.

Classroom-based videoconferencing

For learners and the instructor to easily communicate and share content in a manner similar to a single classroom environment, our hybrid instruction occurs in CVC rooms equipped with microphones, cameras, monitors and/or screens, a document camera, and a computer. On many campuses, these technology-equipped rooms were in buildings outside of the language center and were largely underused. In some cases, the videoconferencing equipment was being used primarily for special meetings and events. Thus, at minimal cost, classrooms were modified with the necessary equipment for CLP classes that meet four times per week for 50–60 minutes. The CLP now monopolizes the use of many of these equipped classrooms. Because few others use this space, some instructors have covered the walls with posters and bulletin boards related to the target language and culture, an opportunity not typically found in traditional university classrooms that are shared by other disciplines.

The extensive use of and focus on verbal and auditory exchange in the communicative process of language learning brings to light the shortcomings of the CVC system. With each class session, some time is lost due to the delay inherent with the use of interactive two-way video technology and the occasional loss of audio or video. Although the delay is minimal, it does make choral response a less desirable activity, and some time is lost simply due to waiting for responses from connected sites. In addition, the instructor cannot clearly hear the individual speech of students working in groups or pairs. Facilitators at the receiving sites assist with pronunciation and the flow of activities, organize drills locally at the direction of the instructor, and report areas of struggle for students to the professor. The facilitator ensures learner focus during class sessions. These facilitators are highly proficient or native speakers of the target language who work as student employees; they have no formal teaching background, nor do they necessarily hold any interest in language teaching as a profession.

Despite the fact that CVC instruction has shortcomings inherent to the technology, our experiences demonstrate some unanticipated benefits. In a nondistance face-to-face classroom, instructors and students spend a significant amount of time simulating situations to practice language. Although this is also true in CVC classrooms, simulations are not as necessary at times. For example, when UW-Oshkosh Japanese professor, Dr. Fumiko Fukuta, teaches students to reference the locations of objects, students practice "this one" (*kore*), referring to an object close to the speaker; "that one" (*sore*), an object away from the speaker, but closer to the listener; and "that one over there" (*are*), referring to an object at a distance from the speaker and the listener. Although this example may seem quite simple, with a number of students at a great physical distance from each other, no "simulation" is necessary. Curtain and Dahlberg (2004) described an ideal environment for students to develop communication skills as one that allows experiences providing a context with real meaning and content to which they have an emotional connection (p. 25). These and many other linguistic challenges are easily brought to life in a hybrid course, simply as a result of the distances, differences, and diversity of the students. Therefore, connecting to other campuses also has diversified the classroom in ways that were not previously possible. Not only do students come from a variety of backgrounds, but the way in which they live and the cities in which they are living are quite different, with some being more urban and others more rural. Moreover, different universities have different program strengths that draw in students. These differences make for very real conversations and genuine curiosity because students want to get to know each other better. As one might imagine, a student needs to describe in much greater detail their favorite place to spend time when numerous classmates have never been there before.

Another advantage to our CVC classrooms is the addition of the native-speaker facilitator, a peer to the students, who typically is of a different background and generation than the instructor. These facilitators share their experiences and beliefs about their homeland with the students. Their regular contributions provide learners with additional perspectives on the target culture beyond that of their professor. Thus, the learning environment for many of our courses has proven to be much richer than that of a classroom with a single professor and a more homogeneous community of learners.

Overall, students at both origination and receiving sites seem pleased with their experiences in the CVC classrooms. A second-year Russian origination-site student noted the following in his midsemester survey:

> It's a good program. It obviously benefits the students at the universities without a Russian program to begin with much more than us, but it's not at all detrimental to us. So, I would have to give the program a thumbs up.

A receiving-site student from Stevens Point sent an e-mail to his professor stating the following:

> You made class fun and I was surprised how effective you were long-distance. I was skeptical at first of the technology but now I believe it works. I am glad we had the opportunity to speak Japanese often. I liked the pace of the class which was slow enough to absorb a lot of information but quick enough so that I was never bored.

Online media-rich environments

In a hybrid course, our online components extend the classroom. The use of both synchronous and asynchronous technologies outside of class sessions not only compensates for the time lost during the CVC, but also increases the amount of time students are exposed to and are working in the target language and with target-culture content. Although the majority of hybrid courses focus on the use of a course management system as the means for student interaction outside of class sessions, for CLP courses, the course management system primarily manages the course structure. The course management system is not used to improve student language proficiency. Instead, online voice tools and wiki assignments are the primary components outside of class sessions that contribute to growth in student language proficiency. These tools are ideally suited to providing students with ample opportunities to practice the target language and explore the target culture and student connection to it. They also are used to build a community of learners through activities that promote interpersonal communication. Furthermore, the integration of these tools directly impacts the CVC environment. Students become intimately familiar with each other even across sites, building the same personal connections found in face-to-face classrooms. Students in a traditional classroom settings are engaged in regular interaction with each other as they use the target language to practice talking about themselves. It is common in face-to-face classes for students to develop friendships as well from this more intimate personal sharing. Their in-class interactions often take on a more humorous tone as a result of this familiarity. While the students in a CVC classroom setting do not have as much physical contact with each other, the use of online voice tools and wiki assignments still allow the students to develop a similar level of intimacy and friendship. The humorous tones are now found in the CVC sessions, which was not the case prior to the use of these additional technologies outside of class.

Building oral proficiency using online voice tools

With the goal of preparing learners to interact with speakers of the target language in increasingly diverse communities, workplaces, and world, spoken language must be practiced in meaningful contexts. Furthermore, sufficient speaking opportunities and feedback prior to testing situations must be available for all learners. With substantial practice prior to midterm and final oral proficiency tests, students will be more comfortable with and successful in these summative assessments, which typically simulate authentic contexts.

Wimba Voice Tools is a suite of tools for both synchronous and asynchronous online communication and is an important tool—but only one of a set of technological tools used in our hybrid courses. They provide the necessary practice opportunities and oral testing environment that ensures that all students are tested in the way that they have learned and are tested equally regardless of being at an origination or a remote location during CVC. This suite of tools includes voice chat, threaded voice discussion boards, voice e-mail, voice announcements that can be added to Webpages, *Podcaster (a tool that* teachers can use to create podcasts), and *Oral Assessment Builder (OAB)*, which functions as a Web-based language lab.

For the purpose of CLP courses, the voice chat, the voice discussion board, and the OAB are the most useful for promoting the growth of oral proficiency when combined with the other components of our courses. Unfortunately, the Wimba Voice Tools suite does not integrate directly with our course management system, D2L, as it does with Angel, Blackboard (WebCT), and Moodle. However, by hyperlinking to voice-tool activities from D2L, students still have relatively easy access to assignments. The disadvantage is that students need to log in first to the course management system and then into the Wimba server. Although not preferred, this has not proven to be problematic when students are forewarned that the tools require them to log in multiple times.

With the integration of voice tools, students have more opportunities for listening to and speaking the target language. This better prepares them to understand and respond appropriately in real-life situations. Extensive practice also leads students to achieving higher levels of oral proficiency as defined by the American Council on the Teaching of Foreign Languages proficiency guidelines (Stansfield & Harman, 1987). In addition, these tools provide students at receiving locations the same access to materials and oral-proficiency assessments as their peers at the origination site.

Wimba voice chat and discussion board

Synchronous communication used outside of CVC class sessions, as found with the voice chat, most closely simulates face-to-face interactions. Once the chat room has been created, participants arrange to meet online at their own convenience. This tool provides students with opportunities to speak outside of class, thus increasing the amount of time that they are communicating interpersonally in the target language. One important feature of the chat session is that it can be archived. Its archived form is an asynchronous threaded voice discussion board that the instructor can view and listen to at any time.

Chat rooms are particularly useful for small groups practicing speech outside of class (see Figure 1) and for holding office hours. Students log into a chat room created by the instructor, click a hand icon to speak, and are heard by all others participating in the chat session. Unlike a normal conversation, the application requires participants to take turns, which can seem unnatural. Participants must wait until the current speaker clicks an "X" icon to release the microphone before the next speaker is heard. This eliminates voice interruptions and participants talking over each other as is common in face-to-face conversations. Despite the awkwardness, experience demonstrates that more provocative topics promote the most extensive conversations.

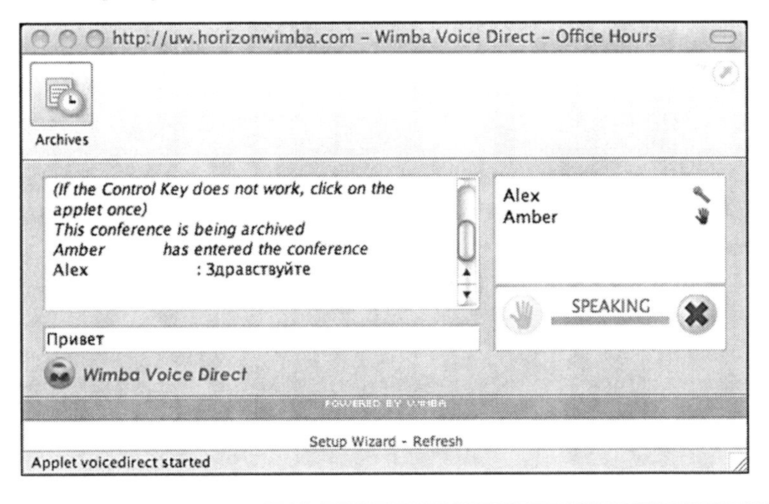

Figure 1: Wimba voice chat.

The chat tool also provides a text-chat option. Although students may use the textbox to type comments at any time, archives indicate that the text feature is primarily used for single-word utterances, not full conversations. This may be due to the difficulty for beginning language students to learn the keyboard in the target language, whereas voice chat allows them to concentrate on spoken language. Jepson cited Herring

(1999) and Werry (1996) who indicated that "the text-chat environment may promote more of a need for repair moves due to breakdowns in communication related to topic incoherence" (2005, p. 81). Characteristics of a text chat include a tendency for some participants to abandon a topic while others are still addressing it, thus altering the natural sequence of a conversation. On the other hand, face-to-face communication includes additional body and vocal cues that allow participants to know when it is appropriate to move on to the next topic. In comparing text and voice chat, Jepson concluded that voice-chat participants use significantly more strategies to negotiate meaning for repairing errors. In general, learners in a voice chat are more apt to negotiate meaning than those in a text chat. Jepson's conclusions strongly support the use of voice chat as a technique to develop students' speaking skills, particularly in the area of pronunciation, because the environment is void of nonverbal cues (p. 92). Despite this lack of cueing, interpersonal communication in the target language outside of class sessions for most students is rare. Increasing these opportunities through online chat can only help students improve their speaking proficiency. Additionally, Sanders' (2006) research holds that chat participants converse for longer periods of time when they control the time of meeting in an electronic chat room (p. 71). This appears to hold true for voice chat as well as text chat, despite the seemingly artificial environment of forced turn taking found in Wimba's voice-chat tool.

Many instructors in traditional classroom environments claim that students do not use their office hours, and similar results are common with online office hours. The success or failure of online office hours appears to be directly related to the consistency and dependability of their use. In other words, the hours need to be specified, and students need to be reminded of the times at which an instructor will be available online. If the instructor cannot be present on a given day at the scheduled time, students need to be informed of this absence exactly as is the case with traditional office hours. Nothing is more disappointing to a student needing assistance than to show up during scheduled hours and discover an office door closed or an empty chat room and no assistance to be found. Students are less likely to seek assistance during those times in the future if they fail to make contact on their first attempt. Nonetheless, instructors who do keep online office hours find that local students also use the online connection instead of visiting a professor's office. This may be because students are already working at a computer when they have questions, it is a comfortable medium for them, or it is faster than taking the time to go to a specific location in search of their instructor.

Most instructors choose to archive chat sessions. Archived sessions structure participants' comments in a threaded format identical to that of an online discussion board. The chat session then can be reviewed at any time, and all comments are date and time stamped. In instances where asynchronous communication is more appropriate, a voice discussion board is created (see Figure 2). A typical use of a voice discussion board instead of a voice chat is when students need to consider their beliefs prior to in-class activities and need to take the necessary time to formulate their thoughts rather than speaking spontaneously. With the voice board, students are often grouped to make the discussion more manageable. Much like chat sessions, with respect to quality input, the most successful topics are those that connect to students' lives and draw on their opinions.

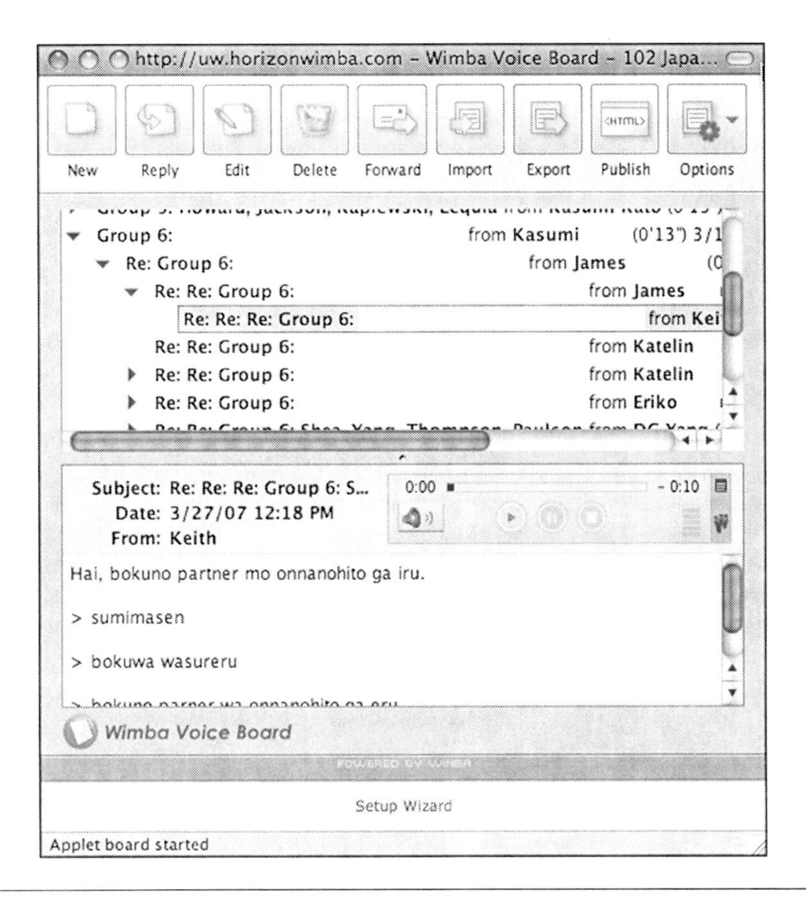

Figure 2. Wimba voice discussion board.

Wimba discussion board

Students using a voice discussion board commonly first write what they plan to say, followed by using the microphone to record their voice comments. Due to the asynchronous nature of a discussion board, students can spend more time focusing on their input prior to posting it than they can in a synchronous voice chat. In the voice discussion shown in Figure 2, students have described their ideal partners using vocabulary and structures learned during class sessions. Following the instructor's model, students shared their ideas and opinions about the topic on the discussion board and then revisited the topic in the CVC environment during pair work and final oral assessments. Using discussion-board content that reflects themes practiced during classroom activities and oral assessments further supports meaningful contextualized practice and provides a forum for students to become better acquainted as they make connections between the content studied, their own lives, and those of their classmates.

Survey feedback from novice-level students indicates a preference for using these online tools over speaking into a microphone in the CVC classroom. Although they are still heard by other students and/or the instructor, the group to whom they speak is smaller, and they are physically alone in environments that are comfortable to them while participating in these interactions. Beginning language learners feel less self-conscious about speaking in the target language when their peers are not in the immediate vicinity. This initial insecurity for most students is less prevalent as students become better acquainted with their peers at distance locations and using the in-class microphones becomes second nature. However, student comfort with speaking in an online environment may contribute to speaking at greater length in that setting due both to the additional opportunities and the lack of time limits. Further research in this area is necessary.

Wimba Oral Assessment Builder

Although chat rooms and discussion boards provide students with opportunities to practice interpersonal communication outside of class sessions, they are not appropriate platforms for feedback directed to individual students. Because this personalized feedback and guidance is essential throughout the development of oral skills, CLP instructors extensively use the Wimba OAB. This tool most resembles a Web-based language lab for practicing listening, speaking, and reading. It provides a mechanism for instructors to give directed oral feedback to individual students for each recorded utterance. Because issues of pronunciation are best addressed using sound and not writing, the OAB is an invaluable tool. The question types include vocal dialogue, vocal multiple choice, multiple choice, and matching. All questions require both written and oral prompts; images can be added for additional support. The two most useful and interesting question types, according to CLP instructors, are the vocal multiple-choice (Figures 3 & 4) and vocal dialogue questions (Figure 5).

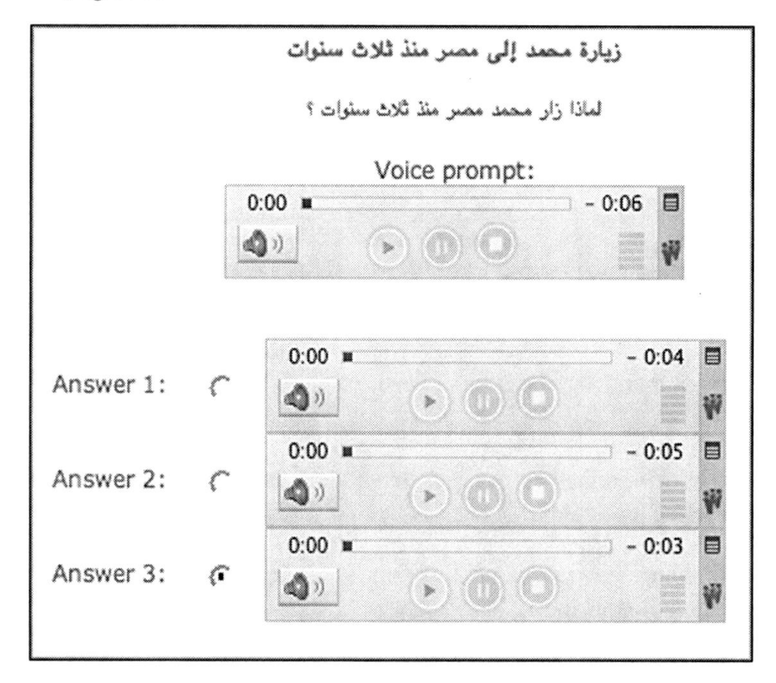

Figure 3: Vocal multiple-choice question.

As illustrated in Figure 3, a vocal multiple-choice question requires students to first read and listen to a prompt and then determine the best answer by listening to the recorded options. This listening-comprehension practice may be a common occurrence in most language labs. In fact, in many cases, these types of exercises allow students to e-mail their responses to instructors or, as is the case with Wimba's tools, store responses on a server that is accessible through a login to instructors and students. Although the question shown in Figure 3 may not appear unique, what makes this activity different is that students receive not only right and wrong answer feedback, but they also receive voice commentary from their instructor (see Figure 4). If the instructor uses choices that differ in tone, thus affecting meaning, and the student chooses an incorrect answer, a voice comment is the most effective way of describing those differences to a student.

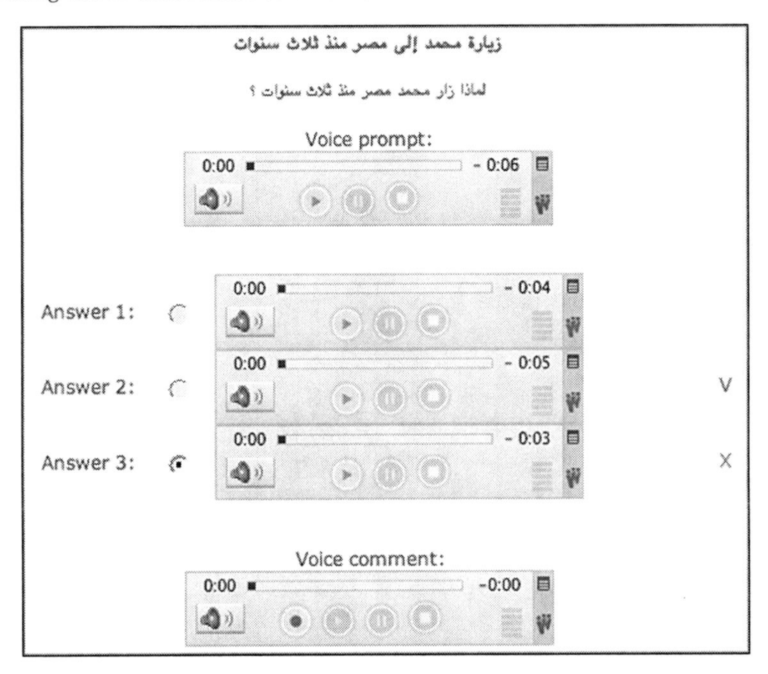

Figure 4: Vocal multiple-choice question with feedback.

The vocal-dialogue question is by far the question type most used by CLP instructors because it provides opportunities for students to speak in longer meaningful utterances in response to prompts. Figure 5 includes a picture, questions in Chinese to prepare the student for recording, and a Chinese spoken prompt with additional details and guidance. In other instances, students may be given a situation and related questions to expand on or react to with no image provided. The "grading" view below demonstrates the instructor's screen for recording a voice comment to the student. After the instructor records voice comments and assigns grades, students log in and review the instructor's directed feedback on their graded assessments.

A UW-River Falls student summed up the experience of many students in stating, "I liked Wimba because it let the professor give feedback to each phrase for each student individually, so they knew how to improve on their speaking skills" (personal communication, December 5, 2007). Students also commented that they liked the option in the OAB of listening to their recordings prior to submitting them and rerecording answers to submit only their best work.

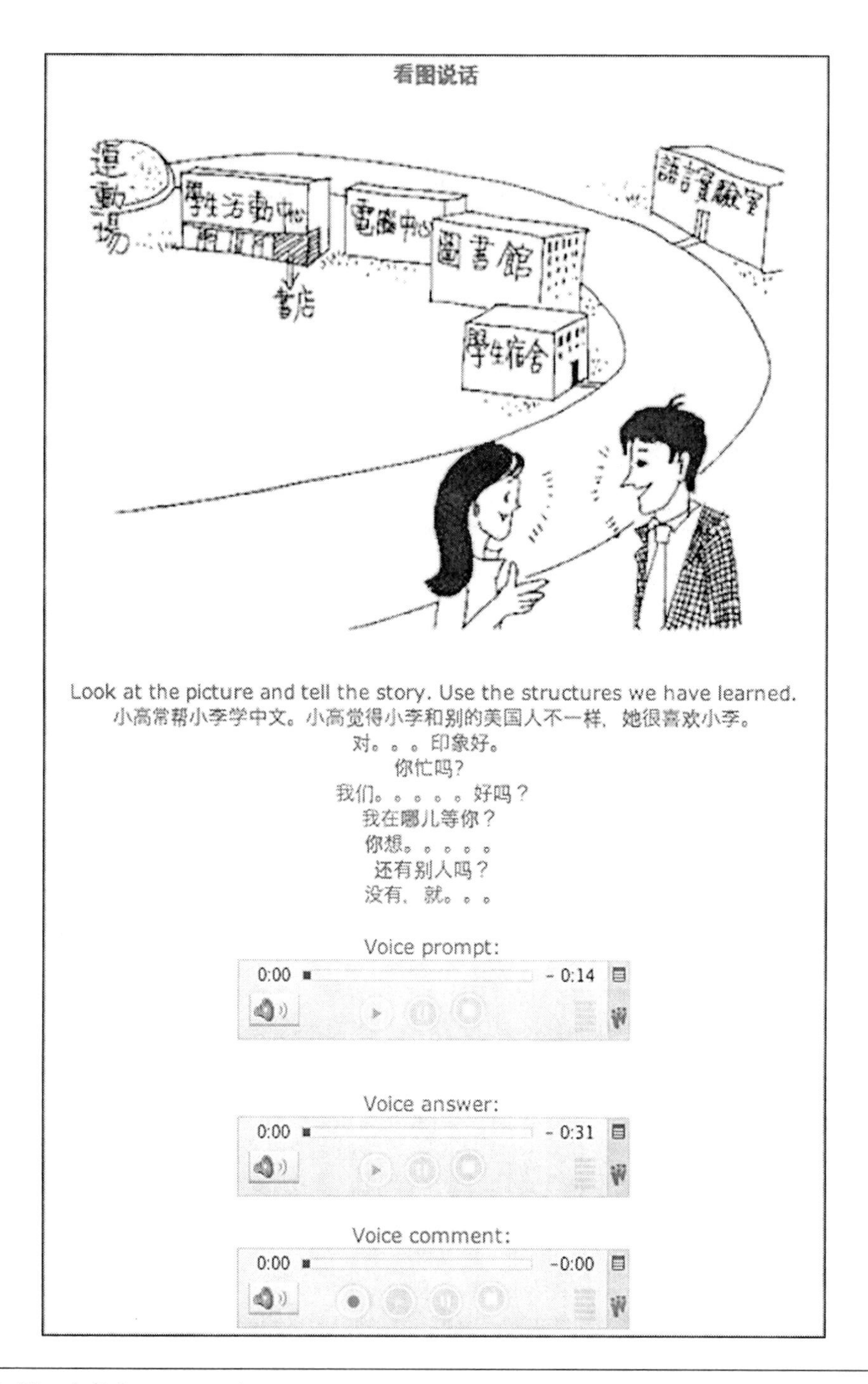

Figure 5: Vocal dialogue question.

For many of our CLP instructors, the OAB provides a place first for students to practice speaking at their own pace and then acts as an oral testing tool. In many cases, for quarterly and final oral assessments, students sign up for specific timeslots, and their testing is proctored. This process ensures that all students have the same testing conditions, each listening to the prompt a specified number of times, with only one opportunity to record an answer. In other cases, where instructors are more interested in students submitting their best, potentially practiced utterances, students are allowed to log in and take the final oral assessment from home on their own time. In both scenarios, the assessment is only made available at a specific time for students to complete.

Most CLP instructors and students find that the voice tools have an intuitive interface, are simple to use, and are very helpful. The complaints most often heard are from those students who need to go to a lab to complete assignments or have to purchase microphones for their own computers. Although students are guaranteed access to the necessary software and microphones in a lab, some students find language lab hours to be inconvenient. Nevertheless, students are arriving at universities more technology savvy each year. Many of them have computers with built-in Webcams and microphones and use Internet telephony services to keep in touch with friends and family. As a result, access to the necessary equipment is becoming less of a barrier. Meanwhile, instructors provide links in the course management system to locations for purchasing microphones. Instructors and students agree that the benefits of using the voice tools, when properly integrated into the course content, far outweigh the inconveniences of locating the necessary peripherals.

Wikis and learncasts

In our hybrid classrooms, the primary goal is increased communicative proficiency, and online voice tools fill the gap in student speaking and listening practice. Despite the distance, instructors regularly monitor student progress. However, the CLP instructors seek more than aural and oral skill development. Students must also increase their reading and writing proficiency while learning content in the target language and about the target culture. The use of additional technology tools is imperative to the development of these skills. Wimba voice tools and classroom videoconferencing alone are not sufficient. Integrating wikis and learncasts offers opportunities for students to connect cultural content to their own lives, which in turn builds community across sites through their similarities and differences.

Discussion boards in the course management system were first used for writing and reading in the target language while connecting students outside of class. Unfortunately, the input and proper display of foreign characters in various areas of a course management system historically are variable at best. In addition, discussion boards use a very linear format that does not easily allow peer correction and the embedding of photographs and other media to support student-created content. Overall, the text-based threaded discussions were deemed a static medium for written communication lacking in both flexibility and interest for students.

Ward Cunningham first developed the wiki in the mid-1990s as a collaborative database. By "the early 2000s, wikis were increasingly adopted in enterprise as collaborative software. Common uses included project communication, intranets, and documentation, initially for technical users" ("Wiki," 2001). Because wiki applications easily handle a variety of language fonts and character sets, CLP instructors decidedly moved to that medium for student online communication and collaboration. Current wikis are collaborative Websites, very dynamic documents, in which one posts text and embedded digitized media. This content is editable by all those who are given access. Arguably, the most well-known wiki is Wikipedia; it is an example of a public wiki that can be edited by anyone who creates a login. Members of its community monitor all contributions for validity.

CLP course wiki sites limit login access to the students in the course and others for whom the instructor provides a login. This limited access maintains privacy for the students, who include pictures and personal information intended for their classmates at dispersed locations. What is remarkable about this online communication tool is the ease with which it allows for self and peer correction and collaboration with proper input and display of language characters and fonts. The simplicity of the wiki has had tremendous impact on the amount that students are both reading and writing throughout the semester. Learners spend time reflecting on their own writing and that of their classmates. They continue to return to the wiki to read more about their classmates and to improve on their own content as they become more proficient in the target language. Furthermore, built into the wiki is a feature that displays the history of the document. This can be used to identify or track the students that contribute to the writing process and exactly what contributions are made. MediaWiki is the wiki engine preferred for CLP courses because it supports many languages, even those that require right-to-left input. Moreover, MediaWiki is free to download, has a large support network, and is relatively easy to use and administer. The interface is familiar and comfortable for most users because it is similar to that of a word processor. This adds to the ease of its adoption.

Using wiki tasks within the curriculum provides students opportunities to write and speak about themselves, their interests, and their beliefs as related to the themes studied. The result is that students want to read about their classmates and tell about themselves; in so doing, they are using more target language than prior to the use of wikis. In particular, they are reading and writing more than with traditional methods, where students write a few focused compositions during the course of the semester. As might be expected, the more students regularly produce content in the target language, the more proficient they become, and thus, the easier it is for them to communicate. In fact, Curtain and Dahlberg (2004) described outcomes as directly proportional to the quantity of time spent communicating in meaningful ways in the target language, concluding that the more time students spend in the target language, the more language they acquire, and the higher their potential level of proficiency (pp. 33, 283).

Projects and learncasts: Two models for wiki use

Two primary structures for wiki assignments have emerged for CLP instructors over the last few years. Some use a class wiki for occasional projects, while others integrate wiki assignments throughout the semester. In both cases, the structure is similar in that the instructor introduces the wiki assignment and explains what a wiki is, how it is implemented, the collaborative goal, and grading criteria for the assignment. On the wiki assignment page, groups of three to five students are identified and given links to their own pages on which to create content.

In the case of a second-semester Russian course, the instructor, Professor Natalia Roberts, needed to overcome a 2-week span of spring vacations because the campuses had different vacation schedules. She chose to use a wiki project as a way for students to remain connected to the content being studied during the time their campus held classes and other campuses were on vacation. In the end, all of the students studied the same theme and demonstrated their knowledge of house vocabulary and describing rooms and objects in a virtual house tour.

For this assignment, the students were grouped by campus so that they could easily work together while their campus was in session. The instructor created a model for each section in the activity, including charts that students needed to complete, adding to the ease of entering content. The students uploaded pictures of their dream-house floor plans with furniture and rooms labeled in the target language, recorded oral walkthroughs of the house, listed contact information for the necessary contractors to build and decorate the house, and developed a budget (Figure 6). Prior to starting the project, the students studied house and profession vocabulary and the structures necessary for describing the objects and rooms.

Following the online project, the groups presented their dream homes orally and visually during class, allowing classmates to ask questions.

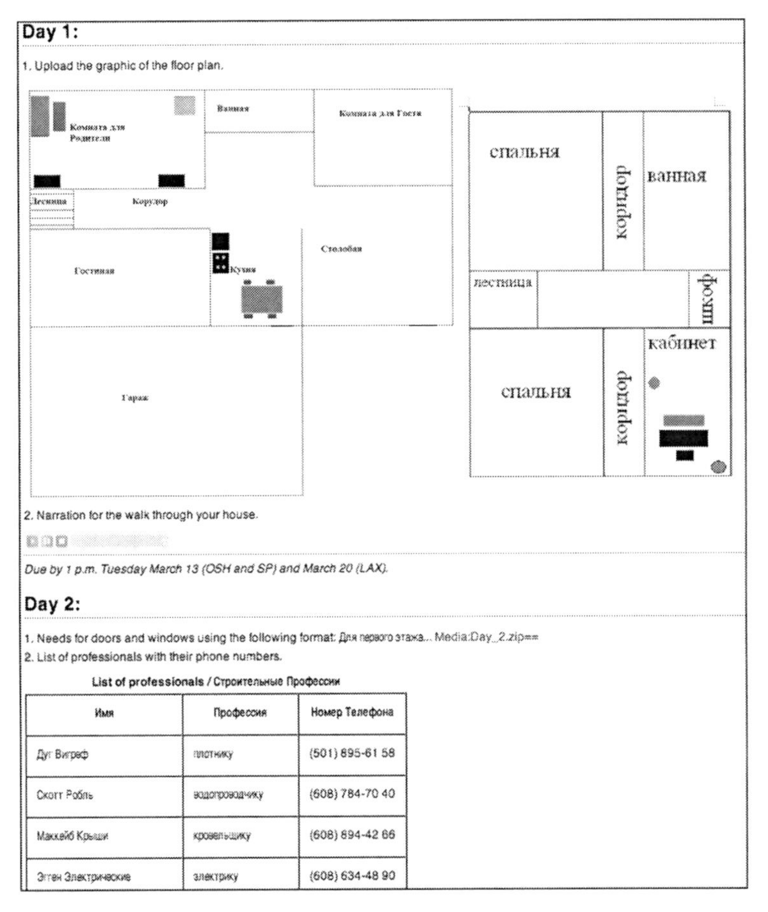

Day 1:

1. Upload the graphic of the floor plan.

2. Narration for the walk through your house.

Due by 1 p.m. Tuesday March 13 (OSH and SP) and March 20 (LAX).

Day 2:

1. Needs for doors and windows using the following format: Для первого этажа... Media:Day_2.zip==
2. List of professionals with their phone numbers.

List of professionals / Строительные Профессии

Имя	Профессия	Номер Телефона
Дуг Вигреф	плотнику	(501) 895-61 58
Скотт Робль	водопроводчику	(608) 784-70 40
Маккейб Крыши	кровельщику	(608) 894-42 66
Эттен Электрические	электрику	(608) 634-48 90

Figure 6: Partial view of Russian dream-home project.

For the Russian project, expectations for each day's assignment were provided to the students prior to the beginning of their work. However, the instructor waited until the last two days of the project to give the actual rubric for grading to the students. Then, the students were given extra time to make any additions or changes to their projects to better meet the criteria as described in the rubric. A number of students took this opportunity to improve their work, and in the future, the instructor will provide this rubric at the beginning of the assignment. The majority of students reported feeling well prepared for the project and indicated that it helped them demonstrate their ability to use the Russian language. They also reported that working collaboratively was very helpful, despite some students' usual preferences for individual work. One student reflected on this assignment in a survey of the course experiences, "GREAT PROJECT!! It was a nice break from the norm." However, others found it difficult to use some of the technology needed for voice recording and posting content to the wiki. Some suggested that more time was needed than was allowed. One student noted that the oral presentation seemed redundant after having posted materials to the wiki, including recordings, because the students had already reviewed the detailed plans of their classmates. Despite some changes

Professor Roberts intends to make in the future, she described this project as the "highlight" of her semester (personal communication, April 3, 2007).

The process for this project requires students to research information based on a theme, collect their materials, and present them to the class, which is similar to traditional projects. However, the wiki gives multiple students a single space to edit a document at their convenience and combine their content. In addition, their content is immediately available to their classmates and instructor as it develops, which provides a wider audience throughout the project, not only for the final presentation. During this process, the students demonstrated both written and spoken Russian-language skills. This is an interdisciplinary project where students also develop budgets and learn to work with electronic media, skills that reach beyond the language classroom.

Another successful model of wiki activities is the semester-long work of first- and second-year Japanese students. This content aligns more with the "learncast" model of online student-created content. Whereas some have described a learncast as a podcast for e-learning or one in which instructional material is delivered to students, our definition focuses on the learners and their demonstration of content learned. By our definition, a learncast is a collection of digitized materials that show evidence of what students have learned. Learncast content is integral to the curriculum; it demonstrates student application of knowledge expanded upon over a period of time, such as a semester or a year. Students and teachers can subscribe to these learncasts for notification when content has been updated and may choose to visit the site to view or add additional related content.

In the case of the CLP learncast model, students use a wiki as the platform for connecting content they are learning to their own lives and the culture studied. The material they post is directly connected to their experiences with the language and cultural content practiced in the CVC classroom. For these Japanese classes, the instructor initiated the assignments and timeline, but the content was all student generated. Professor Kasumi Kato. assigned four to five students to each group, mixing students from different locations and sections. The students had a broad audience, and each assignment required three to four postings, including student responses to each other's postings (Figure 7). The content was flexible and expanded during the semester as new themes were introduced.

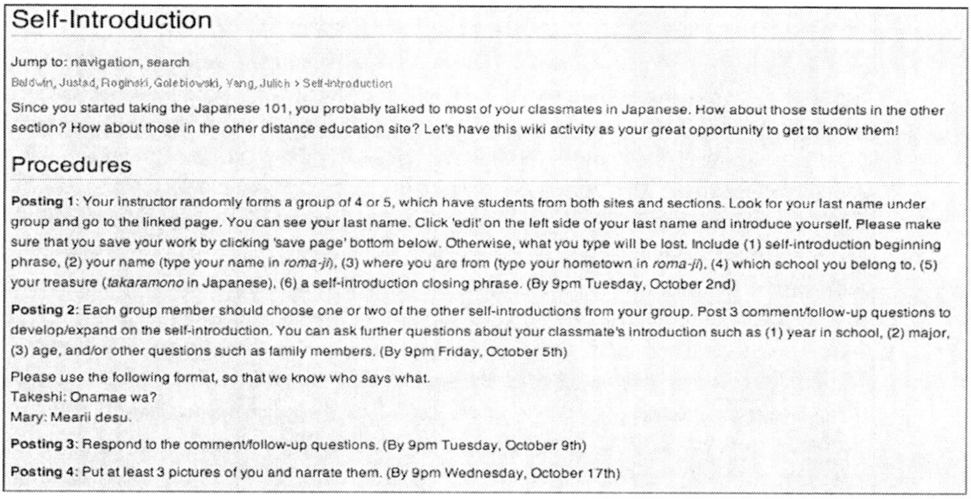

Self-Introduction

Jump to: navigation, search

Baldwin, Justad, Roginski, Golebiowski, Yang, Julich > Self-introduction

Since you started taking the Japanese 101, you probably talked to most of your classmates in Japanese. How about those students in the other section? How about those in the other distance education site? Let's have this wiki activity as your great opportunity to get to know them!

Procedures

Posting 1: Your instructor randomly forms a group of 4 or 5, which have students from both sites and sections. Look for your last name under group and go to the linked page. You can see your last name. Click 'edit' on the left side of your last name and introduce yourself. Please make sure that you save your work by clicking 'save page' bottom below. Otherwise, what you type will be lost. Include (1) self-introduction beginning phrase, (2) your name (type your name in *roma-ji*), (3) where you are from (type your hometown in *roma-ji*), (4) which school you belong to, (5) your treasure (*takaramono* in Japanese), (6) a self-introduction closing phrase. (By 9pm Tuesday, October 2nd)

Posting 2: Each group member should choose one or two of the other self-introductions from your group. Post 3 comment/follow-up questions to develop/expand on the self-introduction. You can ask further questions about your classmate's introduction such as (1) year in school, (2) major, (3) age, and/or other questions such as family members. (By 9pm Friday, October 5th)

Please use the following format, so that we know who says what.
Takeshi: Onamae wa?
Mary: Mearii desu.

Posting 3: Respond to the comment/follow-up questions. (By 9pm Tuesday, October 9th)

Posting 4: Put at least 3 pictures of you and narrate them. (By 9pm Wednesday, October 17th)

Figure 7: Japanese semester I first assignment.

As technology has continued to improve, wikis have become collaborative Websites that allow users to embed audio and video as well as text. They are used in various sectors, including corporate, government, and education. Taking full advantage of the flexibility of this technology for our Japanese students has meant including videos created by students using Microsoft Photo Story 3 and uploaded to YouTube (Figure 8) and audio tracks recorded using Audacity and RecordPad. The ease of doing this is in part due to the ease of editing in the WYSIWYG[6] environment of a wiki and in part to students coming in with sufficient comfort and familiarity with technology to easily adapt to using new software.

Figure 8: First-semester student learncasts.

The students found that the additional media greatly enhanced their learning experience when using the technology. Several students commented that the wiki in conjunction with Photo Story was a great way to become acquainted with other students taking the class. They continued by stating that wiki projects are more interesting and engrossing than other computer projects that they have done (personal communication, November 12, 2007). Their primary complaint was the lack of sufficient access to computers with the Japanese fonts available.

Using a class wiki extends the audience for written work to all students in the class, not only the instructor. It offers a platform for easily editing pages, thus encouraging process writing. The dynamic nature of wikis coupled with their ease of use lends them to activities

6 WYSIWYG stands for "what you see is what you get."

that promote exploration of the target-language community, connecting learners' lives to popular culture in the target country. As students create learncasts based on the themes being studied, the connections between students grow stronger. They learn from each other and compare their own interests with those of their classmates and the culture studied. They point out that wiki assignments provide a platform for learning in creative and personal ways. With learners in dispersed locations, one student stated that the wiki assignments "promoted communication between the two sites," and another stated that they "provided a good opportunity to learn from other students' progress." Comments of this nature illustrate that student interaction includes both sharing with and learning from each other (Kato & Rosen, 2007).

Students also used their class wiki to initiate their own special interest topics. These included suggestions for best practices in learning Japanese and cultural aspects such as music, food, and animé. Although primarily written in English, these extra topics were completely student-initiated and included independent research on aspects of the target culture. This student initiative stems from their motivation to learn and share knowledge with their classmates. Highly motivated students, we believe, are more likely to continue their language studies through classes and/or study abroad. In addition to positive gains for students, this student-directed area of the wiki also serves as a great resource for instructors to learn more about their students and to gain better insight into their interests and concerns. Professors can thereby tailor their course content more directly to students, engaging them in meaningful ways, despite the fact that they are in dispersed locations. No other technology being used in our hybrid learning model is as effective in building these connections. Using MediaWiki's watchlist,[7] students can subscribe to any page in the course wiki. Subscribers receive regular notifications of changes and can very easily log in to include their own input at any time.

CLP wikis are private, although we recognize that many benefits may be gained through outside interaction. Future course wikis may include a select group of outside contacts such as sister-school students or outside experts in an area of study related to the course content. The latter may have an even greater impact in language courses as they relate to other disciplines such as culture, history, politics, and philosophy.

Conclusions

The combination of sound language pedagogy and the use of a variety of technology components to provide practice both synchronously and asynchronously proved to be the key to high performance and low attrition in our hybrid language courses. However, note that one tool alone does not produce high levels of language proficiency in this distance-learning environment. Rather, the combination of opportunities for students to practice and demonstrate receptive and productive skills is what leads to their success.

In instances where there are sufficient students for multiple sections, CLP instructors can compare students in distance courses with those in locally taught courses. In courses where the technologies used outside of class are the same, such that the only difference is the CVC classroom, no significant difference in student performance has been noted. However, in cases where instructors have used some, but not all, of the technologies described in this article in their hybrid courses, the students reported feeling less connected to their classmates on other campuses and having fewer opportunities to practice language production in a variety of ways. This practice is essential for students to be able to perform

7 MediaWiki's watchlist feature allows a user with a login to receive e-mail notifications when changes are made to pages.

at targeted proficiency levels. For example, upon viewing student work in a colleague's wiki, a Japanese instructor who did not use a wiki commented that her students would not be able to write as much as the wiki-using students. Similarly, we found that students who have more opportunities to practice speaking using Wimba Voice Tools are more confident when speaking about similar topics during class. Furthermore, instructors who did not use all of the technologies described commented that they struggled to provide students with sufficient opportunities to demonstrate their proficiency in an environment where the instructor is able to assess their tasks. Finally, we found that using a variety of technologies also helps to more easily reach students with varied learning styles.

Interestingly, when comparing students at the origination site to those at distance sites in the same course, students at a distance did as well as or better than those at the origination site. We have identified a few factors that potentially contributed to the success of our receiving site students: They may focus more closely because they have little opportunity for direct instructor assistance; they may be more dedicated and self-disciplined in general based on the fact that these students have chosen a difficult language that has fewer similarities to English than other languages offered on their campus; they may be highly motivated to learn based on the fact that they have chosen to learn at a distance rather than taking other languages that are offered locally. More research in this area would help clarify this discrepancy.

As with most technology, both the instructors and the students encounter a learning curve. Language faculty made adjustments to visual aids and altered numerous learning activities to better reach students at all locations with sufficient practice in the CVC environment. In the case of both the online voice tools and the wiki, students find the technology more effective when it is regularly integrated into their class rather than used as an isolated assignment. Although more research in this area may find clear insights into student preferences, we suspect that students who do take the time to learn a new tool, much like learning a new language, want to make the time spent learning it worthwhile by using the tool more extensively and becoming more proficient at using it.

Students are entering our courses with more technology skills than ever before. Therefore, pedagogy must be at the forefront in language learning, and any technology used must be integrated into course content to help students truly learn. Language learning must be the focus. The technology should remain a transparent tool providing a mechanism for practice, for communication, and for demonstrating evidence of students' language development over time, not only for summative assessments.

References

Allen, E., Seaman, J., & Garrett, R. (2007). *Blending in: The extent and promise of blended education in the United States.* Boston: Eduventures.

Allen, I. E., & Seaman, J. (2008). Staying the course: Online education in the United States. *Sloan Consortium.* Retrieved May 5, 2009 from http://www.sloan-c.org/publications/survey/pdf/staying_the_course.pdf

Chenoweth, N. A., Ushida, E., & Murday, K. (2006). Student learning in hybrid French and Spanish courses: An overview of language online. *CALICO Journal, 24*(1), 115–145.

Clementi, D. (2007, November). *Focusing Teaching for 21st Century Literacy.* Paper presented at the Wisconsin Association For Language Teachers Conference, Appleton, WI.

Curtain, H., & Dahlberg, C. (2004). *Languages and children—Making the match.* Boston: Pearson.

Herring, S. (1999). Interactional coherence in CMC. *Journal of Computer-Mediated Communication, 4*(4). Retrieved December 12, 2007, from http://jcmc.indiana.edu/vol4/issue4/herring.html

Jepson, K. (2005). Conversations—and negotiated interaction—in text and voice chat rooms. *Language Learning & Technology, 9*(3), 79–98. Retrieved December 11, 2007, from http://llt.msu.edu/vol9num3/jepson/default.html

Kato, K., & Rosen, L. (2007). Improving proficiency, building community: A wiki case study. *The Language Educator, 2*(6), 52–54.

Omaggio Hadley, A. (2001). *Teaching language in context* (3rd ed.). Boston: Heinle & Heinle Publishers.

Sanders, R. (2006). A comparison of chat room productivity: In-class versus out-of-class. *CALICO Journal, 24*(1), 59–76.

Stansfield, C. W., & Harman, C. (Eds.). (1987). *ACTFL proficiency guidelines for the less commonly taught languages.* Washington, DC: Center for Applied Linguistics.

Wiki. (2001). In *Wikipedia*. Retrieved December 31, 2007, from http://en.wikipedia.org/wiki/Wiki

Werry, C. (Ed.). (1996). *Computer-mediated communication: Linguistic, social, and cross-cultural perspectives.* Amsterdam: J. Benjamins.

The Influence of Technology on Second-Language Writing

Raquel Oxford
University of Wisconsin–Milwaukee

Despite a great deal of promotion and excitement about the significance of writing to learning in one's first language and English as a second language (ESL) contexts, writing continues to be the neglected skill in foreign-language curricula (Greenia, 1992a, 1992b; New, 1995; Scott & Terry, 1992) and perhaps not without reason. L2 learners are often challenged to produce fluent writing due to issues with grammar and vocabulary and, indeed, fluency in writing is a skill that develops only through practice (Atwell, 1998; Calkins, 1983; Graves, 1975; Romano, 1987). Although a student might write well in his or her native language, this ability does not necessarily "translate" into a second language (L2); thus, accurate and fluent expression suffers.

Hands-on technology tools, some of which give students immediate feedback, allow individuals to learn by working in what Vygotsky (1962) refers to as the zone of proximal development (ZPD). This requires the presence of an expert other who supports the learner on his or her journey through the ZPD. Learners use the language that they have, working in the area between their native language and the L2 being studied on an interlanguage continuum. On the path of language learning, interlanguage is a learner's use of language to communicate as effectively as possible with the skills that he or she has, that is, the learner's version of the target language. Computer programs that allow students to work at their own pace to learn grammar or writing-assistant programs that bridge the gap between what learners can accomplish at their current level of proficiency only with help and what they will ultimately be able to accomplish independently can enhance the learning process. During composition, for example, students can use programs such as *Atajo* (Dominguez, Noblitt, & Pet, 1999) that combine a word processor with immediately available language reference databases that include a dictionary, grammar reference with examples of use, spell checker, and pronunciation help. This instantaneous accessibility may help students to express more fluidly their ideas, rather than becoming frustrated in their expression by having to wait for a teacher or to stop to use a reference book.

Oxford, R. (2009). The influence of technology on second-language writing. In R. Oxford & J. Oxford, (Eds.), *Second language teaching and learning in the Net Generation* (pp. 85–100). Honolulu: University of Hawai'i, National Foreign Language Resource Center.

Thus, technology may increase student production, fluency, and possibly ability to produce meaningful texts earlier on in language-learning curricula. With such a variety of tools and methods available, technology integration has the potential to provide the necessary scaffolding and individual assistance for students to alleviate some of the anxiety of learning to write in an L2. However, the efficacy of such technological components in instruction must be evaluated to make the best use of the learners' time and efforts in the enterprise of L2 acquisition.

The purpose of this study, then, was to examine the effects of technology-enhanced language learning (TELL) on students' composition skills in an L2 by investigating the differences between students who received more traditional instruction in the classroom with no formal grammar computer practice and students in a technology-enhanced section, which included a minimum of 30 minutes in a lab setting per week with a grammar practice program. That is, does systematic grammar and vocabulary computer practice improve the composition fluency—measured as the number of words produced in a specific period of time and total composition quality—of university-level intermediate Spanish students, and how does said practice affect the students' use of a writing-assistant program?

Research design

The design involved two intact, intermediate-level Spanish classes, each with 30 students, taught by the researcher; one class was the control, and the other was experimental. The classes wrote their first composition as the pretest; the grammar practice was the treatment, and the final composition was the posttest. All compositions were written in a lab setting to ensure that the students did their own work and to control for the actual time spent composing. Group characteristics such as gender, majors/minors, comfort with writing, experience with technology, and pretest scores on compositions were compared to note any significant differences between the groups. A repeated-measures analysis of variance (ANOVA) where the treatment (weekly grammar practice in the lab vs. no weekly grammar practice in the lab) was the between-participants factor and the composition results was the within-participants factor was used to determine measures of improvement on compositions for the experimental group in comparison to the control. The major grammatical point introduced and requiring mastery in this course is the subjunctive mood (both present and past). Although the subjunctive does exist in English, its modern-day usage is much less frequent and generally does not require a completely different verb form. In Spanish grammar, however, the subjunctive is a critical element and always mandates the use of a different verb conjugation

The control group used the text *Puntos de partida* (Knorre, Dorwick, Pérez-Gironés, Glass, & Villarreal, 2001) and the *Workbook to Accompany Puntos de partida* (Arana & Arana, 2001). The *Puntos de partida* text and ancillaries are a widely used, highly regarded program with a range of material from grammar or form-focused activities to communicative tasks. The experimental group used the same text and workbook plus the computer software program *Spanish Partner: Introductory Spanish Exercises for Personal Computers* (Morley & Fisher, 1994). Both groups wrote in-class compositions using the writing assistant *Atajo.*

Spanish Partner is intended for use at the beginning levels of study, but it can be used at the intermediate level for skills practice and/or remediation and is especially viable due to its range of coverage of grammar topics and generic nature. One reviewer of *Spanish Partner* noted that students at various levels of ability in Spanish have used the program with positive reactions and results (Raschio, 1998). VanBuren (1997) described *Spanish Partner* as "practical and user-friendly" and "a beneficial addition to any curriculum in which the acquisition and practice of grammar concepts are principal goals" (p. 528). The program includes 30 main volumes with topics meant to help students review grammar and vocabulary. The vocabulary volume includes a variety of lesson topics that are of personal interest to students or useful to basic, daily communication. The program is grammar-based but with most of the activities presented in contextualized paragraphs or situations. The activities are fill-in-the-blank, multiple choice or matching. All answers receive some type of initial feedback in Spanish, for example, *excelente, bravo*, or *así es*. In most cases, the feedback is accompanied by an affirmation of the correct grammar rule or an explanation of the applicable rule. Students can see the errors they have made on each item and their scores for each exercise and can print out their scores for up to 30 completed lessons in one session. *Spanish Partner* gives help with producing diacritical marks and skipping over troublesome items by using the F10 key to give the answer.

Atajo 3.0, 1st edition, by Dominguez, Noblitt, and Pet (1999), is subtitled *Writing Assistant for Spanish*. (The word *atajo* in Spanish means "short cut" or "cut," as in editing, intimating the resources available within the program.) The *Atajo* writing-assistant program combines a word processor with databases of language reference material, including a sound feature highlighting pronunciation of the core vocabulary, definitions, and examples of usage; a Spanish spellchecker; a core vocabulary of 10,000 Spanish words with English translations and examples of usage; a grammar reference including 250,000 conjugated verb forms with examples of use in context; and a reference of functional phrases including hard-to-define idiomatic expressions and models for correspondence and everyday communication. The user's manual that is provided with *Atajo* reaffirms that the "program supports the creative use of language as you focus on the task of discovering how meaning is constructed in another language" (p. 2) and that "the computer offers information on demand, much like working with a native speaker" (p. 3). Students can compose within an editor section, which is in a split-screen arrangement where the text being written and the dictionary are both available at the same time. Students also have access to a reference screen from which they can search grammar, phrases, or vocabulary and can use a variety of strategies to search for words.

Participants

The participants in this study were 52 students of intermediate-level Spanish at a university. The sample population consisted of two sections of SPAN 2040, each with 30 students enrolled. All of the students agreed voluntarily to participate, and no monetary compensation or extra credit was awarded. One section served as the control group, the other as the experimental group. In the experimental group, 4 students did not complete the course, resulting in 26 participants (12 men, 14 women). In the control group, 3 students did not complete the course, and one doctoral student in English (age range of 31–35) was considered unlike the other participants, who were undergraduates and primarily between the ages of 16 and 25. This resulted in a total of 26 participants (12 men, 14 women). The majority of the students in the course were fulfilling the College of Arts and Sciences language requirement of six credits of a foreign language at the intermediate level (LANG 2040 and 2050), with prerequisites of LANG 1010 and 1020 (four credits each) or credit by examination.

Although the two sections can be considered a convenience sample, having the same instructor for both sections had the advantage of controlling for instructor effects, often stated to be a threat to internal validity. Selection bias (i.e., the comparability of groups prior to participation in the study) was addressed by looking at group characteristics in addition to the quality of the first composition to assess comparability and identify outliers.

Data collection

Data was collected during the course of the semester. On the students' first day of class, they completed an information form that included contact information and each student's personal assessment of his or her ability levels in listening, speaking, reading, and writing and several questions aimed at assessing each student's experiences with and opinions of technology. Instructors in the foreign-language department normally obtain this type of student information at the beginning of each semester with some variation in the forms.

The researcher was the instructor for both classes and selected one as the experimental and the other as the control. The experimental group was allotted regular class time for practice in the lab using *Spanish Partner* once a week during the 15-week semester, barring any unusual circumstances, for a total of 10 sessions, with the primary area of practice being the subjunctive mood. The control group remained in the regular classroom and completed traditional communicative activities. The students could independently go to the lab to practice, and this activity was documented on a sign-in sheet maintained by the staff in the Foreign Language Learning Center (FLLC) and provided to the instructor at the end of each week. A writing sample in English was obtained from the students in both sections to make a comparison of students' writing abilities in English and Spanish.

Early in the semester, both sections received an introduction to the lab facility, *Spanish Partner*, and *Atajo*. During the orientation to the lab, the features of the software programs were described. In another session, the students were given a more hands-on overview of the writing assistant *Atajo* because students often do not take full advantage of the tool without some guidance (Burston, 1991; Scott, 1990). The following is offered as an example of a practice guided composition; students were given the task and then directed to the various databases for information.

> Today, you are going to write a letter to a friend or relative about cars. This can be a true or fictional story about a new vehicle or problems that you are having or have had with your car.
>
> Access the following features to help you with this assignment:
>
> 1. Under Reference: Phrases: writing a letter (informal). Be sure to include the date.
> 2. Under Reference: Vocabulary: automobile. You may also use your text.
> 3. If you are talking about something in the past see Reference: Grammar: Verbs and scroll for imperfect, preterite, or preterite vs. imperfect as needed.

Data sources

Compositions

Three compositions were assigned during the course of the semester, and all writing took place in the language lab, the FLLC, during class time. The three compositions assigned during the semester counted together for 10% of the final course grade. As per the informed consent form, the students were aware that the researcher was "interested in how [her] instruction affects your success" and that she was "conducting a study of the effects of technology enhanced language learning on composition." I have included here in abbreviated form the prompts for the essays.

Composition 1 (pretest): As we brainstormed in our prewriting exercise on Tuesday, you will be writing about a problem or situation that impacts your environment. This could be a social or environmental issue, such as recycling, racism, excess noise, or pollution.

Composition 2 (not included as a data source): Discuss your professional goals. This should include what you are studying now and what type of work you want to do. Talk about what your job will be like.

Composition 3 (posttest): Imagine that you are one of the "rich and famous" and would like to take a trip. Plan your trip, including where you would go, who you would invite, how you would travel, where you would stay, the clothes you would wear, and the things that you would do in that place.

Composition 2 was not used in the data analysis because the time intervals between writing assignments were not equal (thus, a nonequivalent-groups pretest-posttest-only design was used in this study). The topic is included here to illustrate the types of writing topics that students used during the semester. The composition tasks were designed to take advantage of the thematic vocabulary and grammatical structures studied at the particular time in the course and to follow the advice of the National Standards (National Standards in Foreign Language Education Project, 1999), which encourage the learner to discuss personal events and perspectives in writing at the intermediate level. For example, the first composition task elicited writing on an issue affecting the students' environment; this is parallel to the chapter titled *El medio ambiente* (The Environment), with vocabulary terms including the ozone layer, recycling, natural resources, public transportation, crime, and the fast pace of life. This first composition served as the baseline or pretest comparison, and the final composition in the semester served as the posttest. The students were instructed to always use a pseudonym and not to put their name or other identifiers on their compositions.

All essays were collected and randomized prior to grading. The rubric used for composition assessment was adapted from what has come to be known as the Jacobs scale. Originally called the ESL Composition Profile (Jacobs, Zingraf, Wormuth, Hartfiel, & Hughey, 1981), the instrument has been used as a holistic and analytic measure for L2 writing research (Polio, 2003) and modified for use in foreign-language composition evaluation (Hedgcock & Lefkowitz, 1992). The profile contains five component areas, measured using a continuous scale, which can give a measure of overall composition quality. The five areas are content, organization, vocabulary, grammar/language use, and mechanics. Research regarding the factors that influence readers most when evaluating compositions guided the selection of the subscales. Each subscale is weighted according to its estimated contribution to written communication and has descriptors and criteria. The issue of semantics or meaning is addressed in the underlying principle in the design of the ESL Composition Profile—the fact that the reader's overall impression of the message communicated in the writing sample matters most. "The five component scales thus are intended to be regarded as five different windows or viewpoints from which to judge the writer's overall communicative effect" (Jacobs et al., p. 32) with the total score being the most reliable indicator of a writer's ability.

Atajo log

Another valuable tool for data collection was the logging feature of *Atajo*, the word-processing program that the students used in the lab to write compositions. The writing log of *Atajo* provides unobtrusive observation of students' use of the software and details the time that the writing assistant is started, each occasion that the databases such as the dictionary, grammar, or phrases are accessed, and requests to see examples or have verbs conjugated.

The writing time allotted for composition in research studies (as in timed writings for placement and assessment) may be more restrictive in most cases for prewriting, planning, and actual writing than in a classroom setting, but it can also be comparable to in-class exam situations (i.e., students have limited time to complete an essay on a test instead of a homework assignment or take-home composition with unlimited time). No conclusive evidence has shown that the time allowed seriously affects the reliability of scores (Jacobs et al., 1981). The students were allowed a minimum of 30 minutes for writing compositions, a time-limit imposition that is long enough to provide an adequate sample of writing behavior (Jacobs et al., 1981).

Pretest composition 1

An ANOVA was used to test the hypothesis that the means of the two groups were not significantly different on Composition 1. An ANOVA is robust to departures from normality, and this sample population had comparable ranges and means, with a few extreme values deemed not to be outliers. A homogeneity of variances test was used, and the Levene statistic (p=.01) confirmed rejection of the null hypothesis that the variances are equal. An ANOVA is robust to this violation when the groups are of equal or nearly equal size. In this study, the control and experimental groups both included 26 participants. For the ANOVA on Composition 1, the significance level was p=.16, indicating no statistically significant difference in the performances of the two classes on the pretest, Composition 1. This test was intended to give additional assurance as to the comparability of the two groups in terms of composition ability.

Missing data

Statisticians use multiple approaches to handle missing data; most commonly used is the replacement of missing data with the mean, median, or mode. The decision to replace missing values for analysis depends on the reason that they are missing. The best case for replacing data is when data are missing at random. The analysis of the *Atajo* logs revealed that in some cases, students neglected to turn on the logging feature, or there was a technical malfunction. This resulted in missing data for the time spent composing and the inquiries made to the databases, two important issues in this study. To ascertain the best choice for data replacement, the distribution and measures of central tendency were analyzed. Commonly, the mean is used, but the median is less sensitive to extreme scores (the mean is pulled toward the skewness in a distribution). The mean (M=39) was determined to be the best replacement for Composition 1 for the time spent composing for both groups. For Composition 3 for the time spent composing, the control and experimental data were replaced with the medians (*Mdn*=39, *Mdn*=37). As for the total number of inquiries made to *Atajo* databases, the range of usage was very broad, and thus, the median was used for all replacements.

Research questions

Question 1: *How will the scaffolding provided by using a grammar- and vocabulary-practice software program (Spanish Partner) affect quantity in L2 students' compositions as measured by the total number of words per composition?*

Examining this question was the preliminary step in looking at the fluency of the students' compositions with regard to the total number of words produced during a given period of time. Completing a count of words per composition provided the information needed to conduct a repeated measures ANOVA, testing the interaction effects or treatment by occasion (pretest/posttest). Writing sessions during class varied across students, with *Atajo* logs revealing that composition times ranged from 28 to 49 minutes. Thus, to examine the quantity of writing produced, the words per minute needed to be calculated to conduct a repeated measures ANOVA to test the interaction effects or treatment of grammar and vocabulary practice on the composition performance by occasion (pretest/posttest). On Composition 1, the control group wrote M=3.58 words per minute, and the experimental group wrote M=3.74 words per minute. On Composition 3, the control group wrote M=4.27 words per minute, and the experimental group wrote M=3.61 words per minute. Although the control group made a slight gain, a repeated measures ANOVA on the change in words per minute showed no statistically significant difference between the groups, $F(1, 50)=2.54$, $p=.12$.

Question 2: *How will the systematic use of a grammar-practice software program (Spanish Partner) affect the quality of L2 learners' compositions as measured by a total composition score and the subscale areas of content, organization, vocabulary, grammar/language use, and mechanics (spelling, accentuation, and punctuation)?*
The quality of the written product is a measure of composition skill and development of fluency. The American Council on the Teaching of Foreign Languages defines fluency as a flow in the written language as perceived by the reader, made possible by clarity of expression, the acceptable ordering of ideas, and use of vocabulary and syntax appropriate to the context, with words, phrases, and idiomatic expressions that go together by common lexical convention (Breiner-Sanders, Swender, & Terry, 2002, p. 14). The composition rubric measures the five subscale components. Measures of improvement in each area of composition for the experimental group with comparison to the control were determined using a repeated-measures ANOVA design, specifically, a mixed-factor ANOVA. Descriptive statistics such as the mean score, range of the scores for both the experimental and control groups, frequency distribution of scores, and standard deviation were examined. All of the compositions were graded by two graders, and the interrater reliability was .81. In 17 cases where the graders disagreed by more than 10 points on the total composition score, the researcher served as a third grader. The 10-point difference is cited in Jacobs et al. (1981) as the standard for reliability: Scores with greater than 10-point differences necessitate an additional grader. The two closest scores were averaged, and that score was used for analyses. Composition 1 yielded a Cronbach's alpha of .82, and Composition 3, a Cronbach's alpha of .80.

Measures of improvement on the total composition and each component subscale of the composition rubric were examined at two levels. Gain scores were examined on the descriptive level and using independent *t* tests for Compositions 1 and 3. No statistically significant results were found using any of the independent t-tests. However, note that the percentage of change on the mean scores between Compositions 1 and 3 is higher for the experimental group on all measures except for mechanics, which was equal for the experimental and the control.

Evaluation of total composition scores and rubric subscales

A mixed two-factor ANOVA was used to look at the differences between the experimental and control groups over time on the total composition score and the five subscales. Although there were no statistically significant differences found between the experimental and control groups in these analyses, the general trends in the increases for the experimental group are visible in the figure plots for the total composition score and the subscales of content, organization, vocabulary, and grammar/language use. There was a statistically significant difference between the total composition scores for Compositions 1 and 3 for all of the participants in the study, $F(1, 50)=15.52$, $p < .01$. When examining the interaction of effects between the control and experimental groups, there was no statistically significant difference, $F(1, 50)=1.68$, $p=.20$.

There was a statistically significant difference between the content subscale scores for Compositions 1 and 3 for all of the participants in the study, $F(1 ,50)=6.71$, $p=.01$. When examining the interaction of effects between the control and experimental groups, there was no statistically significant difference, $F(1, 50)=0.62$, $p=.43$. There was a statistically significant difference between the organization subscale scores for Compositions 1 and 3 for all of the participants in the study, $F(1, 50)=13.64$, $p < .01$. When examining the interaction of effects between the control and experimental groups, there was no statistically significant difference, $F(1, 50)=1.14$, $p=.29$. There was a statistically significant difference between the vocabulary subscale scores for Compositions 1 and 3 for all of the participants in the study, $F(1, 50)=18.45$, $p < .01$. When examining the interaction of effects between the control and experimental groups, there was no statistically significant difference, $F(1, 50)=0.71$, $p=.40$. Although the differences in gains may not have been statistically significant, the experimental group was making greater gains in vocabulary subscale scores and ended at the same point as the control group despite beginning at a lower point.

There was a statistically significant difference between the grammar/language-use subscale scores for Compositions 1 and 3 for all of the participants in the study, $F(1, 50)=9.57$, $p < .01$. When examining the interaction of effects between the control and experimental groups, there was no statistically significant difference, $F(1, 50)=3.55$, $p=.07$. This p value of .07 for grammar/language-use (the focus of this study's treatment) gains between the experimental and the control groups comes the closest to statistical significance of all of the subscale scores. Although the differences in gains may not have been statistically significant, the experimental group seemed to be making more rapid gains in grammar/language use.

There was a statistically significant difference between the mechanics subscale score for Compositions 1 and 3 for all of the participants in the study, $F(1, 50)=19.15$, $p < .01$. When examining the interaction of effects between the control and experimental groups, there was no statistically significant difference, $F(1, 50)=1.16$, $p=.29$. The differences in gains for the mechanics subscale score were not statistically significant and show a more parallel growth pattern for the two groups.

Although the hypothesis was that students with grammar and vocabulary practice would produce better-quality compositions on the total composition score and the vocabulary and grammar/language-use subscales, there was no statistically significant difference in the total composition score between the control and experimental groups.

Question 3: *What are students' opinions of using technology to learn to compose in an L2?* The student information sheet contained Likert-scale items and open-ended questions that probed the students' opinions of using technology to learn to compose. A description of the student opinions was made using a qualitative analysis of the responses. These opinions gave insight into the students' attitudes regarding computers and technology, which can impact their use. In a first step to determine the participants' experience with and attitudes toward technology, the students were asked to rate their computer skill level at the beginning of the semester, indicating the level as *no prior experience, beginner, intermediate,* or *expert.* In the control group, one student (3.8%) identified as a beginner, 19 (73.1%) identified as intermediate, and 6 (23.1%) claimed to be experts. In the experimental group, one student (3.8%) identified as a beginner, 23 (88.5%) identified as intermediate, and only 2 (7.7%) stated that they were experts.

When asked whether they had previously used technology to learn languages, 88.5% of the control group indicated that they had used technology, compared to 84.6% of the experimental group. Four students in the experimental group and 3 students in the control group said that they had never experienced TELL; one additional student (control group) did not respond to the question. Those students that had used technology to learn languages indicated that they had done so in various ways. Examining the participants as a whole, 22 students cited the use of the *Puntos de partida* textbook CD; 8, prior use of *Spanish Partner*; and 18, prior use of *Atajo*. Only 5 students named video or television as a technology tool to learn languages. The Internet was mentioned by 7 students, with one additional student having taken advantage of an online translator and one student who had taken a 1st-year, second-semester course online at another institution. Four students referred generically to "programs in the computer lab downstairs" or nonspecified vocabulary and grammar lessons.

On the first day of class, both groups were asked their opinions of TELL. The question was open-ended to elicit a range of commentaries. The comments were evaluated and tabulated as negative, somewhat negative, neutral, somewhat positive, and positive. An overview of the responses is provided in Table 1.

Table 1: Student opinions of technology-enhanced language learning

	no resp. n/a	negative	somewhat negative	neutral	somewhat positive	positive
control	4	1	1	3	2	15
(*n*=26)	15%	4%	4%	12%	8%	58%
experimental	4	1	0	4	5	12
(*n*=26)	15%	4%	0%	15%	19%	46%

An example of a negative comment is "I don't like it; I don't remember anything." A somewhat negative comment is "It can be helpful, but it often takes more time than reading the book for almost the same help." A somewhat positive comment is "It helped a little but not a lot," and a fully positive response is "It helps very much." In each class, 4 students' responses indicated they had never used technology in language learning.

Many students used the word "help" or "helpful" in some form. In each class, 17 students (65%) were positive or somewhat positive regarding TELL. The students seemed aware of some of the benefits of TELL and had positive attitudes. The control-group member comments included the following:

> It helps to look at grammar and conjugation procedures when there is no one to help you at the time.
>
> It is nice because you can go at your own [underlining in original] pace & not the pace of 30 other ppl.
>
> It's a great opportunity for us to have and use. I'm more of a visual learner.
>
> I like using it. I believe it is more beneficial than workbook exercises and writing papers.

The experimental group members shared:

> I believe it helps to solidify what you can learn in class.
>
> I think technology is a good study aide [*sic*] for learning a foreign language.
>
> It can make learning easier.

Students' opinions were evidently colored by their experiences and familiarity with various programs, which may account for some of the contradictions regarding the usefulness of technology for learning certain skills. One student in the control group asserted, "It is helpful, especially in helping with pronunciation," while another student in the control group stated, "It's helpful reading, writing, & listening....But it doesn't really help speaking." Yet another student in the experimental group aptly stressed, "In my few experiences using technology to learn Spanish, I think it depends on the program. I've used one program that is really good and another that's really bad."

A few students expressed some reservations regarding the use of TELL. One student who admitted never having used technology to learn a language stated, "I learn much better through other means. Technology doesn't seem efficient enough." One student who said that he or she used *Spanish Partner* in the lab previous to the study commented, "It helps me a little, however I learn more with help from a teacher showing me hands on how to write it and the correct way to speak." Both of these students were in the experimental group.

Summary of results

The purposes of this research were to identify and to describe the possible benefits of weekly, structured, in-class, computer-assisted grammar drills and practice on the writing performance of university learners of intermediate Spanish, to determine whether students accessed a writing-assistant program differently based upon their grammatical practice experience, and to examine whether TELL aids in composition abilities. There were no statistically significant differences between the experimental and control groups on composition quantity and quality. However, the results of this study indicate that both the experimental and control groups improved over time in composition performance. The treatment of grammar practice with *Spanish Partner* showed a small to moderate effect from pretest to posttest, and the experimental group showed greater mean gains in composition quality than the control group. The students in the experimental group accessed the databases of the *Atajo* writing assistant less on the final composition than the students in the control group, with a statistically significant difference.

Practice with a computer-based grammar-instruction software program (in this case, *Spanish Partner*) may enhance written communicative competence in the L2 learning environment. Note that a composition "test" is an imperfect measure of the construct of composition ability, which provides only a sample of writing or language behavior (Jacobs et al., 1981) and that a small sample size can be less sensitive to revealing statistically significant results. In addition, improving writing performance is a lengthy process, and often, a measurable change does not occur during one course (Greenia, 1992b).

Discussion of findings

Fluency

The first two research questions were intended to measure the effects of grammar and vocabulary practice on students' fluency, specifically, composition quantity and quality. First, how would the scaffolding provided by the use of a grammar- and vocabulary-practice software program (*Spanish Partner*) affect quantity in L2 students' compositions as measured by the total number of words per composition? The researcher hypothesized that students with grammar and vocabulary practice would produce a greater number of words during composition after the grammar and vocabulary practice. The results of the analyses are not statistically significant, so the null hypothesis cannot be rejected. The overall words per minute from Composition 1 to 3 showed minimal changes for both groups. The control group's increase was slightly greater, yet less than one word per minute. One reason for the control group's increase in the number of words per minute from Composition 1 to 3 may have been the increased familiarity with and efficiency in using the *Atajo* software.

The decrease in the experimental group's words per minute was negligible. However, data analysis revealed that the total usage of *Atajo* by the experimental group declined by almost 50% from Composition 1 to 3. Although the fluency remained static in terms of the number of words produced, the composition quality increased. Thus, the practice with *Spanish Partner* may have increased the students' facility in accessing their own personal lexicons, which in turn increased automaticity in the production of the vocabulary and grammatical structures needed for their compositions. This concept of technology integration to promote fluency of automaticity of prerequisite skills is supported by Roblyer (2003). The usage of *Atajo* increased slightly from Composition 1 to 3 for the control group.

The second part of the fluency issue was the question of how the systematic use of a grammar-practice software program (*Spanish Partner*) would affect the quality of L2 learners' compositions as measured by their total composition scores and the subscale areas of content, organization, vocabulary, grammar/language use, and mechanics (spelling, accentuation, and punctuation). The researcher hypothesized that students with grammar and vocabulary practice would produce better quality compositions based on the total composition score and the vocabulary and grammar/language-use subscales. There were no statistically significant differences between the two groups on any of the variables related to quality, reflecting the fact that changes in writing improvement are often not seen at the end of only one course of study (Greenia, 1992b). However, the percentage of positive change on the mean scores between Compositions 1 and 3 (including the subscale areas) is greater for the experimental group on all subscales except for mechanics, which was equal for the experimental and the control groups. The vocabulary and grammar/language-use subscales showed the highest percentage gains in mean scores. The trends in the data in the mean plots between Compositions 1 and 3 indicate that *Spanish Partner* did have a small to moderate effect overall and especially on grammar and vocabulary. Krashen (1999) indicated that the successful application of consciously learned rules of grammar involves knowledge of the rule, concern with correctness (focus on form), and sufficient time. The behavior exhibited by the experimental group may, therefore, indicate their formal rule knowledge of grammar gained via computer practice. Findings by Liou, Wang, and Hung-Yeh (1992) showed that instruction plus CALL impacted writing more than instruction plus homework. Their results suggest that classroom instruction combined with grammatical computer-assisted language learning (CALL) is helpful to writing, parallel to the present study.

Additionally, examination of the standard-deviation changes in total composition scores from Composition 1 to 3 reveals a noteworthy finding. The standard deviation decreased by 4.02 for the experimental group from Composition 1 to 3, while the increase for the control group was only 0.56. In interpreting these results, the decreased standard deviation for the experimental group illustrates less variability in the total composition scores on

Composition 3. Greatly improved performance for some students on the final composition may indicate that the treatment of grammar practice was beneficial to the students who scored lowest on Composition 1. This is supported by Frantzen's (1995) intervention study of an intermediate Spanish content course, where the results suggested that grammar review was a beneficial addition despite a lack of significant differences between groups in terms of their scores on writing samples.

Student opinions of using technology to compose

Research question 3 dealt with students' opinions of the usefulness of technology for composing in an L2. Overall, the students from both the experimental and the control groups were positive in their opinions of the usefulness of technology (specifically *Atajo)* for writing compositions in their L2. This enthusiasm was somewhat mitigated by the requirement to write compositions in the lab with time restrictions. In general, the students in the foreign-language program in this research setting were accustomed to writing assignments being take-home with unlimited time. Even with that in mind, the consensus from the students in the control group was quite positive regarding writing with technology:

> My writing and communications skills in this language have vastly improved.
>
> The technology was really helpful w/grammar, writing and organizing my thoughts in Spanish.
>
> This course helped me write & listen in Spanish more proficiently. The labs when we type Spanish compositions really helped a lot.
>
> Doing all the writing in the computer lab helped tremendously in learning how to use the language.

The experimental group appeared somewhat more reserved than the control group in their responses to the questions. Possibly they were disenchanted with going to lab every week (the researcher, for instance, overheard a couple of students groaning under their breath about "having" to go to the lab). Some were positive about the technology experience but missed the connection between knowing grammar and improving writing:

> The focus on technology in this course through intense lab time has helped on writing the foreign language but not so helpful in grammar.
>
> Furthermore, the class had more of a writing slant, which allowed students to focus on applying what we learned from style and grammer [*sic*] to papers and compositions.
>
> Main focus on grammar and especially verb conjugation. Did not look holistically at the language and therefore did not help to think and write in the language, only translating.

The comments by the last student reflect the language acquisition-learning distinction proposed by Krashen (1982); adult language acquisition is similar to the way children develop language, and language learning emphasizes the conscious knowing and application of grammar and grammar rules. Yet, it is important to note that Terrell (1991) stated that explicit grammar instruction may positively affect language acquisition.

The positive attitudes of students regarding the use of technology to write is of great consequence. Gillespie and McKee (1999) defined the successful integration of CALL into the curriculum at their institution by the quality of the student work produced and the degree of acceptance by students. These benchmarks certainly seem reasonable, especially at the university level, because access to technology can often be restricted, and the time available to incorporate it into the curriculum can also be limited. In this study, the students' quality of composition improved across both groups, and they held very positive attitudes with regard to TELL. This echoes the previous work of Scott (1996), who affirmed that computer-aided writing enhances the foreign-language experience. Additionally, Pennington (2003) drew from her extensive research on the writing of English language learners and presented models of positive and negative paths in computer writing effects. Although her models address characteristics of the English as a second language population, the concepts can apply to learners in foreign-language contexts who face writing with computers. Pennington outlined cognitive-affective responses of awareness and attitudes that interact with behavioral responses of quantity, quality, and manner. On the positive path, students have an awareness of computer capabilities for the writing process and a positive attitude toward computers and writing. The behavioral response observed could be writing at length with high levels of content coverage and a physical and cognitive ease in writing seen in recursive patterns. On the negative path, students are unaware or have low awareness of computer potentials for writing. The behavioral response can be limited writing in quantity and quality and a physical and cognitive strain with writing. In the present study, a combination of these effects may have influenced the outcomes of quantity, quality, and use of the *Atajo* databases.

Implications

The effects of technology-enhanced grammar and vocabulary practice on the composition of students in a university-level Spanish course were the focus of this study, which also sought to address the dearth of writing research specific to the foreign-language context. The treatment of grammar practice using *Spanish Partner* showed a small to moderate effect, although with no statistically significant differences between the experimental and control groups. The grammar practice was certainly not detrimental to the students' composition abilities.

The implications of this study on foreign-language instruction are many. For foreign-language writing, TELL, in the form of computer-based grammar and vocabulary practice, can be important for the development of composition skills, especially for weaker students. Students that struggle with a grammatical concept often ask teachers what they can do to improve, and teachers often suggest time in the lab for additional practice. The treatment in this study was for a minimum of 30 minutes per week and showed some promise. Whereas Terrell (1991) supported the idea that explicit grammar instruction may help to speed up the language acquisition process, the process is hampered by the low number of hours of instruction in the university classroom. This limits the amount of input and interaction that a language learner experiences, and additional independent computer-based grammar practice could provide a one-on-one tutorial that would be otherwise unavailable and perhaps prohibitive in cost.

Teachers often focus on mechanics (spelling, accentuation, and punctuation) in foreign-language writing in addition to grammatical accuracy, yet, perhaps this attention is unwarranted. Polio (2001) questioned whether mechanics is a construct at all and whether it is important to writing researchers. In the few writing studies that have included mechanics (typically a secondary focus of these investigations), change over time in learners' abilities to correctly apply mechanics was not statistically significant (Hedgcock & Lefkowitz, 1992; Pennington & So, 1993; Tsang, 1996). Although this study did not focus exclusively on mechanics, the students clearly did not effectively use the available technology tools, such as spell checkers.

With improvements in both the experimental and control groups on the total composition score and the students' positive remarks regarding writing with technology in the lab, support is evident for the integration of computer writing assistants in the foreign-language curriculum, confirming Pennington's (2003) findings. Using *Atajo* for writing facilitates the writing experience by allowing time for reflection, rereading, and cut-and-paste editing techniques.

Another observation during this study with implications for technology integration is that in spite of repeated practice, some students will continue to misuse technology. Several researchers have found that students did not use technology as instructed (Baily, 1993; New, 1995), and the implication is that in some cases, students require more guidance to use technology than might be expected (Burston, 1991; Scott, 1990). Providing more explicit directions and monitoring students is critical if they are to reap the benefits of the activity.

Finally, the composition subscale score gains for grammar/language use and vocabulary of those who experienced the computer grammar and vocabulary practice were higher than those of the control group. Therefore, although there was not a statistically significant difference, the data do suggest that teachers and curriculum planners may need to integrate specific technology tools and activities to better nurture specific abilities in L2 acquisition.

References

Arana, A. A., & Arana, O. (2001). *Workbook to accompany Puntos de partida.* New York: McGraw-Hill.

Atwell, N. (1998). *In the middle: New understandings about writing, reading, and learning.* Portsmouth, NH: Boynton/Cook.

Baily, C. A. (1993). Getting the message across: A study of compensation strategy use in writing by adult foreign language learners using *Système-D* as an unobtrusive observation tool. (Doctoral dissertation, Peabody College for Teachers of Vanderbilt University, 1992). *Dissertation Abstracts International, 53,* 4222.

Breiner-Sanders, K., Swender, E., & Terry, R. (2002). Preliminary proficiency guidelines—Writing revised 2001. *Foreign Language Annals, 35,* 9–15.

Burston, J. L. (1991). Using *Système-D* in a classroom environment. *CALICO Journal,* 8(4), 51–57.

Calkins, L. M. (1983). *Lessons from a child.* Portsmouth, NH: Heinemann.

Dominguez, F., Noblitt, J. S., & Pet, W. J. A. (1999). *Atajo 3.0* [Computer software]. Boston: Heinle & Heinle Publishers.

Frantzen, D. (1995). The effects of grammar supplementation on written accuracy in an intermediate Spanish content course. *Modern Language Journal, 79,* 329–344.

Gillespie, J., & McKee, J. (1999). Does it fit and does it make any difference? Integrating CALL into the curriculum. *Computer Assisted Language Learning, 12,* 441–455.

Graves, D. H. (1975). The child, the writing process, and the role of the professional. In W. Petty (Ed.), *The writing processes of students.* Buffalo: State University of New York.

Greenia, G. D. (1992a). Computers and teaching composition in a foreign language. *Foreign Language Annals, 25,* 33–46.

Greenia, G. D. (1992b). Why Johnny can't *escribir*: Composition and the foreign language curriculum. *ADFL Bulletin, 24*(1), 30–37.

Hedgcock, J., & Lefkowitz, N. (1992). Collaborative oral/aural revision in foreign language writing instruction. *Journal of Second Language Writing, 1*, 255–276.

Jacobs, H., Zingraf, S., Wormuth, D., Hartfiel, V., & Hughey, J. (1981). *Testing ESL composition: A practical approach*. Rowley, MA: Newbury House.

Knorre, M., Dorwick, T., Pérez-Gironés, A.-M., Glass, W., & Villarreal, H. (2001). *Puntos de partida*. Boston: McGraw-Hill.

Krashen, S. D. (1982). *Principles and practice in second language acquisition*. New York: Pergamon Press.

Krashen, S. D. (1999). Seeking a role for grammar: A review of some recent studies. *Foreign Language Annals, 32*, 245–257.

Liou, H.-C., Wang, S. H., & Hung-Yeh, Y. (1992). Can grammatical CALL help EFL writing instruction? *CALICO Journal, 10*(1), 23–44.

Morley, M., & Fisher, K. (1994). *Spanish partner: Introductory Spanish exercises for personal computers* [Computer software]. New York: McGraw-Hill.

National Standards in Foreign Language Education Project (1999). *Standards for foreign language learning in the 21st century*. Lawrence, KS: Allen Press.

New, J. E. (1995). Revision strategies in French as a foreign language: Case studies in computer-aided writing. (Doctoral dissertation, Vanderbilt University, 1994). *Dissertation Abstracts International, 55*, 3489.

Pennington, M. (2003). The impact of the computer in second language writing. In B. Kroll (Ed.), *Exploring the dynamics of second language writing* (pp. 287–310). Cambridge, England & New York: Cambridge University Press.

Pennington, M., & So, S. (1993). Comparing writing process and product across two languages: A study of 6 Singaporean university student writers. *Journal of Second Language Writing, 2*, 41–63.

Polio, C. (2001). Research methodology in second language writing research: The case of text-based studies. In T. Silva & P. K. Matsuda (Eds.), *On second language writing* (pp. 91–116). Mahwah, NJ: Lawrence Erlbaum Associates.

Polio, C. (2003). Research on second language writing: An overview of what we investigate and how. In B. Kroll (Ed.), *Exploring the dynamics of second language writing* (pp. 35–65). Cambridge, England & New York: Cambridge University Press.

Raschio, R. A. (1998). *Spanish Partner*: Introductory Spanish exercises for personal computers [Review of the software program *Spanish Partner*]. *CALICO Journal, 16*(1), 83–88.

Roblyer, M. D. (2003). *Integrating educational technology into teaching* (3rd ed.). Columbus, OH: Merrill Prentice Hall.

Romano, T. (1987). *Clearing the way: Working with teenage writers*. Portsmouth, NH: Heinemann.

Scott, V. M. (1990). Task-oriented creative writing with *Système-D*. *CALICO Journal, 7*(3), 58–67.

Scott, V. M. (1996). *Rethinking foreign language writing*. Boston: Heinle & Heinle Publishers.

Scott, V. M., & Terry, R. M. (1992). *Système-D: Writing assistant for French. Teacher's guide*. Boston: Heinle & Heinle Publishers.

Terrell, T. D. (1991). The role of grammar instruction in a communicative approach. *Modern Language Journal, 75*, 52–63.

Tsang, W. K. (1996). Comparing the effects of reading and writing on writing performance. *Applied Linguistics, 17*, 210–233.

VanBuren, P. E. (1997). *Spanish Partner*: Introductory Spanish exercises for personal computers [Review of the software program *Spanish Partner*]. *Hispania, 80*, 527–528.

Vygotsky, L. S. (1962). *Thought and language*. Cambridge, MA: The MIT Press.

Podcasting and the Intermediate-Level Spanish Classroom

Nancy Bird-Soto
University of Wisconsin–Milwaukee

Patricia Rengel
University of Wisconsin–Madison

Being an effective language instructor requires teaching the target language in the most authentic fashion possible. From beginning to intermediate courses in Spanish, a myriad of textbooks and reading materials are available. However, finding interesting, meaningful, and relevant sources for listening practice may not be as easy. Prerecorded tapes and CDs, although suitable for most introductory language courses, lack the more immediate effect of a lively discussion or conversation. By the end of 2005, podcasting in higher learning had become a new venue for facilitating audio materials for students. As instructors of Spanish, we recognized an absence of relevant listening materials, especially for language learners at the intermediate level. Podcasts,[1] which are easy to produce, allowed us to address this gap. With the goal of enhancing class discussions through direct interviews and conversations with authors, artists, and other outstanding "personalities," we developed a collection of over 25 podcasts titled *Personalidades de la Cultura Hispánica.*[2]

Podcasting, which more recently includes not only sound but also images, is based primarily within the development of digital audio technologies. Sound, with its nuanced physical properties, is a versatile yet complex element, and its digital representation certainly proves so. As explained by Dobrian (1997), "In order for a computer to represent sound accurately, many many samples must be taken per second—many more than are necessary for filming a visual image. In fact, we need to take more than twice as many samples at the highest frequency we wish to record." Although the process of quantization appears rather complicated, using digital audio for podcasting is not necessarily daunting

1 The University of Minnesota's brochure, "Podcasts in Education" (dmc.umn.edu/technologies/podcasting.pdf), provides detailed information and a general overview of pedagogical uses of podcasting.
2 *Personalidades de la Cultura Hispánica* may be found at http://spanport.lss.wisc.edu/new_web/?q=node/152.

Bird-Soto, N., & Rengel, P. (2009). Podcasting and the intermediate-level Spanish classroom. In R. Oxford & J. Oxford, (Eds.), *Second language teaching and learning in the Net Generation* (pp. 101–109). Honolulu: University of Hawai'i, National Foreign Language Resource Center.

for individuals developing an educational program using this technology. Back in 2005, when podcasting in education was an emerging trend, the notion of making learning accessible beyond the classroom superseded any doubts by instructors like us, who at the time, had no formal training in digital audio technology. As Jeff Curto (2006) has explained regarding his photography courses at the College of DuPage, the idea of podcasting as a way to "[open] the door of [the] classroom to the rest of the world and [start] a class discussion that is not constrained by the classroom walls" was readily embraced. The complexities embedded in sound and audio technology notwithstanding, the tools themselves were accessible enough for us to develop a program of interviews in Spanish for our students and beyond.

Aside from implementing new technologies in the world-language classroom, the *Personalidades* project had a much more ambitious reach than merely adding a sample of interviews so that intermediate-level students of Spanish would be able to practice their listening skills and animate class discussion. Although the initial goal was to have between five and eight podcasts as part of the program, the project quickly gained momentum soon after the first interviews—with Dominican musician Pavel Polanco and with Peninsular Spanish Literature Professor Juan Egea—started in January 2006. By April, we had already featured renowned writers such as Mexican author Angeles Mastretta and Chilean poet and human-rights activist Marjorie Agosín. The interviews became increasingly popular, and Patricia Rengel was contacted numerous times by the local Madison newspapers. On May 24, 2006, the *Capital Times* ran an article about *Personalidades de la Cultura Hispánica* on its front page (Nathan, 2006). In its first 5 months, the project had gained a considerable amount of attention. However, more importantly to us as instructors, it was the first semester that we used it for our own Spanish classes. The use of podcasts had a pedagogical and engaging versatility from the very beginning. As we will illustrate, students would not only listen to varied interviews, but they also had agency in choosing questions and producing their own recordings.

Nathan (2006), in a Madison *Capital Times* article, pointed out how in the *Personalidades* project, "lecturers are also journalists, creating an electronic trove of interviews with internationally and locally famous Spanish-speaking personalities." The process itself turned us into professional interviewers because our primary goal was to provide authentic listening material to students by creating podcasts in which they would be able to listen to a variety of recognized writers, musicians, sportspeople, and activists from the Hispanic world. Although designed for our students at the time, the program was envisioned in such a way that it would appeal to a wider audience. Students of the language; Hispanic cultures, literature, and linguistics; and U.S. Latino/a cultures may access the program and use it for practice and for class discussions. *Personalidades de la Cultura Hispánica* is hosted by the Board of Regents of the University of Wisconsin (UW) System and can be accessed via the Website of the Department of Spanish and Portuguese at UW-Madison or via iTunes.

In this chapter, we review the technology, podcasts in general and their place in academia, and several case histories of our use of the podcasts and other pedagogical uses of this emerging technology for the intermediate to advanced Spanish classroom. From the very start, we were to use podcasting as a way to "make a better conversation" (Campbell, 2005, p. 46), in our case, with students of Spanish from the intermediate level onwards. The initial challenge was learning how to use this technology, especially for two literature specialists who were neophytes in this area. Doug Worsham, Foreign Language Technologist/AV Services Coordinator at UW-Madison, was instrumental in our training for editing the audio interviews using Audacity. In fact, Worsham's contribution, as is the case for many technology specialists who work behind the scenes, helped take the project to a professional level in terms of the audio quality and in training us to use recording and editing programs. The following is an overview of what a podcast is and the technology that it requires.

Podcasts: Emerging technology

Regardless of whether someone considers him- or herself a techie (technologically savvy person), early adopter (someone who embraces new technology before others), or simply a Web surfer (someone who visits Websites via the Internet), most Web users have probably heard of podcasts. In fact, newspapers and radio programs, such as National Public Radio and *The New York Times*, among others, routinely offer podcasts covering late-breaking news or feature articles on their Websites. Podcasts are audio files that are compressed into a digital format known as MP3 (**MPEG-1** Audio Layer **3**) that can be played on a computer or a handheld digital player. It is a medium that incorporates the Internet, computers, and portable listening devices. It is also a medium that is especially attractive to the Net Generation, those 88 million individuals in North America who were between the ages of 2 and 22 years old in 1999 and are "fluent" in computers.[3]

The etymology of the word "podcast" reveals the history of this emerging technology. Originally derived from a combination of "i**Pod**" and "broad**casting**," "podcast" became the word of the year when it was added to the *New Oxford American Dictionary* in 2005. In that same year, *Business Week* magazine reported an "explosion" of podcasts downloaded from the Internet, which was compared to the activity of the early days of the World Wide Web.[4] A podcast is defined in the *New Oxford American Dictionary* as "a digital recording of a radio broadcast or similar program, made available on the Internet for downloading to a personal audio player." A unique feature of a podcast is that it is downloaded automatically from the Internet via a syndication format. For this to occur, a user needs to install onto a computer a media aggregator program such as iTunes or Juice, which are free on the Internet. In short, podcasts are audio and video files on the Internet that can be downloaded onto mobile listening devices and personal computers.

The success of podcasts is linked to a type of small handheld digital audio (MP3) players, the iPod, which was launched by Apple in 2001. These audio players are about the size of a deck of cards and originally had the capacity of "putting 1000 songs in your pocket" as the advertising slogans touted while promoting the gadget. Upgraded models of the iPod and other digital audio players have multiple uses, which range from an increased audio capacity to storing photos or a contact list, functioning as a small hard drive of sorts. The introduction of the digital music player started a "revolution" in online music downloads and distribution (Miller, 2007), according to *PC Magazine*, a magazine that serves as a guide to technology.

On campuses, the iPod is ubiquitous and quite popular among students. In a 2006 *Student Monitor* Lifestyle and Media Study, the iPod was ranked as the most "in" thing on campus, toppling beer, which had dominated the list since 1998 (Windham, 2007, p. 4). College-age adults constituted the largest number of owners of this gadget, according to a 2005 survey from Pew Internet and American Life Project, which concluded that one in five adults between the ages of 18 and 28 owned an iPod or MP3 player (Rainie & Madden, 2005).

3 Don Tapscott discussed the concept of the Net or InterNet Generation in his book *Growing Up Digital: The Rise of the Net Generation* (1998). The Net Generation, he claimed, is larger than the Baby Boom Generation, which is 29% of the population, as compared to the Net Generation's 30%.

4 The May 23, 2005 issue of *Business Week* reported that over a 6-month period (December 2004–May 2005), the number of podcasts jumped 25-fold to 5,302 feeds ("Podcasting Explosion").

A distinct feature of the podcast, which was originally called an audioblog, is its ability to be syndicated, subscribed to, and downloaded automatically when new content is added.[5] One way to imagine a podcast is to compare it to an audio magazine that is distributed over the Internet. When someone subscribes, podcasts are routinely downloaded to the subscriber's computer. The audio files can then be listened to on any machine that plays MP3 files, which makes the technology highly portable. Easy access and portability make the podcast a natural fit for the teaching of languages, especially in the absence of relevant listening materials available to students.

A review of recent literature (2005–2007) on the use of podcasts reveals an increased use of this technology at the university level (Bongey, Cizadlo, & Kalnbach, 2006; Brittain, Glowacki, Ittersum, & Johnson, 2006; Lee & Chan, 2007; Rainsbury & McDonnell, 2006; Windham, 2007). Podcasts in the teaching of sciences, specifically, information technology and dental, nursing, and computer science, have provided students with additional resource material that complements their lectures. In a study conducted at the University of Michigan School of Dentistry in the fall of 2004, for instance, students preferred podcasts over videos of lectures (Brittain, Glowacki, Ittersum, & Johnson).

The overarching purpose of using podcasts, according to these articles, was to make lectures available to students so as to enhance their learning experience by making material mobile and ubiquitous (Bongey, Cizadlo, & Kalnbach, 2006; Brittain, Glowacki, Ittersum, & Johnson, 2006; Lee & Chan, 2007), especially for institutions that offer distance learning (Lee & Chan, 2007). The isolation frequently experienced by distance learners who are separated from their instructors and the classroom was diminished in courses where podcasts were offered, Lee and Chan reported in 2007. These researchers cited multiple advantages of podcasts: the ease of delivering instructional material, an enhanced classroom experience by engaging students, community building, and the dissemination of student-generated material.

Podcasts are not the sole domain of professors or instructors: Student-produced podcasts are also effective pedagogical tools. Duke University professor Daniel Foster asked his students to produce a radio-theater podcast for their final project in a course titled "Radio and Theater of the Mind," which was successful in engaging the students (Windham, 2007). Most students embraced the new technology. For instance, in one article, a graduate student described herself as a self-styled "podcast junkie" after successfully using podcasts for a research project in the working-class neighborhoods of Northern Belfast even though she had little experience with the technology (Windham).

In this review of recent articles, we discovered only one mention of the use of podcasts to teach languages. Researchers Lee and Chan (2007) mentioned the use of podcasts as part of a study-abroad program for distance-learning courses offered at Charles Sturt University in Australia. Languages and podcasts appear to be in uncharted territory for researchers, a gap that this article addresses by presenting our own experience and uses of this technology.

Podcasts and academia

Podcasts in the academic world challenge the image of academia as an "ivory tower" environment that is slow to incorporate change. Podcasts, a trendy technology, now form an integral part of many university curricula. A simple search on the Internet produced

5 As Curto (2006) concisely defined it, "Podcasting is a generic name for a method of distributing audio and other multimedia files over the Internet for playback on mobile devices and personal computers."

over 21 million sites that discuss or provide links to "university podcasts," which clearly demonstrates the popularity of the medium in academic circles. This search revealed several lists of "university podcasts" that touted the medium as "free educational podcasts" and provided direct links to the podcasts (see http://www.oculture.com/2006/10/university_podc.html).

An early participant in the podcast trend appears to be Georgia College and State University where various courses, including a number of study-abroad courses, have been "iPod-enhanced" with lectures, audio books, and music (Lee & Chan, 2007). Duke University demonstrated a clear commitment to the technology when in August of 2004, 20-GB iPods were distributed to its 1,650 1st-year students with orientation information (Lee & Chan, 2007). A snapshot view of the uses of podcasts at different universities can be obtained if you visit three large university Websites: Stanford, Duke, and UC-Berkeley. Stanford University provides access to a wide range of Stanford faculty lectures, learning materials, music, sports information, and more, which is available on *Stanford on iTunes*. Duke University also offers music, lectures, and tips on Duke life at *Duke on iTunes*. UC Berkeley divides its Webcasts and podcasts into courses (dating back to the fall of 2001) and recent events, where you can listen to podcasts as varied as a lecture by the President of Chile, Michelle Bachelet, and poetry readings. These audio and video files are available to anyone with a computer and Internet access.

Another way to find educational podcasts is to visit iTunes U, a section of Apple's iTunes Store, where users can download free educational content from many universities. Its content includes: course lectures, laboratory demonstrations, and sports items, and these are available as audio and video files. Podcasts on this Website cover a wide range of topics from many universities. For instance, featured podcasts include *Geography of Europe* from Arizona State University, *Philosophy 185* from UC Berkeley, *60 Second Lectures* from the University of Pennsylvania, and *Engineering Works* from Texas A&M. Institutions that participate in this program include Stanford, UC Berkeley, University of Melbourne, Texas A&M, MIT, Yale, Trinity College, and many more.[6]

Podcasts produced at UW-Madison can easily be accessed through iTunes U or the university Website. At the Apple site, *Personalidades de la Cultura Hispánica* registers as one of the most "popular" (determined by the number of downloads), along with *Earthwatch Radio*, which features science and medical topics, and *Das Treffende Wort*, designed for intermediate German students. Podcasts are also available for classes in folklore, business, botany, linguistics, and psychology.

Interest in podcasts on the Madison campus has been on the rise, as can be seen by the 130 grants distributed over the last few years (2006–2007) to professors and students to develop video and audio podcasts. Lectures, interviews, literary reviews, and even birdsongs are now available to university students and Web audiences alike via podcasts. Jan Cheetham, Project Manager at Madison's DoIt Technology Division, reported that over 120 instructors at UW-Madison have used podcasting since 2006 to enhance learning in their courses, using the medium to produce audio/video case studies, explain concepts in detail, and deliver core course multimedia objects in more compact and portable formats. "The number of podcasting instructors CONTINUES to grow each semester and at the same time, campus life, outreach, and research organizations are now offering podcasts to audiences on and beyond the campus," Cheetham explained (personal communication, October 15, 2008).

6 For more language resources, students can subscribe to podcasts such as Spanish 201, found at http://www.language.iastate.edu/main/podcast.

The advantage of this emerging technology is that students can listen anytime, anywhere to podcasts as an assignment or supplement to their academic courses. This feature is particularly attractive to the members of the Net Generation, who in Tapscott's (1998) words are "bathed in bits," which means that they own computers and are computer literate and extremely active on the Internet. Podcasts are a natural and easily assimilated tool for this group, represented by the majority of our language students.

Part of the wonder of the podcasting trend is that the technology is easy to use and requires very little equipment. Needed to record a podcast are a computer with Internet access, a headset with a microphone, and audio recording and editing software such as Audacity, which can be downloaded for free from the Internet. This free, open-source, cross-platform audio recording and editing software is easy to use and versatile enough for most situations. To produce recordings away from the computer, additional equipment must be purchased which ranges in price from $60 to 400. Finally, once a podcast is produced, it can be placed online for students to listen to, or it can be published (for free) on iTunes, the previously mentioned online audio and music store. UW-Madison has its own Web server called Learn@UW where instructors and professors post the podcasts, and students can easily listen to them in a computer laboratory or using their personal computers or MP3 players.

Personalidades: Pedagogical applications

The use of podcasting in the classroom can be a flexible and creative process, as we discovered with our series of podcasts in *Personalidades*. In the intermediate language classroom, students can implement their knowledge of the language to choose the questions that will be included in an interview. Moreover, they can read about and research the person interviewed before or after listening to the podcast and even be interviewers themselves. In the 5th-semester (intermediate to advanced) language classroom, students are able to respond better to context and becoming engaged with a podcast interview—be it by listening to, preparing for, or conducting it—enables them to meaningfully apply that context. The possibility of listening to the same author or renowned personality that they are reading about brings an important dimension of immediacy and connectedness to class discussion. The following examples are ways in which the students are direct agents in the process of relating to the podcasts accessible via programs like *Personalidades de la Cultura Hispánica*.

One of the reasons that Angeles Mastretta, author of *Mexican Bolero*, kindly agreed to her podcast interview was precisely the fact that this was a project designed for students of Spanish and for people interested in Hispanic cultures and literatures. At the time, Spring 2006, Nancy Bird-Soto was teaching Spanish 226 (intermediate language practice, 5th semester) at UW-Madison, and her students were reading excerpts from *Mujeres de Ojos Grandes* featured in the textbook *Voces y Vistas Latinas* (Levine & Montross, 2002). In one of the class discussions, the students were required to make a list of questions that they would like to ask the author if they had the opportunity to do so after they had read the stories and had conversed about them in class. As a group, they voted on the most relevant questions, and those were the questions used in the interview with Mastretta. This activity, in which students had to reflect upon the readings and then choose pertinent questions for the author, turned this podcast into a mediated dialogue between the writer and the students.

Podcasts can also give students the opportunity to voice their opinions or make presentations in the target language, yet another pedagogical asset for this new technology.

An example of student-produced podcasts occurred in a Spanish 226 class taught by Patricia Rengel, where students became engaged in the immigration issue. In the spring of 2006, immigration-rights advocates marched on campuses nationwide. UW-Madison community organizations were particularly active as students rallied against questionable immigration policies by staging protests on campus and at the Wisconsin state capitol. Students in Rengel's section of Spanish 226 voiced the pros and cons of the immigration debate by producing a Spanish podcast in which the students interviewed a leader of the student organization Movimiento Estudiantil Chicano de Aztlán. In addition to this product (a relevant interview about a current events topic), an in-depth class discussion also ensued. This podcast was entirely student-centered and brought world issues into the classroom, all in the target language.

Another way to engage students in listening activities such as podcasting is to ask them to think about questions that they would like to ask the person in the interview after listening to the podcast. This assignment requires more than basic listening comprehension but also makes the students active listeners who would like to gather more information about the topics discussed in the interview. That is, the dialogue potentially continues beyond the interview itself. This is a pedagogical application that can be implemented at the more advanced level within the intermediate to advanced range because students are required to maintain a certain level of sophistication to further develop the conversation they hear in the podcast with the interviewee.

During the fall semester of 2007, Bird-Soto gave her Spanish 318 (advanced listening and speaking) class at UW-Milwaukee an assignment in which they listened to podcasts that featured folklorist and writer Roberto de la Torre Hurtado,[7] who spoke about Texas/Mexico border issues and cultural symbols of the McAllen, Texas region. Three podcasts were produced from this interview, recorded at a restaurant with *audio vérité*[8] quality. Because Roberto de la Torre was in Wisconsin at the time for a conference, he visited the class and conversed with this group of students. Therefore, the students not only had a listening comprehension activity but also a follow-up class discussion. They had to reflect on the interviews and the notes they took to develop pertinent questions. This is a more advanced type of pedagogical use of podcast interviews. It allows students to enter another level of agency by continuing the conversation in the target language in the classroom with native speakers who are not their regular instructors. This particular course, Spanish 318, while practicing advanced listening skills, is still an intermediate language practice-level course (5th semester) at UW-Milwaukee.

For obvious reasons (mainly scheduling and finances), bringing an interviewee to class is a rare occurrence for a project like *Personalidades*, given the various international voices in the program. However, for a more local podcasting project, it may be possible to bring the speakers that students listen to in interviews to the classroom to further the conversation. This is an excellent way to target specific vocabulary and to use it in a meaningful context, thus strengthening the students' confidence in applying the knowledge that they have been acquiring. A possibility for a local podcasting program is a series of interviews with successful community leaders in a specific city or region, conducted in the target language.

7 Roberto de la Torre Hurtado is author of the short-story collection *El Vampiro del Río Grande* (2008).

8 This is a term used by Campbell (2005, p. 34) when describing impromptu or "offhanded" recordings. When Roberto de la Tore and Arturo Zárate were interviewed, they knew that they were going to be asked about "the border" but had not seen the questions. Recording it at a restaurant added to the *vérité*, which required a meticulous approach when editing and turning the interview into three podcasts.

This would certainly enhance class discussions and emphasize a sense of immediacy and relevance to the language studied.

Bird-Soto surveyed her students of Spanish 318 (Fall 2007) as to which podcasts they found most enriching. The majority mentioned the ones with Roberto de la Torre because they enjoyed being able to continue the dialogue in person. In this case, instead of preparing questions for a podcast, the interview itself triggered questions from the students as a follow-up conversation in person after listening to the interviews.

Other pedagogical uses

Students responded positively to the podcasts in the intermediate- to advanced-level Spanish courses taught by Bird-Soto and Rengel at UW-Madison and UW-Milwaukee. Students quickly embraced the technology. For instance, in the spring and fall of 2007, students produced their own podcasts in Spanish 226 at UW-Madison. In these podcasts, the students chose topics ranging from music (merengue, salsa, bachata, Tex-Mex), to artists (Pablo Picasso, Jennifer López) and politics (human rights violations during Argentina's *Guerra Sucia* and Chile's Augusto Pinochet regime). They produced 7- to 10-minute podcasts outside of the classroom. These were placed on Learn@UW, a Web server for UW students and faculty. The students listened to the podcasts and led a discussion in class on their podcasts. These podcasts allowed the students to research, write, and orally produce presentations on topics that interested them. Both oral and listening skills were targeted in this activity, and students diligently participated in the student-led discussions.

Personalidades, although produced at UW-Madison, is readily available to the UW system and to the Web in general as a higher-learning podcasting program. This technology can be used in a variety of linguistic, cultural, and educational scenarios, and it is already evolving into an audio/video means of communication. These audio and video podcasts provide for a wide variety of pedagogical activities in language courses in Spanish language and cultures from the intermediate level onwards. Indeed, expanding the use of this technology has much potential for further research of personalities and topics of interest by both instructors and students. For example, a podcast focusing on a country or a region may include interviews, images, videos, and questions that may lead into an interactive class discussion targeting specific vocabulary. In any case, as the technology evolves, *Personalidades* maintains the primary goal of offering authentic listening material in Spanish as a springboard to dynamic dialogues and as a way to engage students in their own educational process.

Conclusions

Our experience with podcasts revealed multiple pedagogical benefits of using them in the language-learning process. First, the podcasts complemented the assigned readings, allowing students to "dialogue" with renowned authors such as Angeles Mastretta and Marjorie Agosín by formulating the questions that were asked in podcast interviews. Second, students were exposed to a variety of accents (ranging from Latin American to Peninsular) of native speakers at the speed and rhythm that would be found in a natural linguistic context. Finally, the students were able to produce their own podcasts, an opportunity that produced a more dynamic and engaged classroom environment. Podcasts are a technology that is accessible to students. Their response to it in the cases we have highlighted in our own intermediate language classrooms has been positive.

Indeed, we as instructors discovered that the podcast listening and production process was democratic, engaging, and creative. As a way to enable students to become more active in their education, meaningful and contextualized technological applications in the classroom—such as the use of podcasts—are conducive to an invigorating learning environment.

References

Bongey, S., Cizadlo, G., & Kalnbach, L. (2006). Explorations in course-casting: Podcasts in higher education. *Campus-Wide Information Systems, 23*, 350–367.

Brittain, S., Glowacki, P., Ittersum, J., & Johnson, L. (2006). Podcasting lectures. *EDUCAUSE Quarterly, 29*(3), 24–31.

Campbell, G. (2005). There's something in the air—Podcasting in education. *EDUCAUSE Review, 40*(6), 33–46.

Curto, J. (2006, October 5). Globalizing education one podcast at a time. Retrieved April 15, 2008, from http://www.thejournal.com/the/newsletters/smartclassroom/archives/?aid=19369

Dobrian, C. (2007). *Digital audio.* Retrieved April 15, 2008, from http://music.arts.uci.edu/dobrian/digitalaudio.htm

Iowa State University. (2006). *World Languages and Cultures Podcasts.* Retrieved April 15, 2008, from http://www.language.iastate.edu/main/podcast/

Lee, M. J. W., & Chan, A. (2007). Reducing the effects of isolation and promoting inclusivity for distance learners through podcasting. *Turkish Online Journal of Distance Education, 8(1)*, 85–105.

Levine, E. L., & Montross, C. M. (2002). *Vistas y voces latinas* (3rd ed.). Upper Saddle River, NJ: Prentice Hall.

Miller, M. (2007). "Forward thinking… Internet music's 3rd revolution." *PCMag.com.* Retrieved May 4, 2009 from http://blogs.pcmag.com/miller/2007/10/internet_musics_3rd_revolution.php

Nathan, A. (2006, May 24). Accent on the Internet. *The Capitol Times.* (A1). Retrieved April 15, 2008, from http://www.madison.com/archives/read.php?ref=/tct/2006/05/24/0605240372.php

PC Magazine. (n.d.). PC Mag.com Encyclopedia. Retrieved April 15, 2008, from http://www.pcmag.com/encyclopedia

Podcasting explosion. (2005, May 23). *Business Week.* Retrieved April 15, 2008, from http://www.businessweek.com/technology/tech_stats/podcast050523.htm

Rainie, L., & Madden, M. (2005). Podcasting catches on. *Pew Internet & American Life Project.* Retrieved April 15, 2008, from http://www.pewinternet.org/pdfs/PIP_podcasting2005.pdf

Rainsbury, J. W., & McDonnell, S. M. (2006). Podcasts: An educational revolution in the making? *Journal of the Royal Society of Medicine, 99*, 481–482.

Tapscott, D. (1998). *Growing up digital—The rise of the Net Generation.* New York: McGraw-Hill.

Windham, C. (2007). Confessions of a podcast junkie: A student perspective. *EDUCAUSE Learning Initiative, 42*(3), 51–65.

Podcasting in the Language Classroom: Inherently Mobile or Not?

Lara Ducate
Lara Lomicka
University of South Carolina[1]

Of recent focus in computer-assisted language learning (CALL) is the idea of mobile learning. Portable learning holds much potential for language teaching and learning, especially at a distance, and offers new and exciting paths for educators to explore. In fact, students immersed in such technological innovations in recent decades have been referred to as "digital natives" (Prensky, 2001, p. 1). For these students, mobile learning represents "personalised, learner-centric educational experiences" (Low & O'Connell, 2006, p. 2)—instruction that differs from previous pedagogical tools in that it offers "convenience, convergence and connectivity" (Low & O'Connell, p. 2). Mobile devices that are commonly used by these "digital natives" include iPods, MP3 players, handheld computers or personal digital assistants (PDAs), USB flash drives, cell phones, and handheld games (Corbeil & Valdes-Corbeil, 2007). These portable devices, according to Chinnery (2006), can also be "social staples" (p. 9). Thus, although as educators, we envision using these mobile devices for pedagogical purposes, on a practical level, we must keep in mind that students may choose to use them primarily as social tools.

The most popular social applications, according to Corbeil and Valdes-Corbeil (2007), include e-mail, the transfer of files, and movie/music downloads. Lorenz (2007) also mentioned Facebook and instant messaging as taking precedence in popularity over e-mail. Students now seem to prefer to "Facebook" (send a message through Facebook or MySpace) or to text a friend over e-mailing or calling. Many of these social applications can, in fact, be used with mobile devices, which in turn, hold the potential to impact learning and teaching. For educators, the portability factor of these mobile devices can take learning beyond the traditional boundaries of the classroom because learning can ideally take place anywhere and anytime. Another consideration of these popular social applications is cost: An iPod, for example, is relatively inexpensive as compared to a laptop or Tablet PC (Pasnik,

1 The authors contributed equally to the manuscript and are listed alphabetically.

Ducate, L., & Lomicka, L. (2009). Podcasting in the language classroom: Inherently mobile or not?. In R. Oxford & J. Oxford, (Eds.), *Second language teaching and learning in the Net Generation* (pp. 111–125). Honolulu: University of Hawai'i, National Foreign Language Resource Center.

2007). Therefore, as noted by Chinnery (2006), mobile devices such as MP3 players are less expensive for students and especially schools to purchase than standard equipment such as desktop computers. If students are forced to purchase both, however, these devices might appear less attractive in terms of their cost.

As we consider the variety of mobile tools available to students, whether for social purposes or to enhance learning, and the expenses associated with them, we must look more closely at mobile learning. Although many definitions of mobile learning or m-learning exist, it is often referred to as "learning as it arises in the course of person-to-person mobile communication" (Nyíri, 2002, p. 4), as occurring across locations, or as deliberate attempts to capitalize on learning opportunities that result from mobile technologies. However, what language teachers should consider, as pointed out by Sharples, Taylor, and Vavoula (2005), is that the learner is mobile, perhaps more so than the technology. If we think about mobility in this sense, as learners move from one setting to another, they adapt to the technology that is provided to them. Thus, because learners continuously change settings and contexts, we could advocate that learning has always been mobile; learners simply use new devices that allow them to adapt their learning to the relevant technology in today's world.

Although m-learning has gained significant popularity in recent years, Corbeil and Valdes-Corbeil (2007) recognized that "frequent use of mobile devices does not mean that students or instructors are ready for mobile learning and teaching" (p. 51). Maag (2006) suggested that audio files may be accessed as easily from a computer as from a mobile device; in other words, MP3 players are not really necessary to listen to podcasts. In fact, Maag found that about 55% of the students who participated in her research project listened to files on the computer rather than using mobile devices. This finding supports information from Dixon and Greeson (2006), who pointed to the fact that four out of five podcasts are not listened to on a portable device at all. They advocated that portability constitutes a benefit rather than a necessary feature of podcasting. Considering these findings, we offer a rather simplistic and concise definition of mobility: learning away from the computer.

Keeping the above findings and assertions in mind, the portability of mobile devices has specific benefits and challenges. The benefits include the following:

- Learning is extended learning beyond the classroom (Corbeil & Valdes-Corbeil, 2007; Oloruntoba, 2006; Pasnik, 2007).
- Content and information is continuously available on demand and in the hands of the user (Corbeil & Valdes-Corbeil, 2007; Oloruntoba, 2006; Young, 2007).
- Flexibility and interaction are increased (Oloruntoba, 2006).
- The devices can be a motivating factor for certain types of learners, such as the tech-savvy.
- Learning is in a more personalized form that is less expensive than a desktop/laptop (Pasnik, 2007)

Although the benefits are numerous, considering the challenges of mobile devices is important:

- They are often small, which means reduced screen sizes and viewing capabilities (Chinnery, 2006).
- Their availability may not be widespread in educational settings (Chinnery, 2006).

- Connectivity issues may arise, and feelings of isolation could occur (Chinnery, 2006; Corbeil & Valdes-Corbeil, 2007).
- Additional technical training may be required for students not familiar with technology, and formatting issues for media could cause problems (Chinnery, 2006; Corbeil & Valdes-Corbeil, 2007).

Podcasting

Now that we have examined mobile learning and briefly mentioned its benefits and challenges, the remainder of this chapter focuses on one tool that can be used in mobile learning—podcasting. In the next section, we will take a closer look at the literature surrounding podcasting in the field of language learning. Thorne and Payne (2005) suggested that podcasting represents an "interesting addition to the text-based computer-mediated environments we have described thus far. Indeed, one of the principal critiques of textual CMC [computer-mediated communication] has been that speech and aural comprehension are not explicitly exercised" (p. 386). Podcasting can add to the literature surrounding CALL and mobile-assisted language learning in ways that have not been easily attainable in the past: namely, in listening comprehension and oral production.

The origins of podcasting are in blogs and the Web-based publication formatting called Really Simple Syndication (RSS) around 2004, although podcasting has been integrated into language teaching only more recently. One of the first universities to explore podcasting in foreign-language teaching was Duke University, with its freshmen iPod initiative. As part of this innovative program, Spanish classes used listening materials and audio flashcards and created oral-production portfolios using their iPods (cited in Thorne & Payne, 2005). In another project, students at Middlebury College used iPods and recorders, preloaded with vocabulary and dialogues for language practice, to learn Chinese and Russian. At the University of Wisconsin, learners of Spanish used iPods to listen to interviews and cultural news and to complete grammar-based tasks. It is important to recognize, as Young (2007) pointed out, that even though iPod use is popular among students, the use of podcasting in the field of education remains in a relatively early stage.

Although most of the literature in podcasting and language has focused on the technical aspects, how to podcast, and ideas for using podcasting in the classroom (e.g., Godwin-Jones, 2005; McCarty, 2005; McQuillan, 2006a; Stanley, 2006; Young, 2007), a few articles have considered the theoretical aspects of podcasting (Lord, 2008; McQuillan, 2006b; O'Bryan & Hegelheimer, 2007; Rosell-Aguilar, 2007). Podcasting has several theoretical underpinnings in second-language acquisition research. Swain and Lapkin (1995) recognized output as essential for second-language learning. One strategy they suggested is having students listen to themselves as they edit their output and then to go back, listen again, and revise as necessary. They can receive feedback from other students and their instructor. This type of approach could be quite useful in podcasting because it is easy to record, rerecord, and listen to various segments of a podcast. After students record podcasts, they can listen multiple times, edit their podcasts, and comment on their classmates' recordings (see also Lord). McQuillan (2006a) suggested that output produced via podcasting can be recorded by students both for personal and educational purposes. Opportunities for oral production are thus increased because students can use this tool beyond the walls of the traditional classroom.

Podcasting can also provide opportunities for listening comprehension and increase motivation. O'Bryan and Hegelheimer (2007) proposed that podcasting represents a rich source of input via audio and potentially, video, because it uses multiple modes of input. This input can help to reinforce class instruction by offering an input mode to students different from the textbook or teacher. Although he did not offer any findings based on empirical research, Dervin (2006) suggested that podcasts can help to develop autonomous learning and motivation (see also Stanley, 2006). Motivation can be increased, speculated Stanley, because students are creating content for a real audience and not merely for the teacher to grade. Further, Dervin pointed out that students can, for example, take the initiative to ask questions of, interact with, and communicate with podcasters via e-mail, thus demonstrating both autonomy and motivation.

Numerous language educators have implemented podcasting projects in their teaching since 2004, as mentioned above; however, empirical research is clearly lacking on the benefits that this tool affords. Essentially, teachers need to keep in mind that these projects should be designed around sound pedagogy. Young (2007) underscored that we must use knowledge of second-language acquisition to design effective podcasting tasks to create activities that are "engaging, problem-solving and task-based, and that encourage authentic self expression for a purpose, are more appealing than listening to mechanical discrete-point verb conjugations or prefabricated audio files" (p. 45). Additionally, Colpaert (2004) reminded us to focus on the learner rather than the technology. He stressed the importance of developing the language-learning environment before deciding on the role of mobile technologies.

Methods and results

In this section, our focus is to examine students' opinions about various types of podcasting projects including commenting on their classmates' podcasts and their perceived benefits of producing and listening to podcasts and to explore the mobility factor as it applied to these projects. We first describe the setup of each project, including students' assignments, and then reveal students' reactions to the projects. Each of these projects attempted to follow Young's (2007) advice concerning effective podcasting tasks by providing students with task-based assignments that promote self-expression. The projects progress from more to less controlled through teacher involvement. In the first two projects, for example, the teacher monitored each task, including listening to and producing podcasts. In the remaining two projects, the students chose their own podcasts to listen to regularly throughout the semester. At the end of each of the projects, the students completed a survey in which they reported on their perceptions of the podcasting and blogging assignments, what they learned from the assignments, and how they approached the assignments (whether they subscribed to the podcasts, downloaded them to portable listening devices, etc.). The results of these surveys, including the students' reactions to the mobility aspect of the assignments, are discussed below.

Life in your home state (Project 1)

For the first blog/podcasting project, a fourth-semester German class (11 students, 18–21 years old) and a fifth semester French class (12 students, 18–21 years old) each maintained two blogs. Half of the students maintained one of the class blogs, and the other half of the class maintained the other blog, although each task was completed individually. The students were required to contribute to the blog four times during the semester and to visit the other class blog and comment eight times during the semester. Life in their state (history, food, geography, university life, weather, scenery, important sites, politics, religion, diversity, and sports) was the theme of each of the blogs. The audience included the classmates and native German and French speakers. The students were encouraged to keep their audience in mind as they wrote their postings and recorded their podcasts.

For two of the postings, each student was asked to write 200–250 words, including questions for the audience, a picture or link to support the argument, and citations of any sources that were used when writing (a link to the Website, for example). For the other two postings, they each produced a 3-minute podcast for the audience. The podcasts were recorded in the form of personal commentaries, skits, or interviews and posted to their blogs. For the purposes of this chapter, we will now focus on the podcast postings.

Before producing their own podcasts, the students in both courses listened to authentic (produced by native speakers for native speakers) podcasts in class. This pretask activity was used as a listening comprehension task, an opportunity to glean cultural information from the podcasts, and as a chance for the students to become familiar with podcasts and their characteristics.

After becoming familiar with podcasts, the students were asked to create their own. For the first assignment, each student recorded a radio advertisement showcasing a city in his or her state. Each student was assigned a different city, asked to research different tourist attractions of the city, and then to create an advertisement to encourage the listener to visit. For the second assignment in the German class, because the textbook topic was multiculturalism in Germany, each student was required to conduct an interview with another German speaker (native or nonnative) about diversity and immigrants in their state. This gave them the opportunity to engage in discussion with another German speaker using their German in context outside of the classroom. For the French class, each student was asked to present a 3-minute description of a certain area of campus, including pictures. Descriptions of locations such as the student union, sports centers, dormitories, library, and stadium were posted as podcasts by the students. They chose areas of campus that they thought would be of interest to their French keypals and that would familiarize them with the campus before their visit.

At the end of project 1, in which the students made recordings and wrote blogs about their state, 18 out of 21 students (86%) agreed that producing the podcasts was a positive experience, and 16 (76%) reported they learned new information about their state. A total of 17 students (81%) replied that they read their classmates' comments and responded to them, but the majority responded more neutrally when asked how much they enjoyed commenting (see Table 1). In addition to Likert-scale questions were four short-answer questions, which revealed the following. Many students enjoyed the speaking practice: "The podcasts gave me a chance to hear what I was saying and correct it. It also helped to listen to people's podcasts that were the same level as I am." They also appreciated that they had time to prepare before recording: "When given time to prepare your ideas, they seem much more intelligent." Another student commented that being able to plan what he wanted to say also allowed him to "build new vocabulary words," while a classmate reported that she appreciated having time to "check vocabulary which I was unsure of in class." None of the students reported that they subscribed to the podcasts, likely because they were required to comment on their classmates' podcasts and wanted to comment directly on the blog immediately after listening to the podcasts.

Table 1: Questions and results of Survey 1

question		mean	standard deviation
1	Producing a podcast this semester was a positive experience.	4.00	0.89
2	I read my classmates' comments.	4.12	0.57
3	I made comments in response to classmates' comments.	3.80	0.81
4	I enjoyed interacting with others through the comment function.	3.60	0.68
5	I would enjoy listening to podcasts in another language class.	3.80	0.73
6	I learned things from reading/listening to the blogs/podcasts that I did not know about my state.	4.20	0.95
7	Podcasts have academic value.	4.20	0.52
8	I would enjoy creating a podcast in another language class.	3.75	0.72

Study abroad (Project 2)

During the next semester, 19 fifth-semester German and 10 fourth-semester French students (ages 18–21 in both classes) participated in a podcasting project. The students first listened to native-speaker podcasts before producing their own, as they did the previous semester. When the production of their own podcasts began, the context of study abroad was used to encourage them to consider and prepare for international study. For this project, each student produced three podcasts and one blog. The first assignment was two-fold: a written study-abroad application in which the student provided details about him- or herself and why he or she wanted to study abroad and a podcast about an intercultural misunderstanding or experience he or she had undergone either abroad or in the US. The next task required each of them to interview someone in the target language who had studied abroad to learn about where the person lived, what he or she did there, and what he or she liked and disliked about the experience. The final assignment, similar to the first assignment in the above project, was to create an advertisement for the city in which the student hoped to study abroad to encourage friends to visit. The student had to research the city and discuss the tourist attractions, the university, and where to eat and sleep. As in the previous semester, each student was required to comment on three classmates' work after each task; they received extra credit for responding to comments.

For projects 1 and 2, each student podcast was evaluated using a rubric (see Appendix A) that included content, coherency and organization, pronunciation and fluency, accuracy, creativity, and comments. The students were encouraged not to read from a prepared text for their podcasts, but to plan what they wanted to say and then speak freely when recording. We hoped that this would allow them to speak extemporaneously, although in an organized, fluent (for their level) manner.

After the second project, the study abroad context, 26 out of 28 students (93%) identified the podcasting project as a positive experience and even rated the podcasting portion of the project higher than the blog aspect; they reported that it helped them to improve their speaking skills and pronunciation (Table 2). Unfortunately, only half of the students responded to their classmates' comments for extra credit, the majority was neutral about podcasting in another FL course, and only 7 students (25%) subscribed to the podcasts using iTunes. The other 21 students (75%) listened to their classmates' podcasts directly from the class blogs. The reason for this is probably that they were required to comment after listening, as in the project about life in their home state (project 1). If they had downloaded podcasts and listened to them away from their computers, they would have had to remember to comment when they returned to their computers.

Table 2: Questions and results of Survey 2

question		mean	standard deviation
1	Producing a podcast this semester was a positive experience.	4.00	0.89
	Maintaining the class blog with podcasts this semester was a positive experience.	4.00	0.54
2	Producing a podcast this semester was a positive experience.	4.20	0.69
3	I enjoyed the topics of the podcasts.	4.00	0.47
4	I listened to my classmates' podcasts regularly.	3.60	0.89
5	I read my classmates' comments.	4.10	0.52
6	I made comments in response to classmates' comments.	3.40	0.99
7	I enjoyed interacting with others through the comment function.	3.50	0.81
8	I would enjoy listening to podcasts in another language class.	3.60	0.84
9	I feel the podcasts helped me to improve my speaking.	3.90	0.85
10	I feel the podcasts helped me to improve my pronunciation.	3.70	0.96
11	I would enjoy creating a podcast in another language class.	3.50	0.64
12	I will consider creating a podcast on my own after the semester ends.	3.60	0.68
13	I used iTunes to subscribe to and download the podcasts to my computer automatically.	2.70	1.34

In the short-answer section, students discussed the reasons that they liked the project and how they felt that it helped them learn the language. Students commented that their participation in this project encouraged them to pay more attention to pronunciation and helped them to practice speaking in a continuous stream. More reserved students responded positively to opportunities to practice speaking without the pressure of talking in front of their classmates. One student reported, "it was easier because it allowed time to gather thoughts and practice," and another commented, "for me I liked the podcasts because you can correct your thoughts. In a direct conversation you can be easily interrupted. Also you can correct your mistakes with the podcasts." Students also appreciated that they could plan what they wanted to say and self-correct. As in Project 1, the students were encouraged not to read their podcasts, but they could record as many times as they wanted before uploading the podcasts.

French news (Project 3)

In the next project, 9 students (ages 18–20) in a fifth-semester French class were required to listen weekly to a French news podcast, available from the *Langue Française* section of *Radio France Internationale*. They completed a worksheet (see Appendix B) as part of their listening journal three times per month and turned in the journal every month with a log of the topics, new vocabulary, and cultural information that they had learned. A transcript of the news programs was available from the Website for the students to read as they listened to the podcasts, but they were encouraged to listen at least once without the transcript to comprehend as much as possible on their own. The goal of this project was to help the students make gains in listening comprehension that would better prepare them for a 10-day class trip to France. By following the news in France for 8 weeks prior to their departure, they would know more about current events in France (and elsewhere outside the US) and be better prepared to discuss these events with their French counterparts. In France especially, where the discussion of current events and politics is common, this background knowledge would benefit students greatly in their comprehension and participation in day-to-day conversations.

After completing the French news listening project, the students were asked to participate in a short survey (*N*=9). Of the 9 students, 8 (89%) agreed that their learning increased with regard to current events in France and world news and reported that they appreciated hearing the news from a different perspective. They also reported that their listening comprehension and vocabulary increased.

Table 3: Questions and results of Survey 3

question		mean	standard deviation
1	I learned more about current events in France by listening to podcasts this semester.	4.44	0.73
2	I learned more about world news by listening to podcasts this semester.	4.67	0.50
3	I enjoyed the podcast listening project.	3.33	1.12
4	I improved my listening comprehension by participating in this podcast listening project.	4.00	0.50
5	I increased my knowledge of French culture by listening to podcasts.	3.33	1.12
6	I expanded my vocabulary by listening to French podcasts.	4.00	0.71
7	I will continue listening to the French news podcasts after class is over to maintain my listening comprehension skills.	3.22	1.20
8	I subscribed to the French news and it was downloaded automatically to my computer via iTunes.	3.56	1.51
9	I regularly used the "script" that was available in French to help me understand the podcasts.	4.00	1.00
10	I had not listened to a French podcast before this class.	4.22	0.97
11	When I traveled to France or conversed with native speakers, I felt the listening podcast journal project helped me to feel more prepared for conversation and discussion of political/ current events.	2.67	1.12
12	I appreciated listening to the news from a different perspective than in news coverage in the US.	4.22	0.67

Although 6 out of 9 students (67%) did subscribe to the podcast, all but one student listened to it on the computer (one listened on an iPod). Those who did not subscribe said that they felt that listening from the Website was more convenient: "It was much easier to listen to it on my computer and answer the questions at the same time. Also, for a while, I couldn't figure out how to subscribe to it through iTunes." Another student wanted to keep her iTunes player clear of extraneous information: "I didn't subscribe because I didn't want it filling up my iTunes, and it wasn't that difficult to listen to it every week (or however often we did it) without subscribing." It seems that these students felt that listening to their required podcast was easier on their computers due to the task associated with the listening assignment; they wanted to complete their listening journal at the same time as they listened. Others may not have had the technical knowledge to subscribe and download to their iPods, even though this procedure was explained in class. Of the 9 students, 5 owned an iPod or MP3 player but reported that they used these machines only for listening to music.

Target language podcasts (Project 4)

In the final project, 7 students (all 21 years old except for one 24-year-old) in a beginning teaching-methods course for future foreign-language teachers were required to find, from a list provided by the teacher, a target-language podcast that interested them; they were instructed to listen to this podcast weekly and turn in a description of what they learned, including specific vocabulary or new cultural information. The goals of this project were to expose students to the target language and culture because the methods class was taught in English and to help provide students with ideas for how to use listening texts/podcasts in their future foreign-language classes as teachers.

Students in the methods class who participated in the target-language podcast project responded that they also enjoyed choosing and listening to weekly podcasts, so much so that 5 out of the 7 students (70%) agreed that they would continue to listen after the semester ended and that they would subscribe to other FL podcasts in the future. Six students (86%) commented that they learned more about their target culture, and 5 (70%) felt that their aural comprehension improved from listening to authentic podcasts.

Table 4: Summary of four podcasting projects

project name	class	context	listening/ speaking assignment	written assignment
Life in Your Home State	11 4th-semester German and 12 5th-semester French students	city advertisement, diversity in state, controversial topic,	2 podcast assignments of 2–3 minutes	comment 4 times during semester
Study Abroad	19 5th-semester German and 10 4th-semester French students	preparing for study abroad	3 podcast assignments of 2–3 minutes	comment 6 times during semester
French News	9 5th-semester French students	listen to French news	listen 3 times per month to French news podcast	maintain listening journal with new topics, vocabulary, cultural information
Target-language Podcasts	5 undergraduate and 2 graduate students in teaching-methods class	listen to TL podcast of student's choice	listen to TL podcast once per week	turn in journal with new information, vocabulary, cultural topics

Only 2 out of the 7 students (29%) actually subscribed to the podcasts; when the others were asked why they did not subscribe, they responded that it was easier to listen on the computer rather than first figuring out how to download the podcasts to the iPod and letting it take up space there (similar reasons as those of the French students): "I am also not that tech savvy so I didn't want to deal with trying to figure out how to put them on my iPod," or "I am just not a very technologically advanced person, so it was easier for me to just sit at my computer and listen there." Another student responded that it was easier to listen on the computer because she had to write a summary for class: "Since I had to do that I liked to sit at my desk and take notes while I was listening to the podcast. I did however listen to it on my iPod a few times, but the majority of the time I was at my computer." That same student, however, responded that she subscribed to "This American Life" from National Public Radio after learning about podcasts in this class and enjoyed listening to that when walking to class or taking the bus around campus. This student's comment supports the claim that students use these mobile devices primarily as "social staples" (Chinnery, 2006, p. 11). Because an assignment was associated with listening to these podcasts (as in the above podcast projects), it was easier to listen at home while sitting in front of the computer than on a mobile listening device.

Discussion

As we have seen with each of these four projects, the majority of students responded positively to their podcasting projects. Out of the 68 total students, 59 (87%) responded that they enjoyed podcasting, whether listening or producing; they were able to improve their listening comprehension and/or speaking in the target language and increase their knowledge of the target culture. Many even responded that they would enjoy doing a similar project again in a future language class. Students who produced their own podcasts felt that their speaking, pronunciation, and vocabulary improved during the semester and appreciated having time to self-correct and record multiple times if they chose. As Swain and Lapkin (1995) pointed out, editing their output after listening to themselves and then revising accordingly can help students improve their speaking. In addition, the simple task of recording several times was likely a factor in helping students improve their pronunciation because each time they recorded, they focused more on their speaking and pronunciation. Students who regularly listened to podcasts commented that they improved their listening comprehension and learned more about the target culture. The results from these four different podcasting projects illustrate that according to student feedback, podcasting can be an effective way to increase competence in regard to speaking, listening, and pronunciation. Further empirical research should be conducted to test and further prove these findings. Pedagogically sound ways to take advantage of and encourage mobility should also be further explored.

Contrary to the real-life use of podcasts, the students in our projects did not take advantage of the mobile aspect of podcasting, which is similar to the findings reported by Maag (2006) and Dixon and Greeson (2006). Although the tasks in this study were not designed specifically to take advantage of mobility, which could offer a possible explanation as to the lack of motivation on the part of the students, it was interesting that the inherent mobile nature of podcasts alone was not enough motivation for students to listen on the go. Although the inherent ease of making podcasts mobile would alone seem to encourage students to capitalize on this function, the results of this study do not support this idea. Even though the students were offered MP3 players on loan for the semester, all declined. As evident in this study, educators must specifically organize tasks so that students will be encouraged, if not required, to take advantage of the portable aspects of podcasts if mobility is a goal. Because our students were required to turn in assignments or post comments associated with the podcasts, they understandably found it easier and more convenient to listen on the computer and complete the written portion of the assignment at the same time.

In addition to designing tasks specifically for mobility, foreign-language teachers also need to train their students: how to subscribe to and download podcasts. The fact that most students did not subscribe to their class podcasts contradicts the predictions of Godwin-Jones (2005): "The popularity of MP3 players among students means that students could easily download podcasts in the target language (e.g., from a newspaper site, blog, radio program) for listening on the go" (p. 11). Some students did not know how, nor did they want to learn how, to subscribe to a podcast and download it to their portable listening devices; furthermore, some did not want what they considered to be "academic" content taking up space in their iTunes programs. Although subscribing and downloading may be easy procedures for students, whether they automatically receive podcasts may depend on the accompanying pedagogical task and their familiarity with the technology.

Conclusion

When reflecting on the idea of podcasting and the added benefit or challenge of mobility, we must first and foremost consider the pedagogical design, framework, or model for this type of learning. What implications does a device being portable hold for task design? Mobility can take learners out of the classroom and into the real world, affording them opportunities to access others and materials around the world, and mobile devices can allow learners to be immersed in authentic contexts and with native speakers. Keeping that in mind, Low and O'Connell (2006) suggested that "teachers provide the structure and framework for learning to take place, where learners use mobile devices to interact with each other and the world around them; collaboratively navigating and connecting information" (p. 4). They proposed that by using this learner-centric activity model of mobile learning, "the resulting application of mobile devices to learning is personal, social, and connected with information, both as a contributor and consumer. Mobile devices take on the attributes of a Personal Learning Environment—learner-centric, personal portals that serve as gateways to rich, highly contextualised activities" (p. 8). Although their framework was not specifically designed for language learning, it could be applied to task design for mobile learning in second-language classes.

When designing a task with a possible mobile component such as podcasts, however, language educators should first consider whether students should be encouraged to take advantage of the mobility aspect of podcasts and if so, to think about the effect mobility would have on the pedagogical aspect of tasks associated with podcasts. If students are not required to complete listening logs, answer specific questions about the podcasts, or be accountable to their peers with comments, will they attend to podcast projects with the same degree of concentration, dedication, and seriousness? If students are not required to reply to their classmates' podcasts, will they listen at all? Does this remove the motivating aspect of completing the task for an audience (a benefit of podcasting mentioned by Stanley, 2006)? As Colpaert (2004), Rosell-Aguilar (2007), and Young (2007) pointed out, the task associated with technology should be more important than the actual technology. If we hope to take advantage of the mobility aspect of podcasting, we must ask ourselves what types of tasks lend themselves best to being mobile while not sacrificing the pedagogical purposes of the tasks.

Although the results of our study indicate that the majority of our students enjoyed the podcasting assignments and felt that they benefited from them, they also prompt us to think about how "digitally native" our students actually are. Several of the students involved in these projects chose not to download the podcasts because they did not know how. This finding suggests to foreign-language teachers that we cannot assume that our students are "digital natives" (Prensky, 2001) with regard to technology for education's sake. Although the students were provided with directions for subscribing to podcasts and even offered portable listening devices "on loan" for the semester, they chose what seemed most convenient: listening on their computers. As mentioned in the introduction, although our students are familiar with many different types of technology, including mobile devices, most are content to use them mainly for social and entertainment purposes (Chinnery, 2006). Even though the majority of our students owned personal MP3 players, they preferred not to load them with educational materials.

Research still needs to be conducted on the types of tasks most conducive to mobile-assisted language learning, while not losing sight of the pedagogy and learning task. Although it was not in the scope of this study to examine how podcasting contributes to gains in the target language, further research could compare gains in listening comprehension and speaking among students who engage in podcasting projects with those who do not. In future projects, we might also explore, for example, the use of audio comments and how they may encourage mobility. Additionally, mobile blogging may hold implications that could encourage students to use technology for learning on the go. Equally important is to explore the mobility factor at different levels of language learning and in different settings (distance learning vs. more traditional learning). Finally, it could be interesting to explore these mobile devices as both social tools and in educational environments and to examine how to encourage students to implement the devices they are already using as social tools in the context of language learning.

References

Chinnery, G. M. (2006). Going to the MALL: Mobile assisted language learning. *Language Learning and Technology, 10*(1), 9–16.

Colpaert, J. (2004). From courseware to coursewear? *Computer Assisted Language Learning, 17*, 261–266.

Corbeil, J. R., & Valdes-Corbeil, M. E. (2007). Are you ready for mobile learning? *EDUCAUSE Quarterly, 30*(2). Retrieved April 15, 2008, from http://connect.educause.edu/library/abstract/AreYouReadyforMobile/40029

Dervin, F. (2006). Podcasting demystified. *Language Magazine*, 5(8), 30–31. Retrieved April 15, 2008, from http://www.languagemagazine.com

Dixon, C., & Greeson, M. (2006, March 23). Recasting the concept of podcasting: Part I. Digital Trends. Retrieved April 15, 2008, from http://news.digitaltrends.com/talkback109.html

Godwin-Jones, R. (2005). Skype and podcasting: Disruptive technologies for language learning. *Language Learning and Technology*, 9(3): 9–12.

Lord, G. (2008). Podcasting communities and second language pronunciation. *Foreign Language Annals, 41*, 364–379.

Lorenz, C. (2007, November 14) The death of e-mail. Slate. Retrieved April 15, 2008, from http://www.slate.com/id/2177969/

Low, L., & O'Connell, M. (2006, September). *Learner-centric design of digital mobile learning.* Paper presented at Learning on the Move, Brisbane, Australia. Retrieved April 15, 2008, from https://olt.qut.edu.au/udf/OLT2006/gen/static/papers/Low_OLT2006_paper.pdf

Maag, M. (2006). Podcasting and MP3 players: Emerging education technologies. *Computers, Informatics, Nursing, 24*, 9–12.

McCarty, S. (2005). Spoken Internet to go: Popularization through podcasting. *JALT CALL, 1*(2), 67–74.

McQuillan, J. (2006a). iPod in education: The potential for language acquisition. [White paper]. Retrieved April 15, 2008, from http://edcommunity.apple.com/ali/galleryfiles/12071/iPod_Edu_Whitepaper_Language_Aquisition.pdf

McQuillan, J. (2006b). Languages on the go: Tuning in to podcasting. *The International Journal of Foreign Language Teaching, 2*(1), 16–18. Retrieved April 15, 2008, from http://www.tprstories.com/ijflt/IJFLTWinter06.pdf

Nyíri, K. (2002). Towards a philosophy of mobile learning. In M. Marcelo, U. Hoppe, & J. Kinshuk (Eds.), *Proceedings of the IEEE International Workshop on Wireless and Mobile Technologies in Education* (pp. 121–124). Växjö, Sweden: Teleborg Campus, Växjö University.

O'Bryan, A., & Hegelheimer, V. (2007). Integrating CALL into the classroom: The role of podcasting in an ESL listening strategies course. *ReCALL, 19*(2), 162–180.

Oloruntoba, R. (2006, September). Mobile learning environments: A conceptual overview. Paper presented at Learning on the Move, Brisbane, Australia. Retrieved April 15, 2008, from https://olt.qut.edu.au/udf/OLT2006/gen/static/papers/Oloruntoba_OLT2006_paper.pdf

Pasnik, S. (2007). iPod in education: The potential for teaching and learning. [White paper]. Retrieved April 15, 2008, from http://www.apple.com/education/rethink/ipodwhitepaper

Prensky, M. (2001). Digital natives, digital immigrants. *On the Horizon, 9*(5). Retrieved April 15, 2008, from http://www.marcprensky.com/writing/Prensky%20-%20Digital%20Natives,%20Digital%20Immigrants%20-%20Part1.pdf

Rosell-Aguilar, F. (2007). Top of the pods—In search of a podcasting "podagogy" for language learning. *Computer Assisted Language Learning, 20*, 471–492.

Sharples, M., Taylor, J., & Vavoula, G. (2005, October). Towards a Theory of Mobile Learning. Paper presented at mLearn in Cape Town, South Africa. Retrieved April 25, 2008, from http://www.mlearn.org.za/CD/papers/Sharples-%20Theory%20of%20Mobile.pdf

Stanley, G. (2006). Podcasting: Audio on the Internet comes of age. *TESL-EJ, 9*(4). Retrieved February 24, 2009, from http://www-writing.berkeley.edu/TESL-EJ/ej36/int.html

Swain, M., & Lapkin, S. (1995). Problems in output and the cognitive processes they generate: A step towards second language learning. *Applied Linguistics, 16*, 371–391.

Thorne, S. L., & Payne, J. S. (2005). Evolutionary trajectories, Internet-mediated expression, and language education. *CALICO Journal, 22*(3), 371–397.

Young, D. J. (2007). iPods, MP3 players and podcasts for FL learning: Current practices and future considerations. *NECTFL Review, 60*, 39–49.

Appendix A: Podcast grading rubric

5 points—content ______________

4–5 points—topic fully discussed with several examples from your experiences and research

2–3 points—topic only cursorily discussed with only one example provided

1 point—topic barely discussed with no examples provided

5 points—coherency and organization ______________

4–5 points—coherent and well-organized, includes title

2–3 points—somewhat difficult to follow, includes title

1 point—not organized, no title

5 points—pronunciation and fluency ______________

4–5 points—few errors in pronunciation; conversation flows well

2–3 points—a fair amount of pronunciation errors, but still comprehensible; many starts and stops in conversation

1 point—meaning unclear due to pronunciation errors

5 points—accuracy ______________

4–5 points—few errors in spelling and grammar

2–3 points—many spelling or grammar errors, but still comprehensible

1 point—meaning unclear due to spelling or grammar errors

5 points—creativity ______________

4–5 points—creative presentation of topic including music, pictures, background, special effects, and/or energetic presentation

2–3 points—semi-creative presentation without additional effects

1 point—completely uncreative presentation

5 points—impact ______________

4–5 points—voice is engaging, voice sounds natural, includes natural pauses and hesitations, variation in voice intonation

2–3 points—voice is not very engaging, little variation in voice intonation, parts of podcast sounds read aloud

1 point—voice is not at all engaging, monotone voice, entire podcast sounds read aloud

total points ______________/30

Comments (2 required)

5 points—content

4–5 points—demonstrated that you read the posting by reacting to or asking about what your classmate wrote

2–3 points—questionable whether you read or understood classmate's posting

1 point—no demonstration of having read classmate's posting

total points ______________/5

Appendix B: Listening journal worksheet

Podcast project—Listening to podcasts

Listen to one podcast a week (12 weeks total)
http://www.rfi.fr/communfr/dynamiques/podcasting.aspx?rubrique=lffr

- Date of podcast:
- Length of podcast:
- In your podcast journal, take notes as you listen.
- What did you learn about French culture by listening to the podcast this week?
- Summarize the podcast below, including major news items.
- Discuss one story in detail below.
- Find and include a related link to the story you commented on in detail above.
- Write down something new you learned from listening.
- List 5 vocabulary words that are new to you this week. Be sure to identify if the words are nouns, verbs, adjectives, etc. Include the sentence or phrase in which they are used.
- Write down 2–3 questions you have from listening to the podcast.

The Coalescence of Spanish Language and Culture Through Blogs and Films

Vanessa Lazo-Wilson
Clara Inés Lozano Espejo
Eastern Washington University

Language is motion. Regardless of the language, language is in a state of constant transformation as interlocutors continue to interact with each other, negotiate meaning, and discover the representation of ideas, thought, and understanding through differing modes of production. In the case of this chapter, the modes of production are the written and spoken communication through differing levels of Spanish conversation and composition courses offered in the traditional space of the classroom and extend outwards to include online classroom blogs. Because the teaching and learning of language is delicately intertwined with the linguistic variations represented throughout more than 20 Spanish-speaking countries, lexicon, grammar, and representations of culture through popular music, films, and postings on YouTube, the meaning and understanding reached among all participants in this foreign-language learning experience is one of a new rhetoric. Web 2.0 has created a new means of communication through offering more ways of exchanging information that can build upon a common understanding of both language and culture. This chapter addresses curricular and instructional innovations through traditional face-to-face meetings with Spanish students, while at the same time highlighting aspects of popular everyday culture in Spanish-speaking countries through using contemporary films viewed in class, video clips posted on blogs, and exchanges with native Spanish speakers in Colombia that permeate student writing. Through these activities, students will become more informed citizens as they continue to explore the meaning of the language, deeply integrated into the culture and made more accessible and immediate through online social networks.

What is meant by "coalescence"?

Traditionally, coalescence is understood as a process of assimilation and deletion between a dominant and a subordinate language. However, coalescence is also defined as a coexistence of two languages and cultures and the way they influence each other. Based on the latter, the definition of coalescence adopted for this paper consists of the relationship between

Lazo-Wilson, V., & Lozano Espejo, C. I. (2009). The coalescence of Spanish language and culture through blogs and films. In R. Oxford & J. Oxford, (Eds.), *Second language teaching and learning in the Net Generation* (pp. 127–139). Honolulu: University of Hawai'i, National Foreign Language Resource Center.

language and culture as a unity in which aspects of language related to use are being enriched by the process of interaction of experiences and competencies through blogs. The end result of such an interaction is the development of intercultural competence, which involves knowledge, skills, and attitudes (Sercu, 2005).

Theoretical framework

The use of blogs and films as teaching tools to integrate into existing instructional practices links to Vygotsky's (1978) sociocultural theory of higher mental processes. In *Mind and Society* (1978), Vygotsky espoused that "all phenomena be studied as processes in motion and in change" (pp. 6–7). Vygotsky further postulated that through carefully studying human behavior, important changes can be traced and then attributed to human nature based on changes in society and material life (p. 7). Vygotsky is considered one of the pioneers of connecting the Marxist notion of development with concrete psychological questions. In so doing, Vygotsky elaborated on Engels' concept of human labor and tool use with the idea that once a human interacts with nature, nature and the human are transformed.

Vygotsky (1978) proposed a theoretical position called the zone of proximal development (ZPD), best defined as "the distance between the actual developmental level as determined by independent problem solving and the level of potential development as determined through problem solving under adult guidance or in collaboration with more capable peers" (p. 86). The ZPD defined the areas that are in the midst of development or maturation. Within this framework, the stage of development comes before the learning process. After the mastery of a concept is the point at which learning can actually begin. In regards to this study, one can adhere to the maxim that teachers alongside students are lifelong learners.

Background literature

A review of the literature on the use of technology in foreign-language classrooms could be expansive and yet not exhaustive. What follows is a historical overview of technology use in foreign-language education, followed by the most pertinent studies in terms of the use of blogs in education.

Historical overview

Discontent with the audio-lingual method and language laboratories paved the way for the widespread appeal of computer-assisted instruction (CAI) in the late 1960s. The introduction of CAI afforded teachers and students the option to embrace a more integrated curriculum by incorporating CAI activities into the rest of the foreign-language curriculum, potentially leading to more sound pedagogical practices (Brink, 1986, p. 42; as cited in Salaberry, 2001, p. 44). However, CAI was doomed to the same fate as the foreign-language laboratory, and its popularity rapidly subsided due to its high start-up cost, a lack of technical staffing, a dearth of proper courseware, and the negative attitudes of many teachers as to the effectiveness of CAI (Dunkel, 1987, p. 252, and Olsen, 1980, p. 345, as cited in Salaberry, 2001, p. 45). The 1970s and 1980s gave rise to the more promising computer-assisted language learning (CALL). Researchers continued throughout the 1990s to look for further improvements in CALL that would allow teachers to implement certain tasks not as easily implemented without the use of computers, such as drills that compared student answers to those stored in a computer. Intelligent CALL went a step beyond CALL and provided students with feedback that tried to emulate feedback given by a teacher. In turn, this new era brought computer-mediated communication (CMC) to the foreground, allowing students to experience a wealth of computer-based interaction (Salaberry, 2001), which had been somewhat limited by CALL uses in the past.

CMC in foreign languages

CMC offers two modes of communication: synchronous (SCMC) and asynchronous (ACMC). Each modality has benefits and drawbacks in the foreign-language classroom. Synchronous communication can mimic the oral production of language as it occurs in a face-to-face interaction, setting the stage for a face-to-face conversation in a live context. SCMC offers more potential opportunities for students to participate in discussion than does a traditional classroom setting (Kelm, 1992), but may result in the production of more mistakes because the utterances are more immediate, yet not as immediate as in face-to-face communication (Abrams, 2003). Some second-language acquisition experts, however, do not see mistakes as a drawback because they are taken as signs of the interlanguage of the learner. However, more miscommunications may occur during synchronous communication than asynchronous because sociocultural misunderstandings may be more rampant. On the other hand, asynchronous communication allows students more time to monitor thoughts, ideas, and language and provides planning time for students to consult outside sources for content-based meaning. Blogs have the potential to use both SCMC and ACMC.

Use of media in foreign-language instruction

More current research has looked at student perceptions of the use of video materials in the classroom (Garza, 1996; White, Easton, & Anderson, 2000), whether different types of media can actually improve language students' abilities in the foreign language (Herron, Corrie, Dubreil, & Cole, 2002), how the use of media can alleviate some of the affective factors that seem to accompany the language-learning experience in the classroom (Garza, 1996), and how language learning can become more enjoyable and entertaining when technology is incorporated in the classroom (Chiquito, Meskill, & Renjilian-Burgy, 1997; Garza, 1996; Liskin-Gasparro & Véguez, 1990).

Blogs in foreign-language instruction

Although blogs have existed for over 10 years, the increase in popularity for use in the foreign-language classroom has only surfaced in the last few years. Educators are now constantly redefining what literacy instruction means at a time when technologies and access to the Internet are not only changing at a rapid pace, but are also profoundly impacting *how* teachers teach, changing the ecology of the classroom toward a student-centered one, where a constructivist view of education may prevail (Chen & Bonk, 2008; Leu & Kinzer, 2000). Concurrent with these pedagogical changes has been the evolving culture of online social networking, which will continue to drive a newfound understanding reached among members of differing language and culture groupings as they develop digital fluency, (re)defining a new literacy (Witte, 2007).

Methodology

Three differing Spanish courses are under discussion: (a) an intermediate language course; (b) Spanish conversation and composition, a bridge course between the intermediate and advanced Spanish courses; and (c) Spanish composition and conversation, an advanced-level course. The objectives of the intermediate course are to review grammar, expand vocabulary, and broaden cultural awareness. The main goal for the bridge course is to provide a venue for students to begin to produce language in the spoken form while further strengthening their written skills. Because the main outcome for the advanced course is to hone Spanish formal academic writing skills, the blog was incorporated to provide students with a means to exercise language production in a more relaxed setting than in a formal composition, while uniting the two sections of the course. A classroom blog for the bridge course was the first blog created in this department to expand the conversation past traditional classroom walls, while at the same time providing a portal for students to express themselves and practice language while jointly creating an awareness of culture, thus unifying three sections of the course. Attention to form is not the main focus for the bridge course; however, paying attention to form and monitoring are strongly underscored in the intermediate and advanced courses. The instructor for the intermediate course requested that students e-mail the comments before "publishing" them on the blog so that the instructor could carefully monitor student form. The other instructor for the advanced courses simply required that students post comments when new content was made available in context with the chapters being covered in the varying textbooks.

In the case of the intermediate class, a difference between the formal and the informal styles of writing can be clearly observed. The articles posted by the creators follow a structure previously defined and conducted by the instructor. Lozano-Espejo provided clear guidelines for her students on how to post blog comments when students went to the language laboratory, as exemplified by the following:

Clase marzo 13 de 2008
Cinco puntos extra en Quiz 3 por comentar uno de los blogs. [Five extra points on Quiz 3 for commenting on a blog.]

- Identify yourself: name, age, university, and class.
- Highlight positive aspects of his/her English and encourage him/her to continue practicing.
- Give some advice related to the use of language to correct his/her text (find two separate blog postings and make comments).
- Ask questions about culture or related to the content of the articles (find two separate blog postings and make comments).

Students saved their initial drafts, which were then corrected by the instructor. The comments were used as a tool to express feelings and ideas about the topics written about in a free way and as a means for students to help each other. These postings were not corrected by the instructor, but they were submitted to peers, that is, partners in the classroom and teachers or students from Colombia, who gave advice about the style or the use of expressions in specific contexts. In this way, the comments are a helpful element to enhance linguistic and cultural competencies. Finally, some of these comments were taken to class to be analyzed and to resolve doubts resulting in potential misunderstandings.

Discussion

Why choose blogs as a tool for language learning?

Blogs are interactive; they offer the possibility for students to perceive many aspects of language through auditory and visual channels. Blogs can also be commented on and responded to and can function as a persuasive element in reaching an understanding or arguing one's point. Furthermore, the commentary aspect allows the responder to give feedback, ask for clarification, and further scaffold the experience of not only the written word form, but also the function and meaning. Whether the blog is open to the public or password-protected for a customized group of participants, the classroom instructor no longer is obligated to be the sole purveyor of information and feedback in discourse and learning. Other learners, even if they are native speakers of the language, can learn from each other, thus contributing to the more global and social nature of the language experience in the "classroom." This further underscores the importance of the sociocultural potential for development procured through Web 2.0. This evolving way of becoming more literate (Leu & Kinzer, 2000) and learning from each other speaks directly to Vygotsky's (1978) ZPD. Consequently, US-based students can learn from Colombian native speakers of Spanish, and in turn, the Colombian students can learn about (pre)conceived notions of language and (mis)representations of culture and society through exchanges. Through the following example from the US-Colombia blog in the intermediate class, the level of interaction, negotiation of meaning, and cultural awakening can be experienced.

> *¡Hola! Te felicitamos, tienes muy buen manejo del español, y es agradable saber cosas acerca de Spokane. En cuanto a algunas expresiones como por ejemplo jugar deportes y caminar alrededor, tú podrías usar "practicar algún deporte y salir a caminar." No tenemos el smog por "aquí no hay smog." Ir en el centro comercial por "ir al centro comercial." Montar en el transporte por "coger un bus o tomar el bus o transmilenio." Siempre emplea el pronombre "tu" para dirigirte a la persona con quien estas hablando. Puedes preguntar ¿Qué hace el gobierno para proteger el medio ambiente? Reemplazar la palabra "gusten" por "gustan." Continua trabajando, vas por muy buen camino. Chao!*
>
> [Hi! We congratulate you, you are able to handle Spanish quite well, and it's nice to know stuff about Spokane. In terms of some of the expressions like, for example, playing sports or walking around, you could instead use "practice some sport and go out for a walk." We don't have smog, "here there is no *smog*." Go into the commercial center, replaced by "go to the commercial center." Get on the transport, replaced by "get the bus or take the bus or *transmilenium*." Always use the pronoun "you" to talk to a person with whom you are talking. You can ask "What does the government do to protect our environment?" Replace "may like" with "like." Keep working, you're on a good path. Bye!]

This excerpt taken from Lozano Espejo's classroom blog underscores the artful and careful crafting required in reaching a mutual understanding of not only language, but also culture; this further highlights the interconnectedness of culture, grammar, and vocabulary in use, which language comprises, but also the convergence of the participants reaching an accord through the blog. The acceptance of the use of the English word "smog," meaning air pollution, by the native speaker is a clear example of the coalescence and evolution of languages in informal speech. In addition, the advice given about the use of the pronoun *tú* ("you," singular) to address the interlocutor leads us to reflect on the conception of a blog as a means of communication between equal peers, resulting in a style of speech that should be familiar. In addition, the word "transmilenio" was the point of departure in a class about the characteristics of and differences between the systems of transportation in the world, widening the knowledge of the students about the topic.

Blogs help to widen information related to social and cultural (mis)conceptions, as shown in the following excerpt:

> In the order of Colombians problems the security is the problem that worries foreings the most but you lost the best echologic pars in the world and the insecurities less in the parks, and the strange people are the most protected by the police.
>
> Now talk about the rivers in Colombia, it has the coolest rivers in south America, for example is a small city is typical to go on Sundays to eat lunch, sancocho the gallina" and next go to swimming the river, but this rivers are dangerous to swim it.
>
> I had been studying than the foreings like much Colombia than native people, the foreings people are the most careful in my country.

The author presents his point of view about the stereotype of Colombia as a "violent and insecure country" and on how foreigners lose the opportunity to know the positive aspects of the country due to that perception. This excerpt clearly marks the student's interlanguage process as he displays mistakes in the written English; however, the student attains his communicative purpose, which is to highlight the values of his country. This further pushes the native speakers (NSs) of English on the U.S. side to confront their preconceived notions of Colombian life and become more objective in their world views.

Why choose films?

At the outset, films stand as a (re)presentation of culture in its most authentic form. In this case, "authentic film" refers to a product of the culture of NSs of a language for its own consumption (Omaggio Hadley, 2001). Authentic films are a means to showcase issues that are relevant to the country or culture that has produced them. The language represented through films comes alive, is more movable, and may be a real representation of vocabulary, syntax, and common usage not always at the disposal of the teacher in the foreign-language classroom. Finally, Spanish-language films made and produced in a Spanish-speaking country introduce language students to a new aesthetic. Each film chosen for the class underwent careful scrutiny. Oscar-winning director Pedro Almodóvar's film *Todo Sobre Mi Madre* (1999) was chosen for several reasons: This internationally acclaimed film offers a vision of a popular filmmaker that was met with controversy in the Spanish-speaking world; it was Almodóvar's first crossover film to be recognized by the Academy of Motion Picture Arts and Sciences in the US; and finally, the topics and central characters offer grounds for controversy to further provoke conversation and hence push for communication in the classroom. The first time the students viewed a portion of the film was through a teaser on the course blog. The students were invited to speculate as to further content, aesthetic, and storyline through publishing comments. The first viewing of the feature-length film occurred in the classroom as a collective experience among the students in the bridge course. The students were prepared before the film was viewed through reading historical information about post-Franco Spain and about Pedro Almodóvar. The textbook used, *Más Allá de la Pantalla* (Sacchi, Pessoa, & Martín-Cabrera, 2006), contained pre-viewing questions in the *Predicciones y Reflexiones* ("Predictions and Reflections") section of the book. In the *Notas Lingüísticas* section, linguistic appreciation of grammar, linguistic variations, and common vernacular were highlighted. Because the entire film was not posted on the blog, the instructor mediated the film through selecting a clip to post, which was viewed and commented upon for the classroom blog. The instructor monitored comments made by the NSs of English to ensure understanding and to avoid misunderstandings or disconnects between culture 1 and culture 2 as the film as a tool underwent another mediation process: the meaning construction of the blog entries. The following excerpt from the blog highlights a high school student enrolled in an advanced university class making sense of what he has viewed:

> *Yo nunca he visto una oración con "vosotros"! Bueno....Como la otra película, me gusta y no me gusta porque yo pienso que las personas estaban muy diferentes de los vistos tradicionales de Los Estados Unidos. Las películas españoles tienen muchos aspectos de cada día vida; los travestís, las bolleras, y muchos más que son los aspectos de otro tipo de sociedad. Me gustan los diferentes, pero yo creo que la película mostraba los aspectos en exceso, por eso los cosas son cosas de cada día vida están en exceso.*
>
> [I have never seen a film with the "vosotros" form before. Oh well....Like the other film, I like it and I don't like it because I think that the people were looked at as being

very different from those in the United States. Spanish movies show many aspects of daily life: transvestites, lesbians, and many more that are the aspects of another type of society. I like the differences, but I think that the movies showed these aspects in excess, that's why the things of everyday life are in excess.]

Despite some linguistic errors in this posting, it is rich with meaning-making and understanding. This student has recognized, heard, and realized the use of a linguistic form apparent in the Spanish from Spain, but not used in the Americas or Caribbean, that is, vosotros. Furthermore, the student has included the new common vocabulary as part of his lexicon in this posting, underscoring not only the student's interest in more popular language as represented in this popular film, but also the convergence of the language and culture depicted through the entry in stark contrast to other Spanish-language textbooks that tend to be more static and outmoded. The language in the textbook used, *Más Allá de la Pantalla*, is popular and updated, thus piquing student interest and motivation to learn a language that is more current and more movable. Finally, the student has begun to make meaning of the culture of the *Movida* in Spain, that of excess. Movida literally means "movement," and it peaked by the post-Franco era in Spain, when a literal movement of freedom of expression was pursued; a more figurative sense of the word is felt in the movement toward an emancipatory lifestyle marked by a carefree lifestyle popular in the 1980s in Spain.

Films also allow students to perceive, be exposed to, and even possibly appreciate other aesthetics. Almodóvar films are their own genre—some even term it "Almodrama"—with careful attention paid to dialogue, art design, and dramatic acting. Almodóvar, also known as a "women's director," displays a predisposition to work with some of the same actresses throughout his films and prefers roles that highlight female characters. The following bridge student chose to talk about Almodóvar's women, while using a shorthand in Spanish for the word que ("that"), that is, "q." The letter "q" pronounced in Spanish is the first letter of the word "that," which is pronounced and spelled the same way as the letter "q."

Student 1 (S1) wrote:

> *A mí me fascinan todas las películas de Almodóvar y me gusta q sea consistente con los actores q utiliza para cada trama. "Las mujeres de Almodóvar" son extraordinarias actrices q realmente transmiten emociones al telespectador. Se me hace interesante q aunque utilice a los mismos actores siempre logran convencernos y capturarnos en sus personajes dejándonos en el olvido de sus antes personajes en las demás películas. Creo q por esa razón y también porq son buenísimos actores, Almodóvar logra conquistarnos con sus películas.*
> *saludos*
>
> [I like all of Almodóvar's films and I like the fact that he is consistent with the actors that he uses for his plots. "Almodóvar's women" are extraordinary actresses *that* really transmit emotions to the viewer. I think it's interesting *that* even though he uses the same actors he always is able to convince us and capture us in his characters letting us forget the character this person played in all the other movies. I think *that* for this reason and because they are super good actors, Almodóvar is able to conquer us with his movies.
> greetings]

This student is a heritage speaker of Spanish who displays ease with the common usages of the language in its written form. This excerpt combines advanced grammar structures with a high-level usage of the subjunctive mood and gives an introspective look at this student's experience with the film.

An interesting exchange followed several comments down on the blog with another student from a different section of Spanish asking why the heritage speaker had used the "q" in the written form. She wondered if it was a mistake or intentional. Student 2 (S2) commented:

> *Sé que ese no es "en tópico," ¿pero porque usa una estudiante la letra "q" en vez de "que" y "porq" en vez de "porque"? ¿Es un error o es una forma más corta de escribir esas palabras?*
>
> [I know that it's not "on topic," but why did this student use the letter "t" instead of "that" and "b" instead of "because"? Is it a mistake or is it a shortened form to write these words?]

As the course instructor for the blog, wanting to don the old hat of the purveyor of all information, Lazo-Wilson struggled to keep quiet, but this was done to see what would happen. Because the initial student had already fulfilled the class requirements by making the first posting in response to the clip, the instructor was not sure if S1 would answer S2's comment. Ten days later, S1 responded:

> *Contestando a tu pregunta. La razon que utilice "q" or "porq" en vez de "que" o "porque" es por costumbre o error de dedo como lo quieras ver. No es la forma correcta y si es una forma mas corta pero como te comente arriba es la costumbre. Mi intencion no fue confundirte. saludos*
>
> [Answering your question. The reason why I used "t" and "b" instead of "that" and "because" is out of habit or a typo, however you want to look at it. It is not the correct form and it is a shortened from but as I commented above it is a habit.
>
> My intention was not to confuse you.
> greetings]

This is a perfect example of students developing through asynchronous communication with each other and passing through transformational changes as they spiral upwards toward learning in Vygotsky's ZPD. There is turn-taking, negotiation of meaning, and an explanation from a heritage speaker of Spanish of a "common habit" or vernacular sense of word usage that S2, a NS of English, would not have otherwise encountered. Furthermore, S1 has displayed a level of discourse pragmatics by apologizing if she had confused her fellow language student. This interaction would have been impossible in a traditional foreign-language classroom setting, mainly because the students would not have seen the informal usage of the language nor would they have been in the same section of Spanish conversation.

Why use music videos on blogs?

In a way similar to using authentic language films as products of the target-language culture (TLC), music videos also serve the purpose of being able to introduce Spanish-language students to authentic language as heard and viewed in music videos. Through a blog entry posted by Lazo-Wilson for the advanced class, students viewed a video in context with the unit being covered in their textbook, *El Próximo Paso*, on clothes and shopping. In the traditional classroom, students review the vocabulary connected with clothes and shopping and practice the grammar covered in that chapter, prepositions and connectors. For the composition course, students are provided with a list of connectors to incorporate in their formal academic compositions on the course's Blackboard site (see Appendix). The posting on the blog of the Colombian pop singer *Juanes'* video *La Camisa Negra* ("The Black Shirt") presents the opportunity to not only hear a native speaker of Spanish speak, paying close attention to pronunciation and inflection, but also affords students the possibility to experience a deeper cultural understanding of an artist, Juanes, of Colombia, the TLC.

The posting by the instructor has links to the song lyrics and to the official Juanes Website. Students can read the song lyrics while listening to the song and viewing the video. This is language in motion!

The potential with Juanes' song *La Camisa Negra* to be explored for more depth in sociocultural as well as linguistic understanding is enormous. Blog postings, after prompts from the course instructor, have students reflecting on the meaning of the lyrics. Yes, it is the story of yet another broken-hearted man who realizes that his lover has left packed bags at the door. However, ripe with meaning are several utterances and song lyrics that point at sexual innuendo and vulgarities that go unnoticed by students. The course instructor's duty then is to underscore the subtle contextual elements and the connotation of language in action, such as the way NSs play with phonetics to express a possible innuendo or double entendre.

Furthermore, Juanes uses his music and lyrics as a vehicle to show ownership of his language and the way it evolves by combining it with English, a language perceived as the dominant force that drives worldwide communication. The song lyrics are as follows:

> *Tengo la camisa negra*
> *porque negra tengo el alma;*
> *yo por ti perdí la calma*
> *y casi pierdo hasta mi cama.*
> ***Cama cama caman baby,***
> *te digo con disimulo,*
> *que tengo la camisa negra*
> *y debajo tengo el difunto.*
>
> [I have a black shirt
> because black is my soul;
> for you I lost my quiet
> And I even almost lost my bed.
> ***Come on, come on, come on baby,***
> I tell you with pretence
> that I have a black shirt
> and underneath it is the corpse.]

Juanes' artful use of the word *cama* ("bed") in Spanish serves at least two purposes: first, to highlight the sexual innuendo in that verse of having lost his lover and almost losing his bed, representing the loss of sex and even possibly impotence (*el difunto,* "the corpse") and second, to show a phonetic similitude of the Spanish *cama* with the English "come on," as the ultimate representation of coalescence in language.

The use of Juanes in this Spanish course supported the objectives of using authentic materials for instructional purposes in that Juanes refuses to cross over to the mainstream pop culture of the US like Shakira, Ricky Martin, and Enrique Iglesias, artists who have marketed themselves with English-language albums to hit the Top 40. By donning t-shirts that say *Se habla español* ("Spanish is spoken here"), Juanes points at his rich Colombian language culture. He also proudly (re)presents his *paisa* heritage, recognized for its regionalism seen in its language and cultural variations. The musician in Juanes has chosen to mix folkloric Colombian music with electric guitar instrumentation to create a convergence of pop-rock and folk underpinnings to portray his background.

Conclusions and implications

The innovative instructional practices that surround a Spanish blog as not only a communicative device amongst its interlocutors, but also as a means of offering the possibility for language to coalesce with its varying aspects of learnability are astonishing. Kramsch (1999) warned instructors in this new age of information sharing and retrieval to be aware of and to approach with caution the potential hazards or (mis)communications through (mis)representations that are proffered through the chosen medium. The responsibility of representation and meaningful communication, then, is placed on the instructor. Careful guidance and selection of materials posted is required to attempt to narrow the gap of misunderstanding that can ensue in a language-learning environment.

The experience of writing the blogs, regardless of the design by the two instructors for the courses, motivated the students to write more and to self-correct their texts. Working with blogs helped the students to develop social and interdependence skills that were observed in the classroom. As time passed, they felt more confident in expressing their ideas and feelings in the class, becoming organizers of the environment and activities they wished to carry out. One example is a lunch that the intermediate Spanish course experienced at a Mexican restaurant in the middle of the quarter. The students were interacting with the waiters and owners of the restaurant and did short presentations about some authors from Bolivia and Paraguay. This was a successful activity because they were almost completely immersed in Spanish, and their confidence grew noticeably as they spoke. The use of blogs for communicative practice thus facilitated the output of the language in the spoken form. Student interest was tapped to further motivate students via integrative motivation thanks to an environment (the blogs and the Mexican restaurant) where foreign-language anxiety was low and motivation to communicate was high (MacIntyre, 2007). One student who was reticent to speak in class felt herself avoiding situational anxiety and was able to communicate freely with her peers thanks to the online communication and the relaxed restaurant environment.

Students were able to contribute to the course curriculum by co-constructing knowledge with their peers and course instructors through online communication and expanding upon blog conversations in the classroom but only when either the students or instructor integrated these elements into the face-to-face meetings. As a result of the blog use in Spanish courses, the students happily shared how fun writing can be. They felt that more of a purpose surrounded their writing, more "real" communication, topics that tapped into their interests, and expansion of vocabulary; furthermore, they *enjoyed* the feedback that they received from their NS peers in Colombia. A drawback is that some affective factors were still connected with the "saving-face" notion of wanting their published posts to be as perfect as possible when their counterparts read them. However, on a positive note, the instructor's input was still valuable because they revised and edited their postings after her initial feedback, before final publication on their blogs. Students' interest levels were tapped to the extent that they no longer were concerned with the task to receive a grade; they simply wanted to communicate with their peers. The blogs, alongside teacher and student reflections, served as catalysts that changed the "normal" environment of the classroom to make the classroom more interactive, in keeping with the sociocultural perspective of language learning.

Note that the course instructor needs to take an active role and constantly monitor and lead the process to avoid (mis)conceptions about linguistic, cultural, and social aspects involved in language learning. Although knowledge has a great variety of sources, a venue for reflection and analysis is needed to conclude and clarify concepts. This can be easily accomplished in class or online when the objectives have been made clear. When the course instructor creates and organizes a course blog, it is easy to monitor the process and to make the content align with materials covered in a textbook. When the cultural material or blog content posted by the instructor is referred to in class, it is with the assurance that all students know what is being discussed. On the other hand, when the students are given the possibility of presenting their own blogs, they become more creative and develop their autonomy and their ability to work independently. Students can work on the creation of both formal and informal writing texts as they continue to hone varying registers of academic writing.

Directions for further research point at work on identity in terms of the meaning generated through the learning of a foreign language for the learner, the lifestyles represented, and the search for a new "social" identity proffered through the creation of each student's blog. Also, further research on the (mis)representations made through course blogs and through student and instructor postings should be explored in more depth to ensure relevance. Finally, the interaction among students and the course instructor and the roles of the course instructor and students need to be redefined and further investigated. Continued research is needed on the implementation of blogs as another tool to widen students' cultural and linguistic competencies. In that sense, the authors are establishing the advantages and disadvantages of the work developed during the courses under discussion in this paper. A plan for future instruction will be based on the results so that the research can have an immediate and direct impact on teaching methodologies.

References

Abrams, Z. (2003). The effect of synchronous and asynchronous CMC on oral performance in German. *The Modern Language Journal, 87,* 157–167.

Chen, W., & Bonk, C. (2008). The use of Weblogs in learning and assessment in Chinese higher education: Possibilities and potential problems. *International Journal on E-Learning, (7),* 41–65.

Chiquito, A. B., Meskill, C., & Renjilian-Burgy, J. (1997). Multiple, mixed, malleable media. In M. D. Bush & R. M. Terry (Eds.), *Technology-enhanced language learning* (pp. 47–76). Lincolnwood, IL: National Textbook Company.

Garza, T. J. (1996). The message is the medium: Using video material to facilitate foreign language performance. *Texas Papers in Foreign Language Education, 2*(2), 1–18.

Herron, C., Corrie, C., Dubreil, S., & Cole, S. P. (2002). A classroom investigation: Can video improve intermediate-level French language students' ability to learn about a foreign culture? *The Modern Language Journal, 86,* 36–53.

Kelm, O. (1992). The use of synchronous computer networks in second language instruction: A preliminary report. *Foreign Language Annals, 25,* 441–454.

Kramsch, C. (1999). Teaching text and context through multimedia. *Language Learning & Technology, (2)*2, 31–42.

Leu, D. J., Jr., & Kinzer, C. K. (2000). The convergence of literacy instruction with networked technologies for information and communication. *Reading Research Quarterly, 35*(1), 108–127.

Liskin-Gasparro, J. E., & Véguez, R. A. (1990). Teaching listening comprehension through video in first-year college Spanish. *IALL Journal of Language Learning Technologies, 23*(1), 37–49.

MacIntyre, P. (2007). Willingness to communicate in the second language: Understanding the decision to speak as a volitional process. *The Modern Language Journal, 91*, 564–576.

Omaggio Hadley, A. (2001). *Teaching language in context.* (3rd ed.). Boston: Heinle & Heinle.

Richardson, W. (2006). *Blogs, wikis, podcasts, and other powerful Web tools for classrooms.* Thousand Oaks, CA: Corwin Press.

Sacchi, F., Pessoa, S., & Martín-Cabrera, L. (2006). *Más allá de la pantalla.* Boston: Thomson Heinle.

Salaberry, R. M. (2001). The use of technology for second language learning and teaching: A retrospective. *The Modern Language Journal, 85*, 39–56.

Sercu, L. (2005). Teaching foreign languages in an intercultural world. In L. Sercu (Ed.), *Foreign language teachers and intercultural competence* (pp. 1–18). Clevedon, NY: Multilingual Matters.

Vygotsky, L. (1978). *Mind in society: The development of higher psychological processes.* Cambridge, MA: Harvard University Press.

White, C., Easton, P., & Anderson, C. (2000). Students' perceived value of video in a multimedia language course. *Education Media International, 37*, 167–175.

Witte, S. (2007). "That's online writing, not boring school writing": Writing with blogs and the Talkback Project. *Journal of Adolescent & Adult Literacy, 51*, 92–96. Retrieved on February 15, 2008 from http://www.reading.org/Library/Retrieve.cfm?D=10.1598/JAAL.51.2.1&F=JAAL-51-2-Witte.html.

Appendix: List of connectors and transition words for oral and written communication

Conectores y palabras de transición

Secuencia de tiempo	
primero	first
segundo	second
tercero	third
al mismo tiempo	at the same time
desde entonces	from then on/since then
después	after
durante	during
finalmente	finally
luego	then/later
mientras	while
por último	last of all
Resultado	
a causa de	on account of
por lo tanto	therefore
por eso	therefor/for that reason
por esta razón	for this reason/because
Concesión	
a pesar de	in spite of/despite
no obstante	nevertheless
pero	but
sin embargo	nevertheless
Contraste	
al contrario	on the contrary
en cambio	on the other hand/intead
por otro lado	on the other hand
sino	but (rather)
Para añadir	
además/es más	besides
incluso	even
también	also
Opinión	
Desde mi punto de vista...	From my point of view...
En mi opinión...	In my opinion...
Que yo sepa...	As far as I know...
Según...	According to...
Condición	
a menos que	unless
con tal (de) que	provided that
para que	so that
puesto que	since
tan pronto como	as soon as
ya que	since
Conclusión	
Así que...	So...
En conclusión...	In conclusion...
Para concluir...	To conclude...

Pragmatic Variation Among Learners of French in Real-Time Chat Communication

Claire A. McCourt
Pennsylvania State University at Altoona

The ever-increasing use of communication technologies in world-language teaching is providing new opportunities for both learners and teachers to connect to one another and to access existing discourse communities in online, virtual communication spaces. Whereas early on in the history of technology-enhanced language teaching, students were not always familiar with the technologies being used, nowadays many high-school- and college-age students are more proficient with various forms of communication technologies than their teachers. Consequently, language educators seldom need to teach students *how* to use the technologies incorporated into the curriculum so much as they need to prepare students for the types of tasks created around the use of these technologies and to explore the results of these tasks in terms of learner-learner interaction and the making and negotiation of meaning. As Salaberry (2001) noted, "one of the most understudied and perhaps underrated consequences of the use of new technologies has been the interaction among learners generated by activities based on the use of new technologies" (pp. 51–52).

The study reported in this chapter explores the results of learner-learner computer-mediated interaction, focusing specifically on variation in the use of the French second-person pronouns *tu* (T) and *vous* (V). Although several researchers (e.g., Belz & Kinginger, 2002; Kinginger & Belz, 2005) have explored pragmatic development in computer-mediated communication (CMC) environments (see Belz, 2007 for a state-of-the-art review), most previous studies have been qualitative. This corpus-based study aims to complement the existing qualitative research by quantifying the amount and type(s) of T/V variation among learners of French as a foreign language at three instructional levels engaged in small-group chat tasks. The goals of this research are to determine how often students used T/V address appropriately versus inappropriately, to explore in what types of pragmatic categories of utterances T and V were used, and to offer a number of recommendations for using learner-corpus analysis to promote pragmatic development and language awareness.

McCourt, C. A. (2009). Pragmatic variation among learners of French in real-time chat communication. In R. Oxford & J. Oxford, (Eds.), *Second language teaching and learning in the Net Generation* (pp. 141–151). Honolulu: University of Hawai'i, National Foreign Language Resource Center.

Learner-produced CMC corpora

Learner-produced CMC corpora have increasingly been used as tools for promoting language awareness among second-language learners (Belz & Vyatkina, 2008) and providing teachers and researchers with learner language to be used in corpus-based evaluations of the development of second-language sociolinguistic competence (van Compernolle & Williams, 2008, forthcoming-a, forthcoming-b). Although the communication technologies (e.g., chat, e-mail, forums) supporting learner-learner and learner-native speaker interactions are relatively new, the notion of "data-driven learning" (Johns, 1986) has existed for some time. Originally conceptualized to include teacher-prepared native-speaker (NS) corpus excerpts, data-driven learning, or "learning-driven data" (Seidlhofer, 2002), has recently come to include the analysis of learners' own language production. Learner language data can come from any number of sources, such as individual oral interviews with an instructor/researcher, recorded conversations between two or several learners, traditional writing tasks, and so forth. Technology-mediated communication, such as real-time chat, is not a replacement for other types of data, nor does it have any greater intrinsic value; CMC is but an additional tool that teachers can use in and beyond the classroom to promote and enhance language learning and language awareness. Nonetheless, CMC may offer a number of advantages over more traditional oral or written performance data.

Perhaps the greatest advantage to using CMC for constructing learner language corpora is its efficiency. CMC tasks such as small-group chat discussions allow every student to participate simultaneously either during or outside of regular class meeting times. In addition, CMC does not require interlocutors to be physically copresent, which means that tasks can be completed at any time beyond the classroom. This has great implications for task design, creative participation structures, and the like, which can help to broaden learners' discourse options (Kramsch, 1985) and to expand the range of learning opportunities available to them in and beyond the classroom (Hall, 2001). For the purposes of the present study, CMC was necessary because it enabled learners from several classes at different instructional levels to interact with each other on a regular (i.e., semiweekly) basis, which would not have been possible if oral interviews or traditional written tasks had been used to construct the corpus. Incidentally, computer-mediated interaction provided an environment in which learners needed to address several different interlocutors, either individually or as a group. This led to many opportunities to observe the act of second-person address, which may not have been possible in another format.

The efficiency of CMC data also extends to the preparation of learner data for in-class analysis. Collecting and transcribing speech data can be time-consuming endeavors, even when interviews are relatively short and transcription conventions are kept to a strict minimum. This can limit the immediacy of learner language analysis in the classroom because the data are not always available within a short period of time. In addition, transcribing spoken interviews throughout an academic term may not always be practical or feasible for teachers. Likewise, pen-and-paper written data often must be photocopied or digitally scanned before being made available to teachers and learners for analysis. Transcripts of CMC data, on the other hand, are automatically produced in digital format. The digital archives are available for teachers and learners to analyze immediately following the interaction. In the present study, students engaged in seven chat tasks over a period of 12 weeks, producing a true "developmental learner corpus" (Belz & Vyatkina, 2008) showing the learners' progress over this period. Transcripts of each small-group discussion were available for review by the author, teachers, and other collaborators within minutes of the completion of the task.

The remainder of this chapter is organized as follows. The next section provides an overview of the social meaning of second-person pronouns in modern French and why this feature is important for learners of French. Next, the methodology and data are described, and coding procedures are discussed. The analysis is centered on the amount of variation in the use of T and V and the specific types of utterances in which these pronouns were used. Following the analysis, the pedagogical implications of using CMC are explored.

Review of literature

The social meaning of French second-person forms

The use of the French second-person pronouns *tu* (T) and *vous* (V) is influenced by many social and cultural factors that are constantly in flux, thus making the choice between T and V both dynamic and complex. Although T is usually described as a singular, familiar address form and V as having the dual roles of plural address (V-pl) and singular, formal (V-sg) in reference grammars and learner texts, relatively few—if any—hard and steadfast rules govern the use of these pronouns. This is because such factors as a speaker's age, gender, social class, and relationship to his or her addressee, individually or combined, can play a part in determining the choice of one pronoun or the other (Gardener-Chloros, 1991; Morford, 1997). Dewaele (2004) has even described the choice of an address pronoun as a "sociolinguistic tightrope" across which speakers of French must cautiously tiptoe.

In tracing the historical evolution of second-person pronoun use (in French and other languages), Brown and Gilman (1960) described norms for T/V use in terms of a "power semantic" and a "solidarity semantic." The power dimension of pronominal choice was asymmetrical because a person with higher power (e.g., the master of a household or a member of the nobility) used T to address a person with lower power (e.g., a slave, servant, or member of the common people), who responded with V. The solidarity dimension, on the other hand, was described as symmetrical; individuals of "like-mindedness" (p. 258), resulting from, for example, common "political membership, family, religion, profession, sex and birthplace" (p. 258) used either reciprocal T or V with one another.

Although Brown and Gilman's (1960) dimensions of power and solidarity described two fundamental aspects of T/V choice, the scope of their dualistic, semantic approach has since been critiqued as somewhat limited (e.g., Morford, 1997; Mühlhäusler & Harré, 1990). Morford (1997) advanced the argument that it is not simply the relationship between speakers that determines pronominal choice but that individual speaker characteristics also play an important role. After interviewing middle-class NSs of French, Morford argued that two "orders of indexicality" are associated with T/V choice. On one level, pronoun choice indexes, or points to, aspects of the immediate context (i.e., the type of social relationships and the nature of the occasion or setting). At the same time, pronoun choice indexes aspects of the speaker's identity within a wider social context (e.g., social class, education, or political orientation). Most importantly, within this double indexicality model, "pronominal address...does not merely reflect a static social order but repeatedly puts into play and potentially transforms the categories in terms of which social relations, occasions, and identities are defined and redefined" (p. 29).

Previous research on second-person pronoun use among learners of French

Given the rather complex set of rules and parameters that determines a speaker's choice of T or V, this feature of language often poses difficulties for learners of French, especially for those whose first language has no T/V distinction (e.g., English). For Dewaele (2004), learners' appropriate use of T and V is linked to both grammatical competence and sociolinguistic competence. In other words, he attributed more appropriate use of T and V to more grammatical knowledge, while at the same time recognizing that increased socialization in French through contact with NSs in authentic cultural contexts also contributes to learners' command of the T/V system (see also Liddicoat, 2006).

Belz and Kinginger (2002) investigated the cross-linguistic development of address form use in telecollaborative language-learning environments. Fourth-semester students of French and German at a U.S. university conversed with NSs in the target languages via e-mail, threaded discussions, and real-time Internet-mediated chat. In the two case studies the authors present (one student each of French and German), the telecollaborative partnerships resulted in an increased use of appropriate T forms of address because the NS telecollaboration partners specifically questioned the use of V as sociopragmatically inappropriate. Belz and Kinginger concluded that meaningful social interactions with NSs can help L2 students understand T/V usage. In both the French and German contexts, the learners' attention was directed to appropriate T/V forms by the NS partners, and the learners' use of appropriate second-person pronouns increased. The findings appear to suggest that pragmatic competence acquisition is not based on textbook rule-learning or even explicit instruction from language teachers;[1] exposure to authentic discourse, in situations where appropriate T/V use has direct sociocultural implications and consequences, is essential.

Kinginger and Farrell (2004) explored the development of sociopragmatic competence within the context of study abroad. Their main purpose was to emphasize learners' understanding of the social implications of T and V address. They therefore concentrated on learners' questionnaire-based responses to theoretical second-person address situations. The pre- and post-study abroad data indicate an increase in the awareness of the social rules governing T and V use. However, the greatest improvements were reported for those students who had had greater exposure to NSs in authentic sociocultural contexts where inappropriate use of T and V could lead to linguistic ambiguity and/or (negative) social consequences.

Method

Participants

The participants in this study were 81 learners of French enrolled in first- (n=29), second- (n=23), and third- (n=29) semester (U.S. university-level) courses. Their ages ranged from 18 to 38, with a mean age of 21 years (about 95% were under 25). Most participants (78%) were female, and over half were sophomores (n=25) or juniors (n=26), with the next largest group being freshman (n=13). These 81 learners were assigned to one of 27 three-person chat groups for the semester. All but 4 chat groups included one student from each instructional level. This configuration of students at different instructional levels was intended to give learners the opportunity to provide peer assistance (Tharp & Gallimore, 1988) on lexical, grammatical, and sociopragmatic features of language. As Warschauer (1997) pointed out, CMC "encourages collaborative learning in the classroom" (p. 472) because it "creates the opportunity for a group to construct knowledge together, thus linking reflection and interaction" (p. 473).

1 The American students in this study were explicitly advised by their instructor to use the T form in correspondence with their partners. The French/German textbooks used by the U.S. language learners also prescribed the use of T with fellow students.

Data collection

The participants engaged in a series of 1-hour WebCT chat tasks over a 12-week period as part of their normal coursework. Each task involved discussing a particular topic in French among the group members. The students were asked either to discuss a given theme (e.g., "friends and family," Task 2; "your housing and neighborhood," Task 4) or to confer on translation (Task 7) or vocabulary (Task 3) exercises. The topics were related to themes covered in the first- and second-semester course textbook, *Horizons* (Manley, Smith, McMinn, & Prévost, 2006) and the third-semester textbook, *Quant à moi* (Bragger & Rice, 2005).

Data were collected using the transcript-recording function available in WebCT. Following each chat session, transcripts of the chat discussions were downloaded and saved as text files for later review. The students produced varying amounts of data from task to task because not all groups remained stable over the course of the semester due to absences. The entire corpus consists of just over 73,200 words, not including time and date stamps or computer-generated messages (e.g., "Student X has entered the room," "Student X has left the room").

Coding

Following the data collection, each token (i.e., occurrence) of T and V was identified. In addition to subject pronouns, related forms of T and V (e.g., object pronouns, disjunctive pronouns, imperative verb forms) were counted. Because the primary objective of this study is to explore variation in the appropriate use of T and V, each token was coded as either "*appropriate*" or "*inappropriate*." T was considered appropriate when it was used to address a single interlocutor, whereas V was counted as appropriate only when it was used for plural address. This coding was adopted because 1st- and 2nd-year textbooks invariably present T as the appropriate form for addressing friends and classmates, and V is reserved for teachers, strangers, older persons, and so forth. A preliminary review of the data revealed some variation, or alternation, between T and V depending on the type of utterance (e.g., interrogative or declarative sentence, tags). Thus, each token of T and V was also coded for utterance type.

Results and analysis

The first level of analysis aimed to determine the frequency with which T and V were used appropriately. A total of 1,182 second-person pronouns (T=615, V=567) were identified in the corpus. As shown in Table 1, two thirds of T/V tokens were used appropriately (*n*=787, 66.6%). Differences were observed between the pronouns in that T was used appropriately most of the time (88.1%), whereas V was used appropriate less than half of the time (43.2%).

Table 1: Overall distribution of appropriate T and V

pronoun	appropriate uses/total uses	%
T	542/615	88.1
V	245/567	43.2
total	787/1182	66.6

As reported by McCourt (2008), instructional level was not a significant factor. In fact, most students at all three instructional levels appeared to alternate "randomly" between these pronouns. Thus, it appears that appropriate use of T and V does not necessarily increase as learners progress through 1st- and 2nd-year courses given in formal, structured educational settings.

The results displayed in Table 1 indicate that T was used appropriately about twice as often as V, which may lead the reader to believe that T (including related forms) is somehow easier for students to learn. However, given that T was treated as the default pronoun for singular address in this study, the high rate of appropriate T in comparison to that of V may actually be skewed because learners happened to use T. Actually, the few examples of inappropriate T were mostly instances in which more than one other person was clearly addressed, and instead of using V as a plural second-person pronoun, a learner produced T, which can only be used for singular address. V, on the other hand, was counted as inappropriate so often because it was addressed to a single interlocutor. In fact, less than half of the V tokens (*n*=245) were used for plural address. Singular and plural address are shown divided in Table 2.

Table 2: Use of T and V for singular and plural address

	singular		**plural**	
pronoun	*n*	%	*n*	%
T	542	67.2	75	23.4
V	322	32.8	245	76.6
total	864	100	320	100

Variation in singular address (i.e., T vs. Vsg) is of particular interest in the present chapter. Not only do the data show a relatively high rate of inappropriate singular address, but they also indicate that singular address accounts for nearly three quarters of all second-person pronoun use in the corpus (*n*=864, or 73.1%). Thus, even when multiple (potential) addressees were present, most learners clearly opted to address one individual at a time. However, this ratio is actually much lower than what has been reported for nonlearner synchronous CMC, where singular address (i.e., T) accounts for 94.8% of all nonludic second-person pronoun use (Williams & van Compernolle, 2007, pp. 807–810).

One of the most understudied aspects of learner use of T and V (in French and other languages with more than one second-person pronoun) is the analysis of the specific types of utterances in which second-person address occurs. Such analyses have the potential to provide insight into how learners use second-person address in different pragmatic contexts, such as requests for information, advice-giving, joking, and role playing, among others. As Williams and van Compernolle (2007) reported, nonlearner online chat communities engage in a variety of language-play activities, many of which call for the use of second-person address. Williams (2007) noted that learners tend not to engage in the same activities as NSs, such that second-person address is principally limited to task-oriented utterances, such as questions.

To determine in what contexts learners who participated in the present study used second-person address, each token of T and V was coded as one of five token types: interrogative sentence, tag, declarative sentence, object of preposition, and imperative. The distribution of T and V (combined) is displayed in Table 3.

Table 3: Use of T/V by token type

token type	*n*	%
interrogative sentence	760	64.3
tag	328	27.7
declarative sentence	57	4.8
object of preposition	23	1.9
imperative	14	1.2
total	1182	100

Nearly two thirds of all second-person addresses occurred in interrogative sentences, and a further 27.7% were found in tag structures (e.g., *et toi?*, "and you?"). The concentration of T/V use in questions and tags indicates—at least at a superficial level—that the students did not engage in other types of linguistic behavior calling for the use of T/V, such as advice-giving, joke-telling, teasing, and so forth, which are relatively common in NS chat contexts (Williams, 2007). A review of the corpus revealed that the vast majority of interrogatives and tags produced by the learners were oriented to the task. In other words, the learners were not engaging in interpersonal communication so much as they were asking each other questions related to the specific chat task assigned for a given session. This orientation to the task raises doubts about the efficacy of interlearner CMC for pragmatic development, given ever-shifting motivations for participation in CMC tasks (Thorne, 2003; Ware, 2005). Of course, this line of inquiry could be expanded in future studies to quantify the various pragmatic categories of utterances with T and V. In addition, a review of the textbooks used in the beginning and intermediate French classes revealed that nearly every example of T/V use was in a question or tag structure. The few exceptions were in parts of chapters in which advice-giving was introduced. However, this was done within a grammar-based perspective, whereby the main goal (in line with the textbook) was to teach specific grammatical structures (e.g., *il faut que*, "it is necessary" + subjective). Therefore, little emphasis is put on the pragmatic categories of utterances frequently used in noneducational contexts. Thus, learners may not actually know that other options of T/V use exist, or they are at least unfamiliar with how to use them for the purposes of joking, teasing, or giving advice, for instance.

Pedagogical implications

The results of this study clearly show a great degree of variation in the use of T and V among learners engaged in interlearner synchronous CMC. This in itself suggests that the present configuration of learners was not in an environment in which the inappropriate use of T or V had any social consequences. This shortcoming perhaps impeded the learners' development of sociopragmatic competence because experiencing negative social consequences following the inappropriate use of T/V appears to be a key factor in developing learner awareness of the social implications of second-person address (Belz & Kinginger, 2002; Kinginger & Belz, 2005). Another finding of this study was that the vast majority of the T/V tokens were produced in questions and tag structures, most of which were oriented toward the task. This suggests that the learners were unaware of the various types of utterances including T and V used by many NSs in noneducational contexts.

The promotion of language socialization in the foreign-language classroom should be supplemented by exposure to a variety of discourse options within authentic cultural contexts. This ought to include analysis of authentic discourse, such as electronic discourse (for example, chat, e-mail, and forums), transcripts of scenes from films, newspaper and magazine articles, excerpts from literary texts, and advertisements. Such an approach should be multifaceted to include various tasks (or tasks components) fitting within one or more of the "spheres of learning opportunities" outlined by the New London Group (1996). This pedagogy of multiliteracies values not only teacher-led instruction and assistance but also recognizes that learning is a social phenomenon. Thus, for language teachers and learners, the New London Group's framework can be applied as a means of creating a community of learners in which the co-construction of knowledge among learners and teachers is placed at the forefront of language pedagogy (Hall, 2001; van Compernolle & Williams, this volume).

Tasks centered on T and V should incorporate elements of discussion, observation, analysis, communication, and critical reflection. For example, teachers can explain the social implications of using T or V with someone, but they also need to provide students opportunities to observe the (mis)use of these pronouns, switches from V to T, and other phenomena related to second-person address (e.g., pet names, honorifics). This is accomplished relatively efficiently through the use of film, for example. One of the advantages of using film is that the situations represent authentic sociocultural contexts made for NS audiences. In addition, the visual aspect allows learners to recognize not only the linguistic nature of the speech but also the context in which it occurs. Thus, learners should be asked to contextualize a scene they are watching with questions such as "Who are the speakers?", What is their relationship?", "How old are they?", Where does the scene take place?", and so forth. Teachers can then point out some examples of T and V use, and students can note additional examples.

Critical reflection on T and V use should include discussions of patterns of use observed in films or any other type of discourse presented and analyzed in class. The main objective here is to make the familiar unfamiliar. This means reframing what students know about T and V within other (related) contexts, such as the co-occurrence of honorifics (e.g., *madame, monsieur*) or familiar names (e.g., *pote*, "buddy"). In addition, having students look for other features of language that indicate the level of (in)formality or (un)familiarity can also be beneficial in situation T/V use. Students ought also to reflect on how these patterns are both similar to and different from English. For example, although English has only one second-person form, speakers of English use other terms and titles (e.g., *Sir, Mr., Mrs.*) in similar ways.

Students also need opportunities to use T and V in meaningful communication activities. For example, role-playing tasks provide students with a context that determines not only the subject of conversation but more importantly, the level of (in)formality and (un)familiarity required between two or more people who otherwise know each other as classmates. The aim of such tasks should be explicit in that students are aware that appropriate register or language variety is the main focus of the task. As such, any assessment or evaluation will be centered on the use of socially appropriate versus inappropriate language. These types of activities provide learners a safe environment in which to explore the use of new or relatively unfamiliar knowledge, where the teacher and other learners can provide the assistance necessary for development to occur.

Telecollaboration exchanges between NSs and learners such as the one conducted by Belz and Kinginger (2002), although more difficult to incorporate into foreign-language programs, can also greatly facilitate language socialization by allowing learners to experience the direct social consequences of producing inappropriate forms of speech. Learners' electronic discourse could also be incorporated into post-activity tasks in which students analyze and reflect upon their own discourse and its social appropriateness (e.g., Kinginger, 1998). This return to critical reflection on language use is important for raising learners' awareness of what they are doing with the language that they are learning.

Teachers should also be encouraged to incorporate learner-learner CMC interactions as a means for constructing developmental learner corpora. Although learner speech and other more traditional means of data collection can provide much insight for researchers, teachers may not always have time to collect, transcribe, and organize such data. As highlighted in the opening paragraphs of this chapter, CMC data are virtually immediately available for review by teachers and students alike because they can be digitally archived, saved, and later manipulated very easily using widely available text-editing and word-processing software. In many cases, teachers and learners may be able to critically reflect upon a CMC task during a class meeting immediately following the online interaction in a separate session devoted to language analysis. This immediacy has the potential to raise learners' awareness of the language that they are studying and to promote language development throughout an academic term.

Conclusion

Through a corpus-driven analysis of T/V variation among second-language learners of French engaged in interlearner CMC, this chapter has argued that this type of corpus can help teachers and researchers uncover patterns of language use among learners. This window into what learners are actually doing with the language that they are studying is possibly the greatest contribution to world-language teaching made by information and communication technologies (see van Compernolle & Williams, this volume). Future studies ought to investigate how different uses of technologies (Kern, 2006) determine the amount and types of language variation and development on the part of learners. In addition, comparisons of interlearner CMC and telecollaboration with NSs of the language that learners are studying could prove to be insightful in determining the most beneficial configurations for CMC use for achieving specific pedagogical objectives in and beyond the classroom.

Acknowledgements
This chapter is based in part on my MA thesis research (McCourt, 2008), directed by Lawrence Williams (University of North Texas). I am grateful to him for his guidance and encouragement over the past 2 years and for his careful readings and critiques of multiple versions of this research. I would also like to thank Rémi A. van Compernolle (The Pennsylvania State University) for his assistance in the preparation of this chapter.

References

Belz, J. A. (2007). The role of computer mediation in the instruction and development of L2 pragmatic competence. *Annual Review of Applied Linguistics, 27,* 45–75.

Belz, J., & Kinginger, C. (2002). The cross-linguistic development of address form use in telecollaborative language learning: Two case studies. *Canadian Modern Language Review, 59,* 189–214.

Belz, J., & Vyatkina, N. (2008). The pedagogical mediation of a developmental learner corpus for classroom-based language instruction. *Language Learning and Technology, 12*(3), 33–52. Retrieved December 1, 2008, from http://llt.msu.edu/vol12num3/belzvyatkina.pdf

Bragger, J. D., & Rice, D. B. (2005). *Quant à moi...Témoignages des Français et des Francophones.* Boston: Thomson Heinle.

Brown, R., & Gilman, A. (1960). The pronouns of power and solidarity. In T. Sebeok (Ed.), *Style in Language* (pp. 253–276). Cambridge, England: MIT Press.

Dewaele, J.-M. (2004). *Vous* or *tu?* Native and non-native speakers of French on a sociolinguistic tightrope. *International Review of Applied Linguistics, 42,* 383–402.

Gardner-Chloros, P. (1991). Ni tu ni vous: Principes et paradoxes dans l'emploi des pronoms d'allocution en français contemporain [Neither "tu" nor "vous": Principles and paradoxes in the use of personal pronouns in contemprary French]. *Journal of French Language Studies, 1,* 139–155.

Hall, J. K. (2001). *Methods for teaching foreign languages: Creating a community of learners.* Upper Saddle River, NJ: Prentice Hall.

Johns, T. (1986). Microconcord: A language learner's research tool. *System, 14,* 151–162.

Kern, R. (2006). Perspectives on technology in learning and teaching languages. *TESOL Quarterly, 40,* 183–210.

Kinginger, C. (1998). Videoconferencing as access to spoken French. *The Modern Language Journal, 82,* 502–513.

Kinginger, C., & Belz, J. A. (2005). Socio-cultural perspectives of pragmatic development in foreign language learning: Microgenetic case studies from telecollaboration and study abroad. *Intercultural Pragmatics, 2,* 369–421.

Kinginger, C., & Farrell, K. (2004). Assessing development of metapragmatic awareness in study abroad. *Frontiers: The Interdisciplinary Journal of Study Abroad, 10,* 19–42.

Kramsch, C. (1985). Classroom interaction and discourse options. *Studies in Second Language Acquisition, 7,* 169–183.

Liddicoat, A. J. (2006). Learning the culture of interpersonal relationships: Students' understandings of personal address forms in French. *Intercultural Pragmatics, 3,* 55–80.

Manley, J., Smith, S., McMinn, J. T., & Prévost, M. A. (2006). *Horizons* (3rd ed.). Boston: Heinle.

McCourt, C. A. (2008). *Learner use of French second-person pronouns in synchronous electronic communication.* Unpublished master's thesis, University of North Texas, Denton.

Morford, J. (1997). Social indexicality in French pronominal address. *Journal of Linguistic Anthropology, 7,* 3–37.

Mühlhäusler, P., & Harré, R. (1990). *Pronouns and people: The linguistic construction of social and personal identity.* Oxford: Blackwell.

New London Group. (1996). A pedagogy of multiliteracies: Designing social futures. *Harvard Educational Review, 66,* 60–92.

Salaberry, R. (2001). The use of technology for second language learning and teaching. *Modern Language Journal, 85,* 39–56.

Seidlhofer, B. (2002). Pedagogy and local learner corpora. In S. Granger, J. Hung, & S. Petch-Tyson (Eds.), *Computer learner corpora, second language acquisition and foreign language teaching* (pp. 213–234). Amsterdam: John Benjamins.

Tharp, R. G., & Gallimore, R. (1988). *Rousing minds to life: Teaching, learning, and schooling in social context.* New York: Cambridge University Press.

Thorne, S. (2003). Artifacts and cultures-of-use in intercultural communication. *Language Learning & Technology, 7*(2), 38–67. Retrieved May 28, 2008, from http://llt.msu.edu/vol7num2/thorne/default.html

van Compernolle, R. A., & Williams, L. (2008, November). *Analyzing sociolinguistic variation in the L2 community of practice: Performance versus competence.* Paper presented at *New Ways of Analyzing Variation 37*, Houston, TX.

van Compernolle, R. A., & Williams, L. (forthcoming-a). Learner versus non-learner patterns of stylistic variation in synchronous computer-mediated French: Yes/no questions and *nous* versus *on*. *Studies in Second Language Acquisition.* Retrieved November 30, 2008, from http://www.personal.psu.edu/rav137/preprints/SSLA_final.pdf

van Compernolle, R. A., & Williams, L. (forthcoming-b). Variable omission of *ne* in real-time French chat: A corpus-driven comparison of educational and non-educational contexts. *Canadian Modern Language Review.* Retrieved November 30, 2008, from http://www.personal.psu.edu/rav137/preprints/CMLR.negation.pdf

Ware, P. (2005). "Missed communication" in online communication: Tensions in fostering successful online interactions. *Language Learning & Technology,* 9(2), 64–89. Retrieved May 28, 2008, from http://llt.msu.edu/vol9num2/default.html

Warschauer, M. (1997). Computer-mediated collaborative learning: Theory and practice. *Modern Language Journal, 81,* 470–481.

Williams, L. (2007, September). *The acquisition of sociopragmatic competence: An analysis of beginning and intermediate learners of French.* Paper presented at the annual meeting of the Association for French Language Studies, Boulogne-sur-Mer, France.

Williams, L., & van Compernolle, R. A. (2007). Second-person pronoun use in on-line French-language chat environments. *French Review, 80,* 804–820.

These Horses Can Fly! and Other Lessons From Second Life: The View from a Virtual Hacienda

Gloria B. Clark
The Pennsylvania State University, Harrisburg

The other day in class, my students climbed Mayan pyramids, walked on a beach, shopped in an indigenous market, danced on a plaza, explored a waterfall and took a tour of a Mexican island while riding on the back of a big blue butterfly. No, we were not on a study-abroad tour together; we were actually all in our seats in the computer lab. However, the Second Life immersive environment has opened the walls of my basic Spanish classroom to a world that is challenging, fascinating, motivating, and ever-changing. The Second Life world is rich with cultural and interactive possibilities that can be integrated into many different courses. Students can participate in engaged collaboration not only with other students, but also with people from all over the world. Second Life is a global village where students can meet people with similar interests who may live in a totally different home environment. Imagine having a tour of the virtual Alhambra given by a person from Spain or informally discussing rock music with a musician from Mexico. The creative possibilities are endless because virtual technology connects us in ever more meaningful ways. For instance, students can construct their own spaces in Second Life and use them to teach others about their unique relationship to the course material. Education in a virtual space offers students tools to construct meaning and motivates them to a deeper level of understanding course material.

For years, the emphasis in foreign-language pedagogy has been on teaching language in context. Omaggio Hadley (1993), in her seminal book, *Teaching Language in Context*, argued that "language use in the classroom, whether for analytic or experiential purposes, ought to be contextualized" (p. 127). Research has proven that students learn better when language is presented in a logical and connected way. In addition, visual organizers enhance learning because they give students more immediate entrance into the situation at hand. Second Life provides a context for student learning in a way that the classroom cannot. For example, when studying the vocabulary for health and wellness, practice conversations can take place in a virtual hospital setting or even in a virtual doctor's office. Students can dress their

Clark, G. B. (2009). These horses can fly! and other lessons from Second Life: The view from a virtual hacienda. In R. Oxford & J. Oxford, (Eds.), *Second language teaching and learning in the Net Generation* (pp. 153–172). Honolulu: University of Hawai'i, National Foreign Language Resource Center.

avatars appropriately for the situation, which deepens their interaction with the context. Second Life is uniquely suited to foreign-language instruction.

Some Second Life history

Second Life is an online virtual community that is being created by its residents in which they can own land and build houses and either rent or reside in them. Colleges and universities, for instance, have bought land to set up virtual campuses; many college students go to class in Second Life. After class and other times, plenty of virtual shopping can be done. Stores are open 24 hours a day and offer everything from new skin and hair to artwork and music. Residents from all over the world, some 8,500,000 of them, interact in a virtual 3D space through the use of avatars, or 3D characters that represent a resident of the virtual world. Very aptly, the word "avatar" means the manifestation of a god or representation of a god on Earth. In Second Life, avatars explore the environment and become extensions of their owners. Note that Second Life has separate versions available for teens under 18 and for adults, referred to as the teen grid and the adult grid.

Second Life is a relatively new concept. In 1999, Philip Rosedale founded Linden Lab. The first product, called "Linden World," opened to the public in beta form in 2002. In 2003, Second Life had 16 islands covering 16 acres with approximately 250 residents. Today, 15,829,146 residents (avatars) live, work, and play on some 26,539 islands, some of which are incorporated into three mainland continents, and the remaining 4,000 of which exist as separate islands. Second Life has its own economy; the third quarter of 2008 topped $100 million in resident-to-resident trading in Second Life (Linden, 2008). The currency in Second Life is the Linden dollar; the exchange rate varies, but currently is $250.00 L to $1.00 US. Linden Lab considers Second Life an entertainment experience:

> Linden Lab is a privately held company established to develop an extraordinary new form of shared 3D entertainment. Through its first product, "Second Life," Linden Lab offers a truly collaborative, immersive and open-ended entertainment experience where together people create and inhabit a virtual world of their design. (Cited in White, 2008, p. 4)

Although Second Life certainly has an entertainment aspect, it is increasingly being used for education. Currently, at least 250 colleges and universities from around the world have facilities on the Second Life adult grid. The facilities range from educational pilot projects built on land borrowed from Linden Lab for use in one specific course to islands and groups of islands. Here is a mere sampling of American colleges and universities that are active in Second Life: Pennsylvania State University, Loyalist College, New York University, Stanford University, Ohio University, University of Hawai'i, Harvard University, Vassar College, University of Delaware, and George Washington University.

Building the virtual future: Educating in Second Life

The Second Life metaverse is an environment that is both challenging and full of possibilities for creative teaching and learning. Second Life has propelled human life, with all of its diverse identities, into a new arena for collaboration and growth. Whether we are discussing economics, medicine, law, education, science, or one of many other disciplines, Second Life's impact is immeasurable. Michael Schrage, a Research Associate with MIT and a Merrill Lynch Forum Innovation Fellow, in his book *Serious Play* (2000), grappled with philosophical questions about the interactions between people and technology. He expressed a fundamental faith in the positive benefits of those interactions, as follows:

> Today, the media and the marketplace for these expressive interactions are rapidly coevolving in ways that are radically reshaping how people innovate with each other. Tomorrow's innovators will invest more in playing with prototypes, modeling marketplaces, and simulating scenarios because that will become the best way to create new value and profitably deliver it to customers. Innovative models inspire innovative behavior. Even by accident, new prototyping media can create new interactions between people that in turn create new value. (p. 15)

In addition, Schrage (2000) considers such interactions with simulation or modeling as serious play, what he calls the "essence of innovation" (p. 1). Bringing Second Life to the classroom opens that potential for innovation and the connection that is essential for active, immersive education.

Klahr, Triona, and Williams (2007) studied 56 middle school children and their interactions with real and virtual materials in early science education. In this case study, the students built and tested mousetrap cars to see which would go the farthest. Some students built cars with real, three-dimensional materials, and others built with virtual materials shown on a computer (pp. 5–8). The conclusions of the study were that there were "no differences between the physical and the virtual materials in either learning or confidence" (p. 16). The study also found that the virtual experience took up less space, the classroom management was easier, using virtual materials took less time, and virtual materials were easier to replicate and distribute (p. 16). These results are easily transferable to Second Life, which has a whole 3D environment for experimentation. Virtually anything can be built in Second Life, so students can build and manipulate their own objects. Second Life has many public "sandboxes" that are open to anyone for building. Students can get virtual hands-on experience building and then using objects.

Many universities and colleges encourage the intersection of course topics and independent learning in Second Life. Nearly all disciplines have found a connection to Second Life. For medical school training, for instance, Palomar West: The Hospital of the Future has a simulated hospital experience in Second Life, which includes the patient donning a wristband and being taken to a patient room and then to a procedure room. This type of training could be used for hospital personnel and for patients who are about to undergo major surgery to help them understand the processes they will go through. Palomar West will be opening in Southern California in 2011 and will be using robotic techniques and advanced technology in its services to patients. In the humanities, Vassar College has built a replica of the Sistine Chapel on their virtual campus. Avatars can enter the Chapel and view the magnificent paintings reproduced there. The built-in camera capability of Second Life allows you to zoom in on details as you wish. The applications in the sciences are endless. Robert C. Amme, a research professor at the University of Denver, has received a $200,000 federal grant to build a nuclear reactor in Second Life. He wants to use it in training nuclear waste management experts, taking full advantage of the unique possibilities in Second Life. Amme commented on the advantages of using Second Life:

> In a way, running experiments and teaching classes in Second Life offers a number of advantages over real life: students watching from their computer screens won't have to wear expensive radiation badges or obtain clearance to enter an actual laboratory. Instead, they can attend in the guise of "avatars"—virtual likenesses, like personalized computer game characters, whose appearance and features can be customized. (Guess, 2007)

Students using Second Life can interact with other avatars, a key to making a successful virtual classroom, Amme said; collaboration is built-in. He also mentioned that the virtual classroom has a major advantage over more traditional Web-based distance-learning programs:

> We think that a hands-on laboratory experience is the best teacher, and to be able to do this in Second Life is a marvelous breakthrough, a marvelous opportunity.... The Web itself is rather benign by comparison because there's no interactivity.... What's missing in a lot of distance learning is the socialization [among] students. (Guess, 2007)

Dr. Amme highlighted many of the advantages of using Second Life in education, most importantly, that students make connections with the digital environment very easily and adapt quickly to experiencing the virtual world through their avatars. Dresang (2005) proposed a theory of radical change, which she based on three principles of the digital age: interactivity, connectivity, and access (p. 178). Dresang used those principles to examine how young people seek information in the digital environment, specifically, in the library. Many of her findings can be applied to learning in Second Life. First, she defined "interactivity" as "dynamic, user-controlled, nonlinear, nonsequential, complex information behavior and representation" (p. 183). Dresang cited much research that concludes that young students prefer "high visual content and short, simple, textual content" (p. 183). Her next term, "connectivity," refers to "the sense of community or construction of social worlds that emerge from changing perspectives and expanded associations in the real world or in resources" (p. 186). The final term, "access," is used as "the breaking of long-standing information barriers, bringing entrée to a wide diversity of opinion and opportunity" (p. 188). These three terms apply easily to Second Life and give us a clue as to how students of today perceive the digital classroom. Their information-seeking is very different from that of the generations of students before: They seek information in expanded and multilayered environments; they seek information in the company of others and pursue information from diverse sources.

What definition of learning in Second Life can be better than Dresang's theory of radical change? The first term, "interactivity," refers to independent learning, or learning by discovery. Students completing projects in Second Life act independently and/or as groups as they solve problems related to the course material. Second Life also provides "connectivity" as students and instructors build a social network within the virtual world and actively build environments for class use. Dresang related the word "access" to a diversity of sources and opinions. As mentioned previously, Second Life is a worldwide community, which includes a large proportion of Europeans; currently, about 60% of the residents in Second Life are European. Interestingly, 16% of Second Life residents are from Germany; the United States also accounts for 16% of the population (Burns, 2007).

Of course, teaching in Second Life has drawbacks. Some general issues will be discussed below, but foreign-language classes have their own special challenges. For instance, I have been working for 2 years to set up regular conversation tables in Spanish that would be available outside of class time. It is difficult to get native speakers and students to commit to a regular meeting time. Currently, I recommend that students sign up for an *intercambio* [exchange] with a native speaker and then set their own times to meet and practice, usually about 30 minutes in Spanish and 30 in English once a week.[1]

Importantly, Second Life can be a tool used in a hybrid course, which combines the real world and the virtual. Classes meet in a traditional classroom for a portion of the class

1 A Website enables this *intercambio* system in Second Life at http://teachyouteachme.ning.com.

meetings and have the balance in the virtual world. This type of course has advantages and disadvantages, which will be discussed in the next section.

Teaching hybrid courses in Second Life

The demands of a traditional Spanish curriculum in higher education often necessitate the use of a hybrid course that can attend to both the development of language in the physical classroom and experimentation, language practice, and discovery in the Second Life virtual environment. The design of a hybrid course has to take into account the needs of the students for feedback, classroom interaction, assessment requirements, the overall university curriculum, and the integration of virtual experiences into the overall syllabus. The word "integration" is key in designing a hybrid course. Activities in Second Life need to be an essential part of the course pedagogy that enrich and extend classroom activities.

A hybrid course using Second Life presents course material with a combination of in-class activities and assignments in Second Life. Although the time spent in classroom instruction is reduced, students are actively learning material through experiences and projects in Second Life. Instructors strive to give students the best of both worlds: a worthwhile classroom experience and a learning environment that promotes independent, hands-on learning.

Why go with a hybrid course, other than budget concerns by administrators, inadequate classroom space on campus, and enrollment growth? First of all, Second Life enables activities and experiences that are not possible in the traditional classroom. Students can be immersed in the culture of a place; they are able, by extension transference, to walk around, see, perceive, and participate. "Extension transference" is a term used in the cultural theory of Edward T. Hall (Marold, 2002, p. 114), an anthropologist, who proposed that we often participate in an experience by extending ourselves in some way, such as extending our arms with a tool, or our feet with equipment, such as skis or ice skates, and our brains by computers. Marold, in considering electronic tutelage, described the computer as a "'prosthesis'—almost a biological extension of our physical beings. We use it with much the same ease as we use one of our natural limbs" (p. 114). The concept of extension transference is key to understanding how Second Life works and is essential to the design and success of a hybrid course.

Here is an example of extension transference from my classroom: One afternoon we were exploring an island that had large turtles on the beach. One of my students exclaimed that she loved turtles, so I suggested that she have her avatar walk over and sit on its back. Two minutes later, she said excitedly, "I am going to take a picture of myself on this turtle." She did not say that she was going to take a picture of her avatar on the turtle, but take a picture of herself. She was expressing that she perceived the avatar as herself. The same thing happens when your avatar is under the water and you find yourself holding your breath or when you get that sinking feeling in the pit of your stomach when your avatar is in danger of falling.

A hybrid course has many advantages. First, it appeals to students who are looking for a nontraditional approach to learning, while at the same time accommodating those who are more comfortable in the traditional classroom. The Second Life portion of the course often allows the more timid students opportunities to participate in a less threatening environment than the classroom. Also, the combination of in-class and online activities opens up a world of creative opportunities for instructors and students. The online portion increases independent learning on certain projects and facilitates group learning on others. Certain course content can be introduced in the classroom and then practiced in a hands-on, realistic environment. Of course, not all students learn in the same way. In a hybrid course, material is presented in multiple ways, which accommodates all students in some manner.

Using Second Life in the basic Spanish classroom

My first experience with Second Life was a project-based class. Second Life was introduced, and then the students were encouraged to complete a project using Second Life. A comparative literature class, CMLIT153, International cultures through literature and film: Childhood in text and image, compared narrative techniques used by literature and film in portraying childhood in several different cultures, specifically, Latin American and South American. Students read several novels, viewed films, participated in discussions, and completed projects that increased their critical skills as applied to films and narratives and expanded their understanding of the nature of childhood as experienced in various cultures. The class took two field trips to Second Life to visit islands related to Hispanic culture. At the end of the semester, the students had the option of completing a project in Second Life for their final presentation. One project was preparing, on Pennsylvania State's land in Second Life, a slideshow display that gave background information on one of the novels.

Since that small beginning, I have incorporated Second Life into my Spanish courses on a weekly basis. My university has purchased several islands and accepted my proposal to build a Spanish hacienda. My proposal to build a hacienda was based on the rationale that students would learn both language and culture in the Second Life environment. Language teachers have known for a long time that immersion is the best way to learn a second language. However, considering the cost of undergraduate education and the cost of travel, the truth is that most students never get the opportunity to experience Spanish language and culture in a Spanish-speaking country. The virtual environment, however, can creating an immersion-like experience for students that can provide some of the culture and language that is so needed outside of the classroom.

My idea came from a concept that I have had for a long time but that I have never been able to bring to fruition in the real world. I have always wanted to create a resource room that would give students a space to practice the language and interact with materials in Spanish. I would fill this room with newspapers and magazines in Spanish, with art, with computer programs to practice grammar and learn about culture, and with music and food. Students would have a comfortable place to relax, talk to each other, and be immersed for a time in a Spanish that is not in the classroom and not in a book. To date, I have not found an administrator who will give me a room and the funds to fill it with all of the ingredients for a great Spanish experience.

I often teach Latin American literature using books that are set in a hacienda; it always amazes me that students do not have an understanding of this essential Spanish architectural term. Therefore, I proposed to build a moderate-sized building in Second Life that is modeled after a Spanish-style hacienda. With this style, students would begin their virtual experience as soon as they arrived.

Our Hacienda Segunda Vida is built in the shape of a square with the center cut out. Inside the hacienda are four rooms and two entryways, with a garden, fountain, and benches in the center patio. One room provides a classroom setting with floating cushions, a smartboard, and pictures and travel posters on the wall. This room is big enough for students to move around and post their projects. In the future, it will feature some big books of Spanish poetry or quotes from masterpieces of Spanish literature for students to read.

Another large room, the resource room, forms the heart of the hacienda. In this immersive environment, students can access books of Spanish and Latin American literature and read current newspapers from Spanish-speaking countries. Classes will write their own newsletters and have them available for visitors and other students to read. Spanish and Latin American art is on the walls, and each art object will have an interactive component that will reveal information about it. Students will have access to audio files in Spanish for listening to authentic language or music. In Fall 2008, I plan to experiment with having students make podcasts and post them in the resource room so that their classmates can listen to them. They will also be able to listen to live radio broadcasts from Spanish-speaking countries. This environment is perfect for setting up grammar or vocabulary practice that would overlay the Spanish with English or provide the answers to exercises. Students will eventually have opportunities to find out about real-life study-abroad experiences.

All of the above, a student could do alone. However, in Second Life, it is the social networking that is so valuable. In this space, students talk to each other in Spanish. The hacienda will sponsor speakers from Spanish-speaking countries who will lecture on course-related topics and talk informally with the students. Faculty members from other institutions have been invited to give guest lectures and spend time speaking with the students. In the future, I would like to show movies in Spanish on the smartboard in the classroom. Groups of students will complete projects and display them in the building or on the grounds and invite comments from their peers. Faculty members will schedule office hours and talk to students individually or in groups.

One room of the hacienda that is still in development is the kitchen, which is meant for relaxation or group functions. This kitchen will be modeled after the kitchen in Frida Kahlo's house in Mexico City. It will have comfortable chairs, a large table, a fireplace, and art on the walls. I would like to devise some fun things for this room, such as trying on a sombrero, building a taco, or getting a free t-shirt. Students could host social gatherings in the kitchen and learn about Spanish-style cooking. Invited guests would share recipes and cultural differences in cooking.

The last room is an office area where faculty members can hold office hours. The office has a desk, several chairs, computer, rug, lamps, and bookcases. Students can visit the faculty members during their posted office hours to ask questions or chat in Spanish.

These ideas will, of course, evolve over time with new ideas and technologies, but the overall concept is to provide a space filled with ambient information to enhance the language-learning process. The Hacienda learning environment is designed to support the undergraduate Spanish language learner by providing resources that will ensure positive and enjoyable experiences as they are surrounded by the richness of Hispanic language and culture. In Fall 2007, I taught two sections of Spanish 001 (48 students) that had a Second Life component; in Spring 2008, I offered one section of Spanish 002 (24 students) that used Second Life.

Program description

Basic Spanish at my institution meets for three class periods a week: two 75-minute classes and one 50-minute class. Successful students earn four credits for the class. I chose to use the 50-minute class for Second Life and the two 75-minute classes for grammar instruction and in-class communicative activities. This worked out well because the students looked forward to the Friday sessions in Second Life. They were definitely motivated to participate in the virtual world, especially during the weeks that I did extensive pre-Second Life preparation. The assignments in these classes were principally synchronous. Penn State Harrisburg does not have a language lab facility; therefore, the students who visited the Hacienda in Second Life benefited greatly from the practice in written and oral/aural Spanish. Naturally, each student progresses at a different level, but assessments of Second Life assignments throughout the semester show an increased understanding of Spanish language and culture. Transcripts of student comments recorded in focus groups show an understanding of the possibilities of Second Life for sharing language and culture. Here is a student comment on learning in Second Life:

> I was just thinking, um. It is entertaining?, yes. Uh, I mean she [Dr. Clark] can do a lot more with us, like she can show us places. It is kind of a better way than just using pictures, I think, and videos. You get to, like, experience the culture a little bit more, like the way they set it up. You can actually see and tell what they're actually thinking, you're not just looking at a picture and getting a two-dimensional picture of what it is. You have to like look around and you can talk to other people and things like that. (Recorded Spanish 3 focus group)

Another student replied,

> Well to me, Second Life is just, it's a nice getaway. It helps me, or maybe helps all of us, um, just experience new things and it makes, it seems very real. I mean, I would love to be there, but my avatar is there for me (laughter) But definitely, it really feels real, I mean I get to learn more and it's, I feel like I'm right there. (Recorded Spanish 3 focus group)

In addition, all of the Second Life resources were designed to correlate to our textbook, *Mosaicos: Spanish as a World Language* (de Castells, Guzmán, Lapuerta, & García, 2006).

Lindsay (2004) cited two studies in her article on hybrid courses that show positive student reactions to hybrid courses in general:

> Studies have shown that students believe the hybrid approach improves communication and interaction, both between the students and instructors. For example one study showed 66% of the students saw a marked improvement in interaction while 27% felt that communication was the same (Riffel, 2003). Another survey showed that 90% of students in a hybrid course felt they learned as much or more than in a traditional course. (Mueggenberg, 2003, p. 18)

In general, ambient education offers each student the overall experience of being surrounded by language and culture in a way that cannot be reproduced in a traditional classroom; at the same time, a hybrid course offers the familiarity and personal interaction of the classroom.

Designing a syllabus

My goal was to integrate Second Life into the existing syllabi for the Basic Spanish Language Program as a low-stakes part of the courses. I did not want to anchor the courses in an emerging technology because I was unsure of how students would receive it and how it would work on a regular basis in the classroom. A cut-and-paste view of the assessment portion of my syllabus before and after the inclusion of Second Life is shown in Appendix A. The assessment in Basic Spanish is a portfolio approach, with variable credit given for the different aspects of the course.

Because I did not want to simply add Second life to an existing syllabus, I had to consider what items could be adapted to Second Life without overloading the students. The first item was to drop the conversation table requirement. Students had been required to attend a 40-minute conversation table with a native speaker six times during the semester, an assignment done out of the classroom. The new syllabus would include conversation opportunities in Second Life. Oral evaluations could be adapted easily to Second Life, with students presenting role plays in different settings. For Spanish 1, the first evaluation was a face-to-face interview with me; the second oral evaluation was a role play in Second Life. The writing requirement could be effectively incorporated into weekly Second Life assignments.

What syllabus items cannot be adapted to Second Life? Traditional quizzes and tests cannot be taken in Second Life; however, a term project could take the place of the final exam. Some examples are making a movie, building a scene, giving a skit, or preparing a presentation using a Second Life destination, like an art museum. For a hybrid class, where there is a choice, the grammar is better taught in the classroom. Workbook exercises, grammar, and writing practice can be done online, but not in Second Life. However, online material can be linked to objects in the Hacienda. In the resource room is a 3D box on a table, which displays our textbook cover. When you click the box, you go to the Webpage that coordinates with our text. Homework assignments can be a combination of Second Life and the textbook. Reading is improving in Second Life, but is still a challenge because you must wait for the camera to focus on the written word. The development of reading skills is better using written textbooks or other resources. Nevertheless, some reading is possible in Second Life; there are links to Spanish language newspapers, signs in Spanish to follow, and other short texts.

Weekly assignments in Second Life

The Second Life weekly assignments were distributed as a guide to the experience. Appendix B has an example of a Spanish 1 activity that coordinates with the lesson on university vocabulary and the use of the present tense. In my journal entries below, I reflected on the difference between the university vocabulary assignment I used before and the assignment in Second Life, where students practice the vocabulary in an authentic 3D setting and contextualized space, full of visual cues.

The university vocabulary assignment was done in the computer lab on a Friday for 50 minutes with students working independently. Our target vocabulary was university life, including the names of buildings. What was growing in the *tócame* garden: carrots. When you touched each one, a column rose out of the ground containing pictures of one of the buildings of the Escuela Politécnica in Spain. Students could identify such places as the *cafeteria* and *biblioteca*. Following class, students could take their assignments with them to finish and return by the next Wednesday. During the first semester of teaching the hybrid course in Second Life, Fall 2007, I kept a weekly journal. Below is a portion of the entry for the day of our "field trip" to the European university.

Snapshots from the virtual classroom

October 12, 2007

Today I had the students visit the European University, the *Escuela Politécnica Superior.* The task was to learn how to teleport; to practice with the question words (*Mosaicos* 40); to practice description (vocabulary page 91) and the vocabulary of the university (57). It is important to evaluate if this assignment is more effective than the alternative, the textbook assignment. The textbook assignment involves going to the University of Salamanca Website and writing down the names of facultades and profesores, (page 25 in our textbook). In analyzing what is better about Second Life, I have come to the conclusion that the immersive environment is more interesting than a Webpage.

> I have been reflecting on other differences between doing the Salamanca assignment on page 25 of our text and visiting the European University on SL. I think SL involves more critical thinking and problem solving, something that we have to do constantly when we are actually in Mexico. The signposts were in Spanish, for instance, and the campus was a new environment to negotiate. The Webpage is more cut and dry and predictable. SL is different every day, just like real life.

Throughout the time I have been teaching in Second Life, I have been observing and evaluating the benefits of using the virtual environment, particularly in Spanish classes, but much of what I have learned can be applied to any discipline. There is real value for the students to pursue active learning in what might be called a real virtual space; a space that pushes the boundaries of the traditional classroom and extends what is possible in real life.

Second Life assignments should be designed to coordinate closely with real-time classroom material. They need to relate to the real-world classroom in some way and to make sense in the Second Life world.

Activities for Spanish 1 using Spanish 1 topics

Nearly every lesson in a traditional Spanish 1 text can be adapted in some way in Second Life. I have taken the lesson topics from the first eight chapters of the *Mosaicos* text (de Castells, Guzmán, Lapuerta, & García, 2006) and written a Second Life activity to enhance each, as described below. In addition to the target vocabulary, each assignment can include oral or written practice of the grammar points in the chapter. These lessons can be adapted to many other disciplines that require vocabulary acquisition.

Early vocabulary of objects around the classroom: Design a vocabulary scavenger hunt. Plant pictures of objects or the objects themselves around your land or building(s). Have the students find them and write the words in Spanish on a list. Some examples are pen, pencil, notebook, and clock.

Introductions: The students meet in a social setting (a dance floor, for example) and introduce their avatars. Use a written assignment to guide the students and have them fill in information about the people they meet. This could be done on your land or on a visit to one of the many social areas on a Spanish-themed island, like Visit Mexico.

Numbers: The students practice the numbers by shopping for items on a Spanish-speaking island. Provide a written guide for students to follow with space to report what they purchased and how much it was. Because this lesson is early in Spanish 1, the students will have to use a dictionary to report on the items they "bought." Barcelona del Oeste Island has a nice shopping area.

Culture, expressing preferences, colors, likes, and dislikes: The students learn about a Spanish artist in class and visit a gallery in Second Life. For example, Colombiamor has an art gallery with a Fernando Botero exhibition. The students visit the gallery and respond in Spanish, in writing, or in conversation by describing a favorite picture (or pictures) and giving the title.

University life: The students visit a Spanish or Latin American University isle to practice university vocabulary. They draw a map of the campus and label the buildings in Spanish and use it in conversation. The Universidad Autónoma de Guerrero has an interesting site.

Ordering food: The students go to a restaurant on a Spanish isle and role play a restaurant scene. Visit Mexico has a lovely restaurant with a menu posted in Spanish in the Ruta Maya, Campeche section.

Sports vocabulary: The students visit an island that has a lot of sports activities. Provide a guide for students to report in Spanish what sports they tried (Boracay has many sports) or plan a vacation trip to the isle and make a poster or brochure advertising it.

House and furniture vocabulary: Visit a Spanish isle and tour some houses. Students report in writing or orally about what they saw, liked, and disliked. Role play a real estate agent selling one of the houses. Al Andalus Alhambra is a site that has many beautiful houses.

Some experiences in Second Life journal entries

Included here are four journal entries from the last two semesters of teaching in Second Life. Seeing how the experiences of the students have begun to shape my pedagogy in Second Life has been very interesting. This is a new technology to use in the classroom, and there is no roadmap to follow; there is imagination, trial, and error. I kept a weekly journal in the fall of 2007 and posted regularly on a virtual world blog during Spring 2008. Looking back over these entries, I can see how the assignments evolved and how the students' interest grew as the courses proceeded.

The selected entries will highlight a variety of assignments in Spanish 1 and 2. They give a very fresh and intimate picture of our time in Second Life. I have included an entry that describes the experience of shopping on Barcelona del Oeste to explain how the students worked with the assignment described above. The next entry describes a guest lecture by a colleague of mine from Borough of Manhattan Community College, Dr. Carlos Hernandez. Carlos is Cuban American and grew up in a Cuban community in Florida. His avatar came to visit the Hacienda, and he told the students about his cultural experiences in Florida and Cuba. His visit clearly demonstrates the uniqueness and possibilities of Second Life pedagogy. The third entry details the cultural experience of visiting the Al Andalus Sim, which is a reproduction of the Alhambra in Spain. Students found this "field trip" to be fascinating and worthwhile as they explored the virtual ancient buildings and visited a mosque. The last entry, a day on the Visit Mexico Sim, will show the volatility of the medium of Second Life and how students can make it their own.

October 19, 2007

Today we had a shopping assignment. I sent the students to Barcelona del Oeste, an island whose shopping district mirrors Las Ramblas in Barcelona, including the statue of Columbus pointing to sea at the end of the street. The students were to find the Island (practice in teleporting), explore the statue, write a description, and then go shopping. They were to find ten things they wanted to buy and write the item name and the price in Spanish. They also visited the cafe. Several students sat down at a table with some other people who were speaking (text chatting) in Spanish. The students joined in for a little while.

I have used a shopping assignment for many years and it is interesting how it has changed with the advances in technology. Early on I used to give out copies of *El Diario*, a newspaper from New York City. Students would find a page of advertising and we would practice the prices in Spanish. A couple of years later I had enough JCPenney catalogues in Spanish for each student to use. They looked through the catalogues and reported the items they liked and practiced saying the prices. After that, when I had the Web available in class, I would get on a Webpage from Mexico that had advertising. Sometimes I used real estate ads to practice larger numbers. One year I called up the Webpage for Gigante, a Mexican supermarket. We practiced the names of the food and the prices. I have also used overheads that have items and prices. Occasionally, I have brought items to the classroom with prices on them and had students say the prices in Spanish. Now the question is, did students learn more in Second Life? Here is what I think they gain from Second Life. They have to make more decisions, because they have to find things. The Webpage assignments were often question and answer, with me asking most of the questions. The JCPenney assignment was usually done with a partner, a sharing of information. I think SL requires more critical thinking. The students have to find things on their own and then use what they have found to speak or write in Spanish. Their experiences definitely have a tie to the ACTFL National Standards for foreign language acquisition.

November 2, 2007

Carlos visited the Hacienda today and talked with students about growing up Cuban in Florida. His presentation was well organized and we found out that it really works well to have the students textchat their thoughts and questions instead of trying to speak in a large group. I started chatting by inserting comments and questions. The students picked it up and also started writing questions. Because they wrote them, we now have a record of their questions, at least. Carlos felt better because he got a lot of immediate feedback. He also liked that he could look at the chat history and go back to answer questions when he thought it would fit in to what he was saying. I asked the students in each class to write a paragraph about the presentation. I collected them and they are overwhelmingly positive.

I also prepared a Day of the Dead display for the students on Penn State Isle. I bought an ofrenda with candles, pictures and all, that I placed in the Hacienda patio. When students clicked on the ofrenda, they received a sugar skull in their inventory. I made an object that students could click on and receive a note card in Spanish explaining the Day of the Dead. In addition to the ofrenda, I placed six "billboards" along the ocean and applied real photos that I uploaded. The first billboard in the line has a paragraph in Spanish explaining the day of the Dead and the fact that the billboards show real photos. Below the billboard I put a small table with flowers, sugar skulls and candles.

I also bought a Halloween pumpkin candy dispenser that ended up to be pretty funny. It was a large, probably comparably about 5 feet high, orange pumpkin. When touched, it gave out one of 12 different kinds of candy bars, which the students put in their hands. It came with a script that animated the avatars. At first they ate the candy, then started to shake, then convulse and then fell down on the ground, dead, for an instant. It was really comical. At first they were a bit worried, then they got it. It was a fun ending to the Day of the Dead lesson.

April 7, 2008

A week ago, Spanish language students teleported from the now familiar Hacienda Segunda Vida to the Al Andalus Caliphate Project, a sim that covers two islands and re-creates the largest historical site in Andalucía, Spain, the Alhambra. Basically, the Alhambra was the palace and governmental center of Islamic power during the years of the conquest of Spain, from about 711 A.D. to 1492. The actual buildings are in Granada and command a large hilltop with gardens and intricately carved buildings with fountains, receiving halls and hundreds of rooms.

The Al Andalus sim, is a magnificent example of Second Life's ability to provide a setting, an atmosphere and a spirit of place. As I led students on a guided tour of the major parts of the Alhambra, I was struck by the authentic feel of the surroundings. Of course, there is no such thing as an exact copy of the original, but this sim is certainly faithful to the design of the Alhambra in many ways.

To get ready to visit, students visited the Webpage for the Alhambra in Spain and learned what it looks like and what the buildings represent. I also connected the Alhambra to the students' own experiences by noting that our American author, Washington Irving, spent some time living there when the Alhambra was in disrepair, and wrote a book of stories about his experiences called *Tales of the Alhambra.*

While exploring the buildings, the students visited a Mezquita, or mosque. They were instructed to take off their shoes before entering and the women put on veils, (which were conveniently located in a basket by the door), to show respect. The students were subdued and respectful during their visit and came to a better understanding of the place of Islamic culture within the Spanish tradition.

On our Spanish Chapter test a few days later, I included a page-long reading on the Alhambra in Spanish and followed with a series of questions on the reading. Approximately 98% of the class read the passage and answered every question correctly. In Second-language pedagogy, we call this type of series of activities related to a lesson, "scaffolding." Nesting activities together provides a firm scaffold to support students when they risk reading, writing, or speaking a language. Second Life has an important place in that scaffold for student learning.

April 18, 2008

> I just came from Spanish class and wanted to write about our experience this morning while it is still fresh in my mind. Our objective today was to learn more about Mayan Culture by exploring the Ruta Maya, a recent addition to the Chichén Itzá Archeological site on Visit Mexico island (sponsored by the Mexican government) and to practice some discrete grammar points that are related to our language studies, namely comparisons and the preterite and imperfect tenses. The students received an information sheet that detailed a walk along the Ruta Maya with visits to four pyramids. In addition, I noted that there were a number of fun things to do in the area, such as swimming near the waterfall, scuba diving, hang gliding and riding a zipline through the rainforest canopy. The students were to visit four pyramids, read the note cards, do one fun thing and complete a written assignment in Spanish using the targeted grammar points.

I soon found out that I had neglected to mention the fact that that there were also free horse rentals available. A number of students converged on the horse rental barn and soon were exploring the Ruta on horseback. As I was ruminating on the fact that, yet again, Second Life had provided an authentic experience, the students discovered that they could fly with the horses. Soon the sky was filled with flying horses. For the next twenty minutes or so, we found out that, yes, horses can climb the pyramid steps, yes, horses can hang glide and even ride the zipline. I suggested that the students should stay focused on our objectives and remember that they had to complete the written part of the assignment as well. One of the students said, well, can't we write about the horses? Well, what I really had in mind was some explanation of the archeological site, but then again, why not? What mattered was the use of Spanish.

I am still analyzing the experience; what is the lesson here? I was very prosaic in my lesson plan; I had visited the island, ridden the horses and it had never occurred to me to fly, let alone climb the pyramids or hang glide on horseback. Maybe I just don't get it; I get hung up on the authentic experiences and neglect the creative possibilities. Second Life is about encouraging that creative fervor, that crazy "look at what I can do" spirit that is certainly missing from most standard classrooms. I am looking forward to reading their written assignments and seeing the results of the turn class took today. Just maybe Mayan culture and the Spanish language can be learned on a flying horse...

Student responses to Second Life surveys

Preliminary statistics from surveys given in class that focused on attitudes about students' experiences in Second Life are shown in Appendix C. In general, the students surveyed pointed out the strong features of Second Life in the basic Spanish classroom as its facilitation of collaboration and culture lessons and its uniqueness and practical applications. These comments reveal much about this generation of 18- to 25-year-olds. They find it essential to collaborate and necessary to be in constant communication with others. They rely on each other in ways that generations before did not in an educational setting. Education, for them, is not a solo experience but involves working with others. They clearly apply this in their everyday living, using Facebook, cell phones, text messaging, blogging, and other means of communication as daily parts of their lives. They are collaborators and communicators. Our call as guides is to support that need for collaboration while strengthening their independent academic skills. In Second Life, this is easily done by giving assignments that necessitate collaboration and assignments that require independent work.

The students expressed their interest in learning culture in Second Life. This can be a double-edged sword, and instructors must be careful to differentiate between the virtual experience and the real experience. Visiting the pyramids on the Visit Mexico Sim, for instance, will provide a feel for the pyramids and a whiff of that ancient culture, but only a whiff. My hope is that the brief time that they have to explore will whet their appetites for travel. You can learn a fair amount about culture by navigating the islands in Second Life, but the experience is still a virtual one that can help a student to understand, not a substitute for travel.

Many students mentioned the uniqueness of Second Life as a plus. I have thought much about their need for something unique. The problem is that in a few semesters, Second Life will not be unique. I reflected on this in my journal after a field trip to the pyramids of Chichén Itzá:

> This experience at Chichén Itzá was quite profound, in a classroom sense. The students were not just engaged, they were fascinated and enthusiastic. I know that we cannot sustain such enthusiasm on a regular basis, but I don't want SL to become ho-hum either. I think the fact that it (SL) is constantly changing and being improved upon will keep it fresh. I have in mind the Gartner Hype Cycle on the maturing process of emerging technologies how it relates to Second Life.

The Gartner Hype Cycle

Gartner, the world's leading information technology research and advisory company, began observing and commenting on the maturation of technologies in 1995. The Gartner Hype Cycle is a visual way to track emerging technologies as they mature in our culture, and Gartner has isolated five phases of a hype cycle ("Understanding Hype Cycles," n.d.). The first is the release of a new technology that gets everyone excited, the "technology trigger." Following the technology trigger is a period of enthusiasm, where the technology is advertised frequently, and everyone has high expectations for its success. Gartner calls this second phase the "peak of inflated expectations." In time, the interest in the new technology slides into a "trough of disillusionment," Gartner's third phase. In this phase is less publicity because the technology did not solve all of the problems that people thought it would. Although the peak of press attention and publicity is over, some technologies achieve a "slope of enlightenment," in which dedicated groups continue to experiment and apply the technology in different situations. Finally, according to Gartner, a "plateau of productivity" is reached, in which the technology becomes a standard and well-used tool.

Second Life's position in the hype cycle is worthwhile to consider as educational institutions make the decision to invest large sums of money to design, build, and implement virtual campuses. Second Life has had much publicity in the last 2 years, and educators have high hopes for its future as an educational tool. However, technology does not stand still, and new and better approaches are already in the planning stage.

Hybrid courses have a number of drawbacks that should be considered before one is initiated. Any time technology is a core part of a course, the technology itself may have problems. Second Life is occasionally down for maintenance, or there are unexpected grid problems. Second Life is periodically updated, so using installations on large numbers of lab computers may not be practical. Most lab computers require an administrator to download programs, so students are unable to update Second Life themselves. We have been using flash drives with Second Life preloaded on them. The flash drives work well but come with their own set of problems. Students have to remember to bring them and remove them from the lab computers at the end of the class. They are also responsible for updating them, if possible. Those who cannot update them at home have to turn them in to the tech department to be updated.

Planning a hybrid course takes much time. At least one semester of planning and design is necessary before teaching. The assignments for students take many hours to prepare because the instructor must visit the sites beforehand, decide how to use them, and structure the assignments to fit into the overall program. Approximately 6 hours are needed to thoroughly prepare one 50-minute assignment in Second Life.

To use Second Life in a hybrid course, then, the following are needed: technology support, time to plan, an understanding of how the technology portion will integrate with the syllabus, and enthusiasm for the process and patience when it does not work. In addition, a sense of humor is also needed for those days when Second Life freezes and unceremoniously ejects students from your virtual classroom.

Other types of courses using Second Life

In addition to part of a hybrid course, Second Life can be used in other ways. Professors can teach entire courses in Second Life, with the students always meeting, completing activities, and gathering for discussion in-world. This type of course would benefit from the additional use of a course management tool, such as Blackboard or ANGEL, where assignments could be permanently posted, resource links and files could be collected, discussion boards could be set up, and provisions for quizzing and testing could be made. This type of course takes much planning and coordination of resources. In addition, students must have computers that have the capability to run Second Life. These are not insurmountable requirements, but a course of this type cannot be put into place on a short timeline. The immersive 3D environment offers much to online courses because it reduces the near anonymity and isolation that usually accompanies an online course.

Professors can use Second Life as a special activity: a virtual "field trip" several times during a course. In this instance, students would not sign in and have their own avatars, but would view the activities of the professor's avatar on a large screen. A humanities class could visit an art gallery and discuss the paintings or attend a live concert. Second Life has a number of fine art galleries. If a class were learning about the Mexican artist Diego Rivera, for example, the students could visit the Diego Rivera Museum in Second Life. There, they would find a good collection of his works in one space. A guided tour of the museum by the curator can be arranged in English or in Spanish. Live concerts are held regularly in-world; of course, the times would have to correspond to the course schedule. There are artists who will give concerts for a minimal fee, which can be arranged ahead of time. These are only two examples of ways in which Second Life can be used as a field trip. In truth, the possibilities are nearly endless.

Final thoughts

Our students today, with their natural acceptance and use of technology in everyday life, are pointing the way that pedagogy should go in the future; we need to pay attention. Pedagogy is no longer only about knowledge transfer from the expert to the novice. In a recent podcast, a member of the Linden Lab team, known as Pathfinder Linden, reflected on the pedagogical use of Second Life:

> Pathfinder: Academics always talk about "pedagogy," the art of teaching, the instructional methods that educators use to help students learn. Really, the real power of Second Life is in its immersiveness, the ability to have conversations with people in real time while you're immersed in the content. You're in it, you're able to create interactive spaces, spaces that have things inside of them that you interact with and you're surrounded by real people, real students, by real faculty, who are able to interact with each other while they're interacting with the content and it all happens in a real place.
>
> There's no context to the conversation. Everything in Second Life is all about context, it's all about conversations around the content and having contextually relevant conversations. That level of immersiveness, if you look at the sort of art of teaching, it's well-known that that level of immersiveness really engages students. It makes them feel connected to the content more. That, in the end, really helps them in the learning process. (Katt, 2008)

What Pathfinder said about context is essential when we consider the future of classroom teaching. We already know that students learn well in a hands-on environment. This has been readily available to the sciences, in labs; it has been available to other disciplines in the form of experience, like internships, for instance. Now, with the technology that platforms like Second Life can offer, that hands-on experience can be created for nearly every discipline. Students can interact with objects and models in ways that are not possible in the classroom. Imagine walking through strands of DNA or sitting on a molecule. However, taking context even a bit further, environments can be created to simulate real-life situations. In a law program, for instance, a courtroom could easily be built, and students could role play different positions, such as judge, lawyer, and jury members. A foreign-language class could "live" in a community and speak only the target language.

If students are living and working within the Second Life community, they are discovering knowledge on their own. Our role as teachers will change from being authority figures and knowledge-keepers to being guides. The role of guide is essential because someone has to know the parameters of the course, lead the students in the right direction, and assess their progress along the way. Some people think that the time will come when the instructor is irrelevant in the classroom. That is not really what students are seeking. They want to explore, discover, and combine information in creative and unusual ways, but they value the knowledge and experience that an instructor brings to the classroom. Remember that technology, in this case, Second Life, is never an end in itself; pedagogy has to come first and has to sustain the students as they acquire knowledge. Thus, the view from the Hacienda may include flying horses, robots, wolves, firemen, and other objects not normally seen in the classroom. The question for us to consider is, where are they leading us?

References

Burns, E. (2007). Second Life users top 1.3 million in March. *Click Z*. Retrieved April 30, 2009 from http://www.clickz.com/3625769

de Castells, M. O., Guzmán, E., Lapuerta, P., & García, C. (2006). *Mosaicos: Spanish as a world language*. Upper Saddle River, NJ: Pearson/Prentice Hall.

Dresang, E. T. (2005). The information-seeking behavior of youth in the digital environment. *Library Trends, 54*, 178–196. Retrieved May 29, 2008, from http://muse.jhu.edu/

Guess, A. (2007, August 20). In Second Life there's no fallout. *Inside Higher Ed*. Retrieved May 29, 2008, from http://www.insidehighered.com/news/2007/08/20/secondlife

Katt (Host). (2008, May 29). Education in Second Life. *Inside the lab podcast*. Podcast transcript retrieved February 25, 2009, from http://static-secondlife-com.s3.amazonaws.com/media/Inside%20the%20Lab%20podcast-transcript-Education.htm

Klahr, D., Triona, L. M., & Williams, C. (2007). Hands on what? The relative effectiveness of physical versus virtual materials in an engineering design project by middle school children. *Journal of Research in Science Teaching, 44*, 183–203.

Linden, L. (2008). Q3 closed on a high note with an unusually strong September. *Second Life*. Retrieved April 30, 2009 from https://blogs.secondlife.com/community/features/blog/2008/11/12/q3-closed-on-a-high-note-with-an-unusually-strong-September

Lindsay, E. B. (2004). The best of both worlds: Teaching a hybrid course. *Academic Exchange Quarterly*, 8(4), 16–19. Retrieved May 28, 2006, from http://www.rapidintellect.com/AEQweb/cho2738z4.htm

Marold, K. A. (2002). The 21st century learning model: Electronic tutelage realized. *Journal of Information Technology Education, 1*, 113–123.

Mueggenberg, K. (2003). Taking undergraduate students into the online learning environment. *Nurse Educator, 28*, 243–244.

Omaggio Hadley, A. (1993). *Teaching language in context*. Boston: Heinle and Heinle.

Schrage, M. (2000). *Serious play: How the world's best companies simulate to innovate*. Boston: Harvard Business School Press.

Understanding hype cycles. (2007, November 18). *Gartner.com*. Retrieved February 25, 2009, from http://www.gartner.com/pages/story.php.id.8795.s.8.jsp

White, B. (2008). *Second life: A guide to your virtual world*. Indianapolis, IN: Que.

Appendix A: Basic Spanish syllabi, assessment sections

Spanish I syllabus: Assessment before Second Life

Assessment: The assessment components below will be measured according to three major criteria of language performance: accuracy, fluency, and complexity. Testing procedures will be representative of the type of language instruction and activities offered through classroom practice. You will be evaluated based on your achievement of the course goals (above) and the following criteria:

Oral expression:	
Active participation in class activities	15%
Oral evaluations (2)	15%
Conversation tables (6)	10%
Written expression:	
Homework	10%
Writing tasks (2)	10%
Quizzes	15%
Written exams (4)	25%

Spanish I assessment using Second Life

Oral expression:	
Active participation in class activities	15%
Oral evaluations: Second Life (1), personal interview (1)	15%
Completion of weekly Second Life assignments	10%
Written expression:	
Homework (workbook, text, Web)	10%
Writing tasks (2) based on Second Life	10%
Quizzes	15%
Written exams (4)	25%

Appendix B: Sample Second Life assignment

Second Life assignment: La Universidad

Today, we are going to visit the European University on European University Island. This island is a consortium of colleges from several European countries. We are going to visit La Escuela Politécnica Superior de la Universidad Autónoma de Madrid.

When you arrive on the island, find the revolving "i" for información and answer the questions below. The objective is to practice the question words on page 40 and the university vocabulary on page 57 as well as verb structure.

Find the calendario académico:

¿Cuándo comienzan las clases?

____

¿Cuál es el período de vacaciones?

____

¿Cuándo terminan las clases?

____

¿Cuándo son los exámenes?

____

¿Cuándo es la fiesta?

____

Explore the Escuela Politécnica following the signs.

The carrots in the garden say tócame (touch me). Check out what is growing in the garden and write the Spanish name of three things you found.

____

____

____

Make a list of the places you visited at the Escuela in Spanish. Use your dictionary if necessary.

____

____

____

____

____

____

Find the video of the Escuela politécnica available in the outdoor auditorium and watch it. Write a two-sentence description of the Escuela.

____

____

Appendix C: Student responses to Second Life surveys

Students who agreed to participate in a study of Second Life in the Spanish classroom filled out a questionnaire at the end of each semester. This is only the beginning of a 3-year study on the effects of Second Life on basic Spanish instruction; at this point, the statistics are rather informal but do indicate some trends. When asked, "List the strongest features of the use of Second Life in the Spanish classroom. What contributed most to your learning?", 67% of the respondents mentioned interaction with classmates on the computer. Selected written comments follow:

It allowed us to talk to people who naturally speak Spanish

Having to communicate solely in Spanish w/other avatars

Talking to actual people in the world who speak Spanish

For 54% of the respondents, exposure to Spanish culture/realism was important. Selected comments follow:

Gained an idea of some hispanic [*sic*] culture and background

The cultural elements of Second Life contributed greatly to the understanding of Spanish culture

Second life gave a different view of Spanish it allowes [*sic*] us to see Spanish culture

Seeing how they treat holidays (how they decorate)

For 50% of the respondents, the uniqueness of Second Life was important. Selected comments follow:

A break from the routine of class (creative learning)

The fact it was something other than textbook work

Change of learning environment which enhanced interest

It made the course more interesting by providing a unique classroom experience

For 46% of the students, practical application of knowledge, reinforced book learning was important. Selected comments follow:

When we used 2nd Life w/ book vocab & previous lessons I better understood what I was doing & that helped w/ test taking

Writing multiple paragraphs in Spanish on what we did

I got to establish definitions with places, so they stuck in my mind more

It helped us to learn the Spanish equivalent to words that weren't in the book

A New Language for the Net Generation: Why Second Life Works for the Net Generation

Jessamine Cooke-Plagwitz
Northern Illinois University

Oblinger and Oblinger (2005) defined the Net Generation as that group of individuals born between the years of 1982 and 1991. Tapscott (1998) identified a broader timeframe of 1977–1997. Despite the debate surrounding exact dates, this generation is typified by their "connected" lifestyle and their facility with technology. They are at home online; in fact, most of them have never experienced a world in which they were not connected to people and information via some form of technology. For many, technology provides their preferred method of communication. This appreciation for the usefulness of technological tools extends to their education preferences. Some of the learning behaviors that define this group include a strong preference for learning by doing, a demand for quick and easy access to information, and a social nature that prefers to work within groups or teams (Oblinger & Oblinger). All of the above inclinations are best served with the help of technology.

Tapscott (1998) noted that the ease with which this generation adapts to and uses new technologies has resulted in a paradigm shift in the relationship hierarchies in which they exist. For the first time in history, parents (and teachers) want to know about and do things about which their children and students are the experts. This shift in roles has occurred both in the home and in the classroom. The role of the teacher is no longer the sole deliverer of knowledge but rather, has become that of facilitator or coach. Many of today's educators have adopted a more constructivist approach to instruction in which their task involves facilitating students' acquisition and construction of knowledge, but not acting as the all-knowing oracle who feeds information to learners in bite-sized increments. Because Net Generation students are, on the whole, much more comfortable when they can learn by doing, this more informal role is by and large the most effective one for the 21st-century educator.

Virtual environments

As Hay (2000) pointed out, members of the Net Generation have grown up with television, computers, and video games, all designed to help them learn. As a result, they arrive at

Cooke-Plagwitz, J. (2009). A new language for the Net Generation: Why Second Life works for the Net Generation. In R. Oxford & J. Oxford, (Eds.), *Second language teaching and learning in the Net Generation* (pp. 173–180). Honolulu: University of Hawai'i, National Foreign Language Resource Center.

school expecting their education to be entertaining. Additionally, many Net Generation students anticipate that their learning will involve computers and the Internet because so many of them not only rely extensively on these tools, but also excel in their use. Woods (2002) noted:

> They [Net Generation students] rely on the Net to help them with completing their schoolwork. They use it for research, collaboration with other students, and as a resource for information passed on to them by other students or teachers. Students also use it as a virtual guidance counselor and as a way to store important school-related materials. (p.)

One of the more intriguing new Internet technologies, seemingly tailor-made for the Net Generation learner, are 3D multiuser virtual environments (3D MUVEs), where emphasis is placed on promoting participants' social presence and on active collaborative inquiry (Dalgarno, 2002; Dickey, 2005; Jones, 2004; Jones, Morales, & Knezek, 2005). 3D MUVEs can motivate learners to engage in purposeful educational inquiries without losing interest or sidestepping intended learning goals. Many 3D MUVEs include entertainment features such as 3D role playing and animated interactive environments modeled after popular commercial games, where players are placed in realistically rendered animated scenes while participating in a series of challenges or puzzles (Cooke-Plagwitz, 2008). Combining these concepts of animated scenery and challenges, 3D MUVEs can "provide highly collaborative, immersive environments that promote interactions among students and with the instructor" (Jones, Morales, & Knezek, p. 221).

The largest and probably best known 3D MUVE is Linden Lab's Second Life. Second Life is a MUVE currently inhabited by over 15,000,000 people worldwide (Charming, 2008) and that provides users with the abilities to build graphic visual representations of themselves (avatars) and to purchase land in Second Life on which they can build. Additionally, one can experience graphics, video, animations, and audio in Second Life. Generally, Second Life users (residents) communicate via text chat that shows up on the screen for all users present to see, though because Linden Lab has enabled voice-chat capabilities in Second Life, voice communication is quickly gaining popularity among language educators who work in this environment (Cooke-Plagwitz, 2008) and simultaneously drawing new language faculty and their students "in-world."

Second Life as educational environment

According to statistics provided in March 2007 by Pathfinder Linden, over 200 universities or academic institutions are already involved in Second Life (Kelton, 2007). Indeed, graduate-level courses in the use of Second Life as a learning environment have recently begun appearing among the course offerings of a number of top-notch universities. There are several reasons for this enthusiasm. First, and perhaps most importantly, for Net Generation students, Second Life offers several of the learning elements that they crave. Second Life is at once entertaining, visual, hands-on, immediate, and online. It presents a realistic virtual space and visible "classmates," elements that can assist students in gaining a sense of participation and of belonging (Omale, Hung, Luetkenans, & Cooke-Plagwitz, 2007), yet has the fantastic elements of a video game in which students are participating.

The interest in Second Life as a teaching and learning tool is also due to personal reasons. One's avatar can often be seen as the expression of one's "ideal self," and as such, avatars are frequently virtual extensions of their creators. Many Second Life residents become personally attached to their avatars, perhaps because of the time and effort involved in creating them (Cooke-Plagwitz, 2008). Members of the Net Generation have become accustomed to interacting as avatars within virtual worlds—predominantly through video games (Tapscott, 1998). Moreover, because the 3D virtual environment "feels" so lifelike, both students and teachers find it easier to become engaged in the experience: "Once student and instructor meet on the common ground of agreeing that they exist, albeit virtually, in an environment in which learning will take place, that agreement is the cement that ties all parties involved to the learning initiatives" (Kelton, 2007, p. 4).

Along with the choice of one's avatar comes the ability to alter its appearance, to the extent that one's avatar need not necessarily take human form. Although many residents of Second Life fashion their avatars upon idealized versions of their real-life appearances, others prefer to experience this new environment in a completely different form, choosing different genders, races, species, or even nonliving objects. This freedom of expression, it has been argued, offers students a unique opportunity to engage with their environment in a completely new way and to gauge reactions from and interactions with other residents based upon a new set of perceptions and beliefs (Omale et al., 2007). As Tapscott (1998) pointed out: "The fact that you're communicating with a toaster is not important—it's what the toaster has to say" (p. 86).

Many educators who use Second Life for instruction have indicated that communication among their virtual students is livelier and more engaged than in their face-to-face classes (Foster, 2007). Indeed, students entering the virtual world of Second Life for the first time are frequently delighted by their avatars' abilities to fly, walk underwater, and magically teleport from one location to another. Many are excited by exactly how realistic the virtual environment feels and are thrilled with the novelty of participating in a class discussion while virtually seated on fluffy pillows by a roaring fire or on jet-skis at a Mediterranean beach, fantastical elements which add to the entertainment value of the Second Life environment.

Second Life, language learning, and the Net Generation

Oblinger and Oblinger (2005) listed a number of characteristics that typify the Net Generation. The authors described students who are digitally literate, connected, experiential, social, and prefer to work in teams; crave immediacy, structure, and experience; and who are largely visual and kinesthetic learners (p. 2.5). Many of the features of Second Life's virtual environment are ideally suited to these needs and preferences and include several elements that are particularly appropriate for foreign-language learning. For example, Second Life provides connectedness and social opportunities for online students. The actual physical separation of students who interact via electronic communication can be a deterrent to students' sense of belonging within a learning community and can thus hinder their learning success (Doughty & Long, 2003). This can be especially problematic in foreign-language classes where interaction can be crucial to instruction. However, because learners in Second Life are typically represented by avatars they have personally designed, their online experience may be more realistic in the sense that it mimics a face-to-face experience, with learners synchronously interacting with other's avatars. This lifelike experience may give learners the impression that they are in a face-to-face setting and thus enhance their sense of being a part of a group and of participating in realistic face-to-face interactions. More introverted students may even be more comfortable in the virtual environment and better able to participate and learn there than in the real-life classroom (Bradley & Lomicka, 2000; Roed, 2003) because "disguises" afforded by one's avatar often impart a newfound sense of confidence to the timid student (Wallace, 1999).

Virtual environments such as Second Life provide an ideal setting for collaborative language learning by encouraging meaningful communication between students through content-based activities (Schneider & Von Der Emde, 2000) and by emulating learning experiences through the creation of simulated environments. Indeed, Second Life has a variety of environments created to simulate different countries, professional environments, scientific models, literary settings, and so on—areas that allow Net Generation students to immerse themselves (virtually) in the material that they are studying. For foreign-language learners, this plethora of virtual cities can be a real asset to their learning experience and can provide a virtual mini-immersion because native speakers of almost any language can easily be found among Second Life's residents. This large international membership provides numerous resources for language learners and foreign-language educators who have enthusiastically adopted the MUVE as the ideal platform for online collaboration and instruction. Second Life is especially suited to Net Generation language learners because so many of them already see the Internet as a natural place to learn and play, so interacting in this environment often feels quite natural and easily accessible for them.

Language educators working with Second Life attest to the seemingly endless list of possibilities available. Early language learners have an almost infinite variety of surroundings and avatars to describe. The ability to change the appearance of one's avatar provides numerous variations on a theme, not to mention the multiplicity of available movements, gestures, and so on that can provide hours of descriptive subject matter (Cooke-Plagwitz, 2008). More advanced language learners can avail themselves of a vast assortment of realistic virtual cities (Paris, Vatican City, Tokyo, Barcelona, Moscow), and take miniature tours of their landmarks. Second Life's voice-chat feature permits students to improve their oral language skills by chatting with native foreign-language speakers, and students and educators find that residents of Second Life are often willing and eager to talk to them. Because Second Life allows users to record short videos of their travels in Second Life, the creation of their own target-language mini tours is a constructive project for language learners. More advanced (and ambitious) Second Life residents can even design and build their own versions of favorite foreign locales if they have access to land "in-world."

Howard Vickers, who runs the online language school Avatar English, adapted Bernie Dodge's original WebQuest model to the 3D virtual environment using his SurReal Quest (Vickers, 2007). By exploiting the communicative features specific to Second Life, Vickers sends his students on information quests throughout Second Life that require them to interact with native speakers of the target language (in this case, English). In addition, his students pursue "traditional" Internet-based research. Ultimately, the students present their information in an audio podcast or video vodcast. This combination of Web-based research and virtual social interaction allows Net Generation learners to practice their language skills in a pedagogically significant manner using a variety of technologies (Vickers). The mixture of online collaboration with the construction of knowledge through technology-based project creation is ideally suited to the particular preferences of Net Generation students.

The collaborative space of a Second Life classroom permits language learners to discuss and construct knowledge within a safe environment where one may incorporate media from external sources (Webpages, PowerPoint presentations, videos, etc.). Second Life educators frequently blend the interface with other applications, such as Blackboard or Moodle (Sloodle; Kemp & Livingstone, 2006), requiring their students to log into both applications simultaneously, then using the whiteboard or threaded-discussion features of their course management system to reinforce concepts immediately or to provide resources for students to use asynchronously outside of scheduled Second Life meetings. An assortment of media is vital for Net Generation students to hold their rapidly fluctuating attention, but also to provide a variety of educational stimuli (especially visual) for students who crave diverse experiences (Windham, 2005).

A growing movement of foreign-language educators is exploring the potential of virtual worlds. In May of 2008, the SLanguages 2008 symposium organized language educators to share experiences of teaching languages within Second Life and to explore new ways to use the MUVE for foreign-language education. This second annual meeting of Second Life foreign-language educators brought together many educational innovators who are working to make Second Life an even better pedagogical experience for all kinds of foreign-language learners. Presentation topics in this international gathering included a number of virtual field trips. For example, conference attendees had the opportunity to tour a number of virtual cities and were guided through a virtual Spanish house designed to assist students with their vocabulary learning. Attendees were also treated to demonstrations of a variety of educational tools for use within Second Life, given an assortment of "freebies" to try out on their own, shown best-practice examples of Second Life instruction, and even given lessons in building within the Second Life environment. That the number of presentations and conference attendees in SLanguages 2008 had very nearly tripled over the 2007 figures is a testament to the increased interest, both on the part of teachers and students, in the use of Second Life for language education.

Drawbacks to Second Life as an educational environment

Because Second Life is a relative newcomer to the field of foreign-language instruction and was not initially intended for use as an educational tool, some elements remain problematic for those educators unfamiliar with the environment. Part of the present difficulty with Second Life is that it may not be user-friendly enough for mainstream educational use; its interface is not particularly intuitive, and its learning curve is fairly steep. Thus, the amount of time and energy necessary to make Second Life a useful instructional tool is often prohibitive for fulltime faculty. Moreover, unless students have had prior experience with such virtual environments, they, too, will have to devote a certain amount of time to orienting themselves to their surroundings. More advanced students can often accomplish this on their own, but frequently, some class time must be devoted to helping students to establish their avatars and to familiarize themselves with the particulars of the Second Life environment. Additionally, instructors often find it necessary to establish a new set of guidelines for their virtual classrooms because students are frequently distracted early on with changing their avatars' appearances, flying, trying out assorted gestures, and so on. Indeed, maintaining student focus in the initial class meeting can be quite difficult.

Technical issues surrounding memory usage associated with Second Life can prevent users with older machines or insufficient graphic cards from working within the environment. Additionally, broadband Internet access is necessary to run Second Life effectively, and even those working from sophisticated university computing labs may face significant lags if too many users attempt to log in or occupy a single "space" (sim) simultaneously. Excessive traffic can cause Second Life to crash or to arbitrarily eject residents from or deny them entry to overcrowded areas. These problems can be particularly cumbersome to foreign-language learners attempting to interact with native speakers in different time zones and with sometimes unreliable Internet connectivity.

Language learners may encounter problems when working with Second Life's voice-chat function. The most frequent difficulties arise when off-site users are unable to configure the audio on their machines, resulting in a variety of complications including students being unable to hear class discussions; microphones being left in the on position, allowing the entire class to hear one student sneezing, chewing, or slurping soup; and annoying feedback that can quickly shut down a discussion for everyone.

Security in Second Life remains a concern. Although the tools exist to make spaces more secure, educators in Second Life are frequently reluctant to lock down their spaces for fear of shutting colleagues or other legitimate visitors out of their spaces. Unfortunately, the freedom to roam Second Life anonymously can result in some undesirable behavior, and unless one's classroom is well hidden or in a restricted members-only area, residents unaffiliated with one's class or institution may occasionally wander in. Although these visitors are generally harmless, they may at times try very hard to disrupt a class or meeting in progress. The best method of dealing with these "griefers," as they are known, is generally ignoring them, thus denying them the angry reactions they hope to provoke. Users can also "mute" such visitors so that they can no longer be heard. Sometimes, however, the best approach is to have an "Area B" or safe location to which all members of a group can quickly teleport upon a given signal from the teacher.

One of the most valuable tools for foreign-language learning in Second Life is the vast array of target-language areas available to visit. Second Life is, however, very similar to the real world in many ways, and as dangers and undesirable individuals exist in the real world, so too in Second Life do such hazards abound. Educators are advised when assigning virtual field trips to warn students of the potential problems and to ensure that they know how to quickly exit any uncomfortable situation. Because students cannot always be prevented from wandering into questionable situations, however, many educators patrol their student groups periodically to verify that they are not intentionally visiting distasteful locations or studying material not included in the course syllabus.

Conclusion

MUVEs such as Second Life have much to offer the field of foreign-language education and much to offer Net Generation students. They have the potential to change the way students learn and the way teachers teach (Dieterle & Clarke, in-press). Second Life enables classes to meet in a 3D virtual environment in which they can collaborate with other students from around the world. Its international membership provides countless opportunities for language learners to gain oral, aural, and cultural proficiency through interactions with native speakers in lifelike settings, while the realistic nature of the 3D environment provides authentic learning conditions that are difficult to make available in traditional classroom settings (Dieterle & Clarke).

Second Life's lifelike environment and its abundant resources for language learners offer both instructors and students some of the most vital linguistic and cultural immersion possibilities short of actual travel. Moreover, Second Life provides online students the opportunity to be part of a class in a much more tangible way than has heretofore been possible using other online resources. As Second Life continues to grow and its residents continue to create, the number of tools available to educators and their ease of use will doubtlessly increase. Foreign-language educators involved with Second Life are pooling resources and creating immersive virtual environments in Second Life in which language learning can occur through collaboration and exploration. Because Second Life is a world created by its residents, its educational possibilities are only limited by the imaginations of its creators: the residents themselves. Net Generation students, intrigued by the opportunity to learn by doing, are also contributing to Second Life's educational resources. Indeed, this freedom to collaborate and to create the ideal (virtual) educational environment makes Second Life one of the most useful tools for Net Generation language learners to date.

References

Bradley, T., & Lomicka, L. (2000). A case study of learner interaction in a technology-enhanced language learning environment. *Journal of Educational Computing, 11*, 247–368.

Charming, F. (2008, February 23). Second Life Statistics: 22-Feb-2008. Message posted to http://secondslog.blogspot.com/2008/02/second-life-statistics-22-feb-2008.html

Cooke-Plagwitz, J. (2008). New directions in CALL: An objective introduction to Second Life. *CALICO Journal, 25*(3), 547–557.

Dalgarno, B. (2002). The potential of 3D virtual learning environments: A constructivist analysis. *Electronic Journal of Instructional Science and Technology, 5*(2), 1–19. Retrieved April 15, 2006, from http://www.usq.edu.au/electpub/e-jist/docs/Vol5_No2/Dalgarno%20-%20Final.pdf

Dickey, M. (2005). Three-dimensional virtual worlds and distance learning: Two case studies of Active Worlds as a medium for distance education. *British Journal of Educational Technology, 36*, 439–451.

Dieterle, E., & Clarke, J. (in press). Multi-user virtual environments for teaching and learning. In M. Pagani (Ed.), *Encyclopedia of multimedia technology and networking (2nd ed.)*. Hershey, PA: Idea Group, Inc.

Doughty, C., & Long, M. (2003). Optimal psycholinguistic environments for distance foreign language learning. *Language Learning and Technology, 7*(3), 50–80.

Foster, A. (2007, September 21). Professor Avatar: In the digital universe of Second Life, classroom instruction also takes on a new personality. *The Chronicle of Higher Education, 54*(4). Retrieved November 9, 2007, from http://chronicle.com/weekly/v54/i04/04a02401.htm

Hay, L. E. (2000). Educating the Net Generation. *School Administrator, 57*(4). Retrieved November 9, 2007, from http://www.aasa.org/publications/saarticledetail.cfm?ItemNumber=3963&snItemNumber=950&tnItemNumber=

Jones, J. G. (2004). 3D on-line distributed learning environments: An old concept with a new twist. In C. Crawford, D. A. Willis, R. Carlsen, I. Gibson, K. McFerrin, J. Price, & R. Weber (Eds.), *Proceedings of the Society for Informational Technology and Teacher Education* (pp. 507–512). Chesapeake, VA: Association for the Advancement of Computing in Education. Retrieved September 7, 2006, from http://courseweb.unt.edu/gjones/pdf/Jones_SITE_FP_04.pdf

Jones, J. G., Morales, C., & Knezek, G. A. (2005). 3-dimensional online learning environments: Examining attitudes toward information technology between students in Internet-based 3-dimensional and face-to-face classroom instruction. *Educational Media International, 42*, 219–236.

Kelton, A. (2007). Second Life: Reaching into the virtual world for real-world learning. *EDUCAUSE Center for Applied Research: Research Bulletin, 2007*(17). Retrieved October 12, 2007, from http://www.it.udel.edu/SecondLifeERB.pdf

Kemp, J., & Livingstone, D. (2006). Putting a Second Life "metaverse" skin on learning management systems. In D. Livingstone & J. Kemp (Eds.), *Proceedings of the Second Life Education Workshop at the Second Life Community Convention* (pp. 13–18). Paisley, Scotland: University of Paisley.

Oblinger, D., & Oblinger, J. (2005). Is it age or IT: First steps toward understanding the Net Generation. In D. Oblinger & J. Oblinger (Eds.), *Educating the Net Generation* (pp. 2.1–2.20). EDUCAUSE. Retrieved May 2, 2008, from http://www.educause.edu/educatingthenetgen/

Omale, N., Hung, W., Luetkehans, L., & Cooke-Plagwitz, J. (2007). *Learning in 3-D multi-user virtual environments: Exploring the use of unique 3-D attributes for problem-based learning.* Manuscript submitted for publication.

Roed, J. (2003). Language learner behaviour in a virtual environment. *Computer Assisted Language Learning, 16*, 155–172.

Schneider, J., & Von der Emde, S. (2000). Brave new (virtual) world: Transforming language learning into cultural studies through online learning environments (MOOs). *ADFL Bulletin, 32*(1), 18–26.

Tapscott, D. (1998). *Growing up digital: The rise of the Net Generation*. Columbus, OH: McGraw-Hill.

Vickers, H. (2007). SurReal language quests. Retrieved August 19, 2007 http://www.avatarlanguages.com/blog/surreal-language-quotes

Wallace, P. (1999). *Psychology and the Internet.* New York: Cambridge University Press.

Windham, C. (2005). The student's perspective. In D. Oblinger & J. Oblinger (Eds.), *Educating the Net Generation* (pp. 5.1–5.16). EDUCAUSE. Retrieved May 2, 2008, from www.educause.edu/educatingthenetgen/

Woods, B. (2002, August 16). A digital divide between students and educators? *Instant Messaging Planet*. Retrieved May 5, 2008, from http://www.instantmessagingplanet.com/public/article.php/10817_1447791

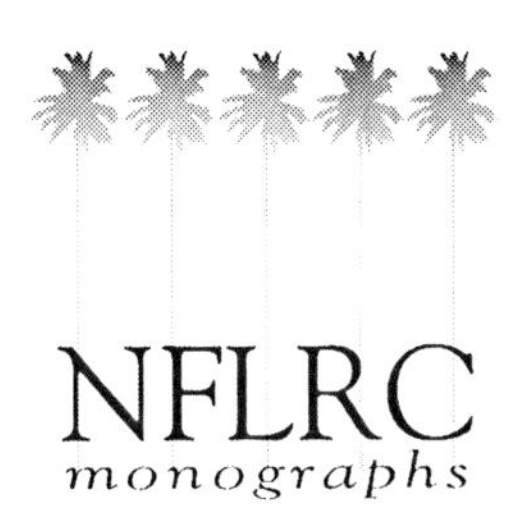

Web-Based Language Portfolios and the Five Cs: Implementation in Foreign Language College Classrooms

Jane Blyth Warren
Kalamazoo College

The past 15 or 20 years have seen great changes in the inclusion of the teaching of culture in the foreign language classroom. Although the language-teaching world has collectively agreed that teaching culture is important (Crawford-Lange & Lange, 1984; Moore, 1996; Omaggio Hadley, 1993; Phillips & Terry, 1999), language teachers have not found an effective way to assess the learning and understanding of culture (Lange, 1999; "Portfolio assessment in the foreign language classroom (n.d.);" Storme & Derakshani, 2002; Wright, 2003). Indeed, the development of the Standards for Foreign Language Learning (SFLL), which place a great deal of emphasis on the integration of culture in the foreign language curriculum, support the idea of the teaching of culture. Appropriate and valid means to assess this understanding must be developed for language teachers to make the claim that culture, as well as language, is being effectively taught. One problem in the assessment of culture is that because the topics of any given culture are limitless, it is virtually impossible to first, list the aspects of a culture that should be required, and second, test the understanding of a limitless number of concepts.

Although the benefits and usefulness of portfolios have been well documented, their use is not widespread (Riggs & Sandlin, 2000). In addition, White (1994) wrote that evidence of the value of portfolio assessment is necessary for it to be considered genuine assessment. This study examined whether having students create Web-based portfolios based on SFLL is a way to effectively implement the learning of culture and assess that learning in the foreign language curriculum.

Portfolios

Digital portfolios have become an increasingly popular, if controversial, method of assessment in a broad range of fields (Gatlin & Jacob, 2002). Teacher education, in particular, has made good use of this method and has paved the way for those in other

Warren, J. B. (2009). Web-based language portfolios and the five Cs: Implementation in foreign language college classrooms. In R. Oxford & J. Oxford, (Eds.), *Second language teaching and learning in the Net Generation* (pp. 181–197). Honolulu: University of Hawai'i, National Foreign Language Resource Center.

disciplines to try portfolios as a means to assess student progress and learning (Wiedmer, 1998). Once considered "alternative assessment," portfolios have become a respected means of assessment (Delett, Barnhardt, & Kevorkian, 2001; Lee, 1997). Web-based portfolios can serve as authentic assessments in the foreign language curriculum. When organized around SFLL, portfolios become a method to align curriculum and assessment with SFLL, ensuring that students' learning and progress follow SFLL. In addition, Web-based portfolios enhance student learning by integrating the learning of culture with the learning of the target language. Although a quiz or test can give the instructor and others a "snapshot" of student learning at a given point in time, a portfolio can provide an instructor and others with "video footage" of student learning over a period of time. This video analogy demonstrates the power of portfolio assessment and how much more it can tell us than traditional forms of assessment.

Importance of culture

Currently, the teaching of culture in the foreign language curriculum is well accepted and used. The American Council on the Teaching of Foreign Languages helped to develop SFLL as guidelines for the teaching of foreign language and culture in the United States. Released in 1996, SFLL clearly shows the integration of language and culture in the curriculum, effectively synthesizing current research on second-language acquisition (SLA) and outlining the core elements of a foreign language curriculum. Whereas language teaching used to focus on the "how" (syntax) and "what" (lexicon) of a language, these standards also focus on when, to whom, and why, or sociolinguistic aspects of communication. These standards, also called the five Cs, are divided into five categories: communication, cultures, connections, comparisons, and communities. As its name implies, the communication standard deals with communication in a foreign language, specifically interpersonal, interpretive, and presentational communication in the four skill areas of reading, writing, listening, and speaking. This standard is what traditionally would have been the focus of foreign language learning. The cultures standard is related to understanding the target-language culture (TLC), and the comparisons standard deals with comparing one's own culture and the TLC. The focus of these two goal areas is for foreign language learners to gain insight into and become competent in another culture while at the same time becoming critical thinkers about their own. The standard titled "connections" encourages students to make connections between the target language and TLC in areas outside the language classroom, such as doing research in another discipline about the TLC. In the communities standard, the focus is on becoming part of a community of speakers of the target language, but also on sharing experience and knowledge as a component of becoming a lifelong learner. Through participation in these activities, students explore areas of the target language and culture that they might not in a traditional curriculum. In addition, they come to understand that communication skills are but one component of language learning. SFLL is based on the concept that language and culture are interdependent and cannot be separated.

To date, research on the use of language portfolios for assessment has been limited, but one article does provide some compelling arguments to support their use. Dellet, Barnhardt, and Kevorkian (2001) explained that portfolios provide authentic communication opportunities in relevant contexts. In addition, portfolios allow students to demonstrate both the process and product of their language learning. Thus, portfolios present an opportunity for students to learn and reflect on their developing language and cultural skills. In addition to constructing their own knowledge, for students to truly learn a foreign language, they need to apply their knowledge in authentic ways to situations that are realistic. Taking a test is not a real application of language knowledge; in visiting a foreign country, we are generally not asked to take a test on grammar. Rather, we are required to perform tasks and functions of everyday and not-so-everyday life. For example, one may need to give directions to one's apartment on the phone. One might need to make a formal introduction of oneself. One also will likely discuss a current movie with a friend. These are all examples of authentic learning that occur in a foreign language. Language portfolios allow students to use these learning scenarios for the purpose of evaluation. In addition, portfolios that include classroom activities, tests, and activities outside of class acknowledge and reinforce that language learning is a combination of functions, conversations, interpretations, presentations, and other scenarios.

Web-based portfolio project

The Web-based language portfolio project aims at integrating student language learning with improving cultural competence. Students create portfolio entries that are tied to SFLL, including cultural products, cultural practices, cultural comparisons, and linguistic comparisons. The communication standard has been divided into the four skills areas of reading, writing, listening, and speaking. Students are asked to reflect on their learning by including a reflective introduction to each entry. The tasks of the portfolio are authentic and represent real-world communication tasks. In college and beyond, one is often required to read a newspaper article and determine the main points or to hold a conversation with someone in another language. The authenticity of these tasks makes this assessment more valid. In addition to providing authenticity, the flexibility of the tasks makes this assessment very interactive. The students are required to interpret the description and then come up with possible ways to satisfy the demands of the task. They need to then complete the tasks and reflect on them. There is constant interaction between the portfolio task and the individual's knowledge of the topic, affective schemata, and language ability.

This portfolio project focused on two skill areas besides target-language cultural competence: technological literacy and language-learning strategies. Technological literacy is essential to life in the 21st century and a gateway to tremendous amounts of information related to other countries. Learning to find this information and use it effectively is a useful skill. In addition, the ability to type a letter or composition on a computer in the target language is a useful skill. Finally, the Web-based digital portfolio project allows students to demonstrate their language skills to any number of people at any given time. Knowing how to choose appropriate language-learning strategies for a given task requires familiarity with strategies and individual learning styles. These are developed through the reflective introductions, where students are asked to reflect on the language-learning process. Having this information gives students the ability to take responsibility for their language learning and learn how to help themselves learn better.

The following research questions guided this study:

1. Do intermediate- and advanced-level foreign language students perceive culture to be an important part of their learning of the target language?
2. Do students perceive the portfolio creation process to be beneficial to their learning of culture?
3. Do Web-based language portfolios increase student interest in the TLC?
4. Do students perceive increases in language abilities from creating Web-based language portfolios?

5. Do teachers perceive increases in student language abilities from creating Web-based language portfolios?
6. Are Web-based language portfolios organized around SFLL an effective way to teach and assess learning of the TLC?
7. What are the problems associated with implementing a portfolio project?

The literature on these topics shows that although many aspects of this study have been addressed singularly, they have not been addressed as an entire topic. There have been studies on using SFLL to organize curricula, studies that relate to teaching culture and the assessment of it, research on the use of portfolios to meet standards for other disciplines and for program requirements, and studies on the use of portfolios in the foreign language classroom. Dugan, Nerenz, Palmer, Peden, and Vostten's 1999 study is the only one on using SFLL as an organizational tool for a portfolio project. However, no studies to date have examined the use of Web-based portfolios, organized around SFLL, for the purpose of teaching and assessing the understanding of the TLC in a foreign language classroom. Thus, this study brings together a number of variables that have not yet been studied. This study will hopefully contribute to the growing literature on portfolio assessment and assessment of SFLL.

Portfolio assessment

In recent years, as second- and foreign language teachers have moved toward communicative teaching, assessments have become more integrative. According to Wesche (1983), communicative language testing should be integrative, direct, criterion-referenced, and assess a variety of language functions. The portfolio project meets all of those criteria. Each of the tasks is integrative, encompassing a number of language functions within one task. The tasks are direct in that they are related to real-life communication tasks, such as having a conversation or writing a letter. The portfolio is also criterion-referenced. As a result, the project can be considered valid based on the current theory of SLA and language-teaching methodology. Bachman and Palmer (1996) suggested six factors that need to be considered when developing and analyzing assessment tools: reliability, construct validity, authenticity, interactiveness, impact, and practicality. Reliability, how consistently an assessment tool measures, is met through the specific tasks of the portfolio that help ensure the measurement of students on a level playing field as much as possible. However, the freedom and flexibility of the tasks that are necessary to motivate students in the portfolio process make it so that student interpretations and products in the tasks will still vary. This is inherent in the portfolio process and is certainly one of the advantages of portfolios. Therefore, task descriptions that give strict guidelines but allow students freedom of choice and expression should be the goal to produce reliable results.

Portfolios have a number of strengths. In terms of validity, portfolios are related to current SLA theory. In addition, the assessment tasks are directly tied to the objectives of a typical college-level course and as such have a high degree of validity. The tasks are authentic and interactive. Overall, a portfolio is a strong assessment tool that can give a teacher a great deal of insight into student learning and the curriculum. When designing language-learning and assessment projects, the teacher needs to ensure that they are meaningful, task-based, and related to authentic communication (Wesche, 1983). Ideally, the learning projects are also assessment tools. Portfolios meet all of those criteria and also allow students to work independently and take control over their learning. The portfolio project is a medium that allows students to demonstrate their achievement in the understanding of language and culture.

This case study followed the piloting of portfolio projects at two locations: in two intermediate college-level Japanese-language classes at a large public university and in one advanced 300-level German-language class at a medium-sized public university, both in the Midwest. Both of the universities have extensive systems of technology and provide wireless access to students in all buildings. Although the large university does not have a foreign language requirement, the medium-sized university does. Calvin and Rider (2004) outlined the process of curricular revision in light of the foreign language requirement, explaining that the focus of the elementary-level language classes is on communicative competence, cultural awareness, and diversity, with students being assessed on their ability to apply this learning in holistic ways. In summary, students who have gone through foreign language 101 and 102 at this university will have a greater awareness, and likely appreciation, of the TLC. Because the Japanese classes at the large university were at the third-semester level, all of the students were there because they were interested in the course, rather than to fill a requirement. This study included three separate classes: two sections of intermediate Japanese, one with 8 students and the other with 16 students, and a German class with 3 students. Therefore, 27 students participated in this case study.

The intermediate-level classes were chosen for this project for a number of reasons. First, the elementary levels at most institutions have a very specific and well-established curriculum that must be followed, making introducing a new project very difficult. Second, intermediate students have better language skills than those in the elementary levels, so at the end of a semester, the students will have sufficient language capability and evidence from classroom activities that they will be able to submit. Finally, instructors of intermediate-level classes often have difficulty finding appropriate materials and activities for students. Students are not yet able to comprehend authentic materials, but they also have generally become frustrated with working with simplified texts and topics. For these reasons, instructors are often looking for activities that will help students move from the elementary skill level to a high-intermediate or advanced level.

Portfolios were created through weekly assignments that were included in the portfolio sections. The weekly assignments were those that are typical in a language class, and each related to one SFLL. The portfolio compilation took about 11 weeks, allowing ample time at the beginning and end of the course to prepare students for the project and to debrief them on the process. In developing Web-based language portfolios, students created eight individual assignments, each related to a standard. These were cultural product and perspective, cultural practice and perspective, cultural comparison, linguistic comparison, and the four communication skills, reading, writing, listening, and speaking. These assignments were published on a free blog, LiveJournal. The student pages included a paragraph or other work that was used as evidence of their work related to each standard and a reflective introduction to the piece. In a reflective introduction, the student introduced the piece of evidence, described the process of creating it, and then reflected on his or her learning, discussing what was learned and what he or she would do differently if he or she was to create it again. The student work was as varied as a link to an online dictionary, an essay written for class, links to language-learning Websites, a film review, and a self-introduction.

The two instructors chose different ways to implement the project in their classes. The German instructor gave the students the typical writing assignments in the composition class and then asked the students to post them online. Therefore, the portfolio was a redundant process because they had already written and turned in the assignment on paper. These assignments were graded on a pass/fail basis. The three students in this class completed the project at varying levels. One student did nothing more than the self-introduction. The two other students included a self-introduction, a cultural comparison, and a self-evaluation. The Japanese instructor, in contrast, had the students turn in the assignments online each week and graded what they had put online. These assignments were not seen by the instructor in any other part of the class.

The implementation of this project took place over the course of the summer and continued through the following fall semester. The project began by e-mail correspondence, phone conferencing, and individual meetings with instructors to discuss the philosophy of the portfolio projects, objectives of the study, and implementation procedures and to provide support for the development of appropriate activities to be included in the portfolio projects for each class. At the beginning of the fall semester, the students were introduced to the project by their instructors and the researcher. The students created preliminary portfolios and then began creating their portfolios through weekly assignments. In the middle of the semester, the students participated in a survey to give feedback on the portfolio project, and the researcher visited the classes to ask if there were questions and to offer assistance. At the end of the semester, the students participated in a survey and interviews to discuss the portfolio project, the instructors participated in a survey to give feedback on the portfolio project, and the researcher met with the instructors to discuss the implementation and study. Throughout the process, the researcher kept in e-mail correspondence with both of the instructors. In addition, the researcher checked the student LiveJournal pages biweekly to keep apprised of the student progress in the portfolio project.

Data collection

Data were collected by viewing student portfolio sections, through surveys completed by both students and teachers, and through interviews with instructors and students. The language and culture parts of the portfolios were used to determine student understanding of the target language and TLC. In addition, the reflective introductions and self-evaluations provided student feedback on the portfolio project and process. The surveys gave information on students' feelings regarding the importance of culture in foreign language learning, how students perceived how much the portfolio contributed to their language skill improvement, and how much students perceived the portfolio increased their interest in studying the culture of the target language. The interviews with students and teachers allowed the researcher to ask follow-up questions on the portfolio process and gave detailed information on student and instructor perceptions of its value and usefulness.

At the beginning of the project, the students were introduced to SFLL and the concept of portfolios. The students were asked to complete a portfolio activity that guided them through establishing a free LiveJournal account and creating a preliminary or baseline portfolio. The students were pointed to a LiveJournal account that served as the home page for the class that they were taking and included links to portfolios that were completed at another college by students of the researcher, so the students in the current study were able to see sample portfolios to get an idea of what was being asked of them for this project. After establishing their own LiveJournal accounts, they were asked to update their journals weekly with their entries. Next, students completed a preliminary portfolio as a baseline measure that was collected and viewed by their instructors. They followed the format of the portfolio and wrote what they would have included in those sections if they were completing that project at the beginning of the course. The first entry that all of the students were asked to do was a self-introduction in the target language. During the course of the semester, the students completed sections of the portfolio at 1- or 2-week intervals and posted them online.

For the purposes of this study, the students created entries for only the culture, comparisons, and communication sections in addition to the self-introduction and self-evaluation. The communication section was further divided into the four skill areas of reading, writing, listening, and speaking. The students needed to choose evidence from their class activities that demonstrated their skills in a certain area. For example, in the communication-writing section, the students included a copy of a writing quiz to demonstrate and document their abilities in writing in Japanese. They also included a written description of what they did and a reflective introduction that explained their thoughts on the activity, what they learned from it, and what they might have changed if they had been able to do it again. In the German class, the instructor chose to make the entries in the portfolio sections uniform for all students. The Japanese instructor allowed freedom of choice for entries in the portfolio. Through the reflective introductions, the students were forced to think about their own responsibility in the language-learning process and what they could do to change or enhance the process.

The data analysis of the portfolios consisted of analyzing and comparing the student responses on their portfolio self-evaluations, surveys, and interviews. The instructors for the courses gave the students the grades for each section of the portfolio. The German instructor chose to grade the students on a pass/fail basis, and the Japanese instructor gave each entry a point value that was part of the total points possible for the semester grade. The surveys from and interviews with the two instructors also provided valuable data to be analyzed. These gave insight into the instructors' perspectives on the value of the portfolio project and the problems that arose from its implementation.

Student feedback also played a large part in the understanding of this portfolio project. Looking at students' reflective introductions and self-evaluations revealed how they felt about the project and what they learned from doing the project. The questions for the reflective introduction given in the portfolio description asked them to report on what they learned from doing specific assignments and what they would change if they were to do the assignments again. The feedback provided by the answers to these two questions supplied information on the students' perception of their own progress in language skills and cultural understanding. More directly, the midpoint and final surveys provided additional feedback regarding the students' perceptions of the value of learning culture, interest in the TLC, and how worthwhile students believed the portfolios to be. The final survey asked the students to rate whether they learned about their strengths and weaknesses in the target language by completing the Web-based language portfolio project. This enabled the researcher to determine whether the portfolio project helped students learn about themselves as language learners. Follow-up interviews and additional comments provided more information about student perceptions related to the portfolio and the portfolio creation process.

Through analyzing the data from the student portfolios, student and instructor surveys, and follow-up interviews, the perception of the value of learning about the TLC and the perception of the improvement of language skills and cultural understanding was determined. In addition, whether the portfolio process assisted the students in their learning about themselves as language learners was determined. Finally, how challenging the project was and the degree to which it was considered worthwhile by the students and instructors was determined.

Results were collected from the students using five sources: the midpoint survey, final survey, interviews, and portfolio reflective introductions and self-evaluations. Data were also collected from the two instructors using three sources: the final survey, interviews, and regular e-mail correspondence.

To highlight the changes in the response averages, a comparison of the student average responses on the midpoint and final surveys is shown in Table 1. On the surveys, the students were asked to respond to six questions, rating their answers on a scale of 1 to 5, with 1 being "strongly disagree;" 2, "disagree somewhat;" 3, "agree somewhat;" 4, "agree;" and 5, "strongly agree." The final question on the survey was open ended and asked students to write their comments about the portfolio process.

Table 1: Comparison of midpoint and final survey responses

question	midpoint survey average (*n*=26)	final survey average (*n*=22)
I believe it is important to learn about the culture of the country or countries whose language one is studying.	4.92	5.0
I am very interested in learning more about the culture of Japan/ German-speaking countries.	4.73	4.8
The portfolio project has helped me learn about Japanese/ German culture.	3.54	3.1
I am more interested in learning about Japanese/German culture after having finished the portfolio project.	n/a	3.4
The portfolio project helped improve my Japanese/German language skills.	3.77	3.8
I have learned about my language strengths and weaknesses from completing the portfolio project.	n/a	3.7
The portfolio project is challenging.	3.85	3.2
The portfolio project is worthwhile.	3.88	3.4

The research questions serve as guidelines for discussing the survey results outlined in Table 1 and the other research results.

Do intermediate- and advanced-level foreign language students perceive culture to be an important part of their learning of the target language?

Overwhelmingly, the students demonstrated that they viewed culture to be an important part of their language study. The average response to the first question, which asked them whether they believed that it was important to learn about the TLC, was 4.92 on the midpoint survey, and the average response on the final survey was 5.0. There was a slight, but not significant, increase in this response from the middle to the end of the portfolio project. In addition, when asked whether they were interested in learning more about the TLC, the student responses had an average of 4.73 at the midpoint and 4.8 at the end of the semester. This question also showed a slight increase in the average response, but it was not significant. The students had likely learned culture through their language classes until this point and were able to reflect on how they believed that it was important to their understanding of the target language. In addition, because they were asked to write on a number of cultural topics, their perception of the value of cultural study may have increased without their being aware of it. In the group interviews, a number of students mentioned that their motivation for language study was an interest in the TLC. Therefore, that these students would value the study of the TLC as part of their language study is not surprising.

Do students perceive the portfolio creation process to be beneficial to their learning of culture?

When asked whether the portfolio project helped them learn about the TLC, the average response for the midpoint survey was 3.54, and the average response on the final survey was 3.1, showing a slight decrease. The figure 3.1 is very close to a general consensus of "agree somewhat" on this question. In the group interviews, the student answers were varied about whether they believed that their cultural understanding improved as a result of the portfolios. One student said that it was difficult to say whether it was the portfolio that benefited learning or whether it was the course work that was later included in the portfolio. Two other students said that they chose to write about what they already knew about the TLC, so it was difficult to say that the portfolio was beneficial to their learning of culture because they were not learning new material. On the other hand, another two students mentioned that they felt that the research aspect, or learning about new aspects of the culture, was beneficial.

In the reflective introductions to the portfolios entries, many students mentioned learning about aspects of the TLC. From the reflective introductions, they clearly did, indeed, learn about the TLC. However, when compared with their responses on the surveys and interviews, it is possible to see that the students did not attribute the portfolio process itself as contributing to their cultural understanding. In addition, many of the students mentioned in the interviews that they chose to write about topics that they were already familiar with, showing that they viewed the portfolio project as a language exercise rather than a cultural exercise. If the students had been specifically asked to write about new topics that they had had to research, then the results for this question might have reflected an increased perception of learning about the TLC.

Do Web-based language portfolios increase student interest in the TLC?

This question was asked on only the final survey, and the average response was 3.4, placing the answer roughly between "somewhat agree" and "agree" on the scale of possible answers. This shows that although some of the students noted an increase in interest, not all of them did. During one group interview, two students mentioned that they were already very interested in the TLC, so they could not become more interested in it. They also mentioned that their classmates felt the same way and that interest in the TLC was the primary motivation for studying the language. In light of these responses, that students would have mixed responses to this question is understandable. Although some of them noted an increase in interest, others who perceived their interest to have peaked did not notice an increase in interest in the culture of the target language.

However, one student mentioned in a reflective introduction that he had learned about one cultural aspect in the process of researching a different cultural aspect for another entry. It seems, then, that students were moved to research unknown areas based on what they had already learned. Although the students were not aware that their interest was increasing, it could have been.

Additionally, the Japanese-language students responded to this question after having done 4 weeks' worth of assignments on their language skills, which were part of the communication sections. Because the cultural entries, that is, the cultures and comparisons sections, may not have been fresh in their minds, they would have not considered them as much as the language skills sections.

In the interviews, some of the students in the Japanese classes mentioned that they thought that the preliminary portfolio activity was for the purpose of planning what they would do through the course of the semester, although the actual intent of the activity was for students to have a baseline portfolio to compare with their final project. This likely impacted their perception of their increases in interest and cultural learning. Having the students look at their preliminary portfolio again at the end of the semester might have changed these results because the students would have been able to see what they had written. The researcher did not have access to these preliminary documents.

Do students perceive increases in language abilities from creating Web-based language portfolios?

When asked whether they believed that their language skills had improved because of the portfolio project, the student average response on the midpoint survey was 3.77, and the average response on the final survey was 3.8, which shows a slight increase. In the group interviews, students mentioned that having the opportunity to practice grammatical structures and vocabulary was one of the best aspects of the portfolio project. Many students also mentioned that they were able to write more in the target language in a shorter period of time toward the end of the semester than at the beginning, showing improved language skills.

The students' reflective introductions and self-evaluations also supported the idea that they believed that their language skills had increased. Some noted that they were able to write more in a shorter period of time than they had in previous entries, which echoes comments from the group interviews. Others stated that they were able to use new vocabulary and apply their learning of grammatical structures to what they were writing for each entry.

Therefore, they appeared to believe that having the opportunity to apply some of their classroom learning in another project was beneficial. This could mean that they did actually feel an increase in language ability even though they did not indicate this on the survey. By discussing the portfolio project more in depth, students may have realized that they did see an improvement in language skills through the project.

When asked to respond to the statement, "I learned about my language strengths and weaknesses from completing the portfolio project," the students' average response was 3.7. This indicates that the students generally agreed with the statement. Generally, most students mentioned how difficult writing in Japanese was, but in the same entry, they also mentioned being able to apply grammar and vocabulary learning in the entry. Although many mentioned improvements in language skills, they did not always attribute this to the portfolio. Also, some students seemed more aware of their learning, especially talking about what they could do well and what they thought they needed to work on. Learning about their strengths and weaknesses helps students become better language learners, so although there was not strong agreement with the question about the improvement in language skills, in subsequent semesters, the students may see an increase in language skills that could be tied to having done the portfolio project.

Do teachers perceive increases in student language abilities from creating Web-based language portfolios?

Both of the instructors answered "agree" in response to this question. Thus, we can see that from the instructor point of view that creating a portfolio improves student target-language learning. It is possible that because the Japanese instructor felt that some of her students were frustrated by the portfolio process, she could not answer the question with "strongly agree." Because the students of German did all of their assignments as homework before posting them in the portfolio, the German instructor may have felt that it was difficult to discriminate between the portfolio itself and the individual assignments in terms of improving student learning in the target language. When asked for further comments, the instructors both mentioned that writing skills were developed from this project. The German instructor also mentioned that the students of German benefited in terms of vocabulary development.

Both the instructors responded "agree" when asked if they thought that the portfolio project was challenging for the students. The German instructor felt that the reflective aspects of the project required students to think critically and that that was especially challenging. The Japanese instructor mentioned that the students were challenged by being required to write about topics of interest and that some students took this as a positive challenge, while others responded negatively to this challenge. Figuring out how to support those who responded negatively to the challenge could have been a source of frustration and concern for the instructor.

Are Web-based language portfolios organized around SFLL an effective way to teach and assess learning of the TLC?

The results of the project, including the data from the surveys, interviews, and reflective introductions and self-evaluations, support the use of Web-based language portfolios to teach and assess learning of the TLC. Students somewhat agreed or agreed when asked if the portfolio contributed to their learning. In addition, the reflective introductions and self-evaluations, where students talked about how much they had learned, show that the students benefited from this project. At the same time, both of the instructors involved in the project responded with "agree" when asked if they felt the project helped the students learn about the TLC. The instructors felt that the students benefited from the cultural comparisons as well as simply learned about aspects of the TLC. As professionals, the instructors were able to see the growth in their students that the students were not always able to see. Although the portfolio helped the students reflect and see some of their own progress, note that the instructors were also able to view this improvement and growth.

When asked whether the portfolio project was worthwhile for the students and what the most worthwhile aspect of the project was, the Japanese instructor responded that the opportunity to practice the language and to learn about the culture was most worthwhile. The German instructor thought that the opportunity for students to think critically about their language learning was the most worthwhile aspect of the portfolio project. This shows that the instructors were able to see the growth of their students in terms of language skills, cultural understanding, and thinking critically about their language learning. The instructors not only saw and noted this growth, but also thought that it was worthwhile.

What are the problems associated with implementing a portfolio project?

Three problems were mentioned by the instructors and students with regard to implementing the portfolio: problems with technology, the time required to implement the project, and student frustration at being asked to complete a difficult task. The Japanese instructor spent a good deal of time helping the students set up Japanese language capabilities on their computers. In addition, a couple of the students in both the Japanese and German classes mentioned having trouble understanding how to post entries in LiveJournal. Even though the LiveJournal interface is relatively simple, some students were not familiar enough with using the Internet to use the site well.

In addition to challenges with technology, the time required to implement the project was a problem. The instructors needed to spend extra time grading the portfolio entries and giving appropriate and useful feedback to the students. The German instructor voiced regret at not being able to take the time to implement the project with tasks clearly tied to the standards and that promoted student reflection. The Japanese instructor mentioned that the time to grade and give feedback to students was somewhat of a burden during the semester. The students had to spend extra time completing the assignments and posting them on the Web because the entries were in addition to their regular homework. The students also mentioned that time was a factor in how much writing they were able to complete in their portfolio entries each week.

Another problem that arose in this study is the frustration that the Japanese students felt when creating the portfolios. It is important to consider what could have been done to alleviate the frustration that the students felt in writing about topics for which they may not have had the vocabulary and grammar. Although challenging students has some value, putting them in situations where they are so frustrated that they want to give up is not helpful. Challenge and frustration level must be balanced. Giving more guidance in choosing topics and providing suggestions could help with this frustration. Giving students suggested topics that are more concrete, such as the use of cell phones in Japan, rather than the tea ceremony, would help with this. Students could be provided with two or three choices for each section so that they could find something that was of interest, but not be allowed to choose something that was too abstract for their language skill level. Students also mentioned that they spent a good bit of time trying to figure out what to write about, so if they were given choices, this would cut down on the time spent deciding what topic to write about.

Implications

Although student learning of language and culture was clear from the portfolio reflective introductions and self-evaluations, the students did not always perceive the portfolios as beneficial to their learning. Therefore, one implication is that the student perception of the portfolio as a benefit needs to be improved. Students need to buy into and feel that their assignments help them learn for those assignments to give them the most benefit as a language-learning exercise. As Gomez, Graue, and Bloch (1991) have shown, simply creating a portfolio is not enough to get students to understand their own learning. Instead, students need to understand the portfolio process, goals, and purpose for the learning and reflection to be meaningful.

Another implication of this study is the realization that specific assignments that are at the student level are essential to the success of this project. This is supported by the ideas of Krashen (1981) and Vygotsky (1986), who both emphasized that student learning takes place when material is at the individual level of the student. Many students in the Japanese class mentioned being frustrated by their feelings of not being able to write what they wanted about the topics that they had chosen. The students in the German class, which was at the advanced level, did not mention this frustration. One reason for this is likely their higher skill level and better command of the target language because they were in an advanced level. Another reason is that they were given very specific guidelines for each assignment that were crafted by the instructor to be at their level. Therefore, the students had less opportunity to choose topics that were too difficult for their individual levels. This shows that guidelines for specific entries could help ease some of the frustration felt by the intermediate students. This would alleviate some of the frustration that the students faced in trying to write about topics that were too abstract for their vocabulary level, such as the Japanese tea ceremony. A topic such as vending machines and their use and availability in Japan is much more manageable for a lower level. This also encourages students to focus more on the daily *culture* rather than the high *Culture* of the target language, which is more in line with the original intent of SFLL.

In terms of guiding students in reflection and critical thinking, we can learn from the German class that participated in this project. Their instructor designed assignments that specifically asked them to reflect on the cultures of the target language. These were then posted in their portfolios. These students demonstrated deeper reflection than the students of Japanese, showing that intentionally guiding the students in the topics for the portfolio project can lead them to reflect on the TLC. However, students will not necessarily lead themselves in this reflection without explicit direction and guidance. There was no indication that the students followed the questions that were given in the reflective introduction of the portfolio description. If the students in the Japanese class had followed these questions, they would have had more depth to add to their reflective introductions.

From the faculty point of view, having clear expectations is important. Developing a clear rubric for the expectations of each class would help the students develop their entries according to the expectations. It would also help the instructors cut down on the time spent grading the portfolio entries and reflections. The grading for the German class was done on a pass/fail basis because the instructor felt that she was not familiar enough with the possible outcomes to develop a rubric. Now that this portfolio has been implemented, both of these instructors can develop a scoring rubric that will make the expectations clear and help reduce the grading time.

Considering that both instructors suggested that they might use the portfolio project in some form for assessing student learning at more than one level, note that a rubric for reading portfolios will need to be developed. In researching writing-portfolio assessment, Condon and Hamp-Lyons (1994) found that without measures to make sure that readers viewed and considered each entry in the portfolio separately, often readers initially formed general impressions of the student writing that later did not vary from that initial impression. When readers were given more direction for reading, they were more likely to consider each work separately, rather than the entire body as a whole.

Recommendations

A number of recommendations can be made based on the research results. Admittedly, these recommendations increase the instructor workload at the beginning stages of the portfolio project, but they should be viewed as an investment in both deeper and more meaningful student learning and the outcomes of the course. First, intentional teaching of reflection is needed for students to make it a part of their portfolios. Most college language classes do not normally involve reflection on the learning process, so the students are not well trained to look at their own learning and consider their own learning processes. Therefore, the teacher needs to devote time normally used for language teaching to assist students in the process of reflection. Furthermore, giving students some examples of reflections and guiding them through the reflective process would increase the value of the portfolio project. The students of German showed much deeper reflection than the students of Japanese, largely because they had been instructed in their assignments to reflect on what they had learned about German and U.S. cultures from completing the assignment. Building time into the curriculum to help students with the reflective process would add to the impact of the project. Although this would take away from some of the time available for language and cultural learning in the classroom, it should be viewed as an investment in student learning. If students are able to reflect on their own learning, they will become better learners during the course and better lifelong learners.

Integrating the portfolio entries and activities with course requirements is another recommendation based on the results of this study. Giving students specific assignments or at least strong suggestions for each entry so that they do not need to spend time choosing topics is an important aspect of this integration. This further ties the activities to the course goals and curriculum so that the portfolio can reinforce what has been taught in class. Making the portfolio entries closely tied to class topics and objectives takes time, but once that time has been spent in creating topics for students to write about and giving them guidelines and resources for finding information, the portfolio project is likely to be better implemented and seen as more valuable by all parties involved. In addition, students are more likely to see the portfolio as beneficial if it is tied closely to the outcomes and topics of the course.

The frustration level of the intermediate Japanese students was a concern for the instructor of that class, so if it were used again at this level, giving students extra support in developing their portfolios would be necessary. Students could be guided in topic choice, as mentioned above. Additionally, students could be given links and resources that are at their level, such as a link to a newspaper written for children in the target language. Although this would be additional work for the instructor, often students at the intermediate level need this type of support in finding sources that are at their level. Finally, helping students through the process could become a class activity, where students would bring typed copies of their paragraphs to class and read their work in round-robin style. The students would be able to get peer feedback and could learn some new vocabulary and structures from this exercise. Another possibility is to have students read their work aloud to a small group while the other group members give comments and ideas for improving the work. The students would be able to see what their classmates were writing so that they could more effectively gauge their own learning.

Another recommendation is to develop a scoring rubric for each course that would use the portfolio project. A good way to begin developing a rubric is by looking at the Indicators of Competence by the American Association of Teachers of French, outlined in Nostrand and Grundstrom's *Acquiring Cross-Cultural Competence* (1996). This book outlines the four "stages" of cultural competence, where Stage 1 refers to elementary competence, which they describe as mainly observing and imitating. Stage 2 describes basic intercultural skills and is explained as the basic skills and knowledge needed to navigate the TLC. Stage 3 is listed as social competence and describes progress in both being able to function in the TLC and having a deeper understanding of the culture. Finally, Stage 4 is socioprofessional capability and stresses the understanding and skills appropriate for professional and social activity in the TLC. According to Nostrand and Grundstrom, college-level students are normally expected to be at Stage 3 or 4 by the end of college, depending on time spent in the TLC. At a minimum, they suggest that college students should complete Stage 2. Using these ideas as a basis and then following some of the sample progress indicators, rubrics can be developed that apply to each level of a program or to one specific level of a program where the portfolio would be used. Developing such a rubric would serve a number of purposes. First, it would show students how they were being graded and what level of cultural understanding was being expected of them. At the same time, it would give the instructors a means to quickly assess the understanding that is being presented through the student portfolios. Having the rubric developed by the individual instructor would ensure that the class objectives and goals were being implemented and measured. Although this would require extra work at the beginning of a course, it would lighten the workload during and at the end of the course. Students would follow the rubric to write their entries, so the work produced should be of a higher quality. The instructor would be able to score the student work more efficiently by using the rubric.

Finally, developing specific guidelines for the self-evaluation section of the portfolio would help students understand the value of the project. For example, having students look at classmates' portfolios and then consider their own again would lead them to reflect on their progress compared to their peers. Asking them to look at their early entries and compare them with their final entries would also give them an opportunity to reflect on their learning. This process is related to Kolb's (1984) ideas about the learning cycle, where concrete experience is followed by reflective observation, then abstract conceptualization and active experimentation. If students followed these steps, then wrote about their learning, what they thought they did well, and what they could improve on, this process would give them some direction in writing their self-evaluations and would likely lead to deeper reflection and improved perception of how much had been learned over the course of the project.

Suggestions for further research

The portfolio project implementation results suggest a number of ideas for future research. One idea that was raised by both instructors was the use of portfolios program-wide. This idea could be implemented at all levels of foreign language instruction. One possible scenario would be to introduce students to the reflection process through learning journals, as were described in Calvin and Rider's (2004) article at the elementary level. This would help cut down on the time needed to introduce reflection at the intermediate level. Students in intermediate classes would use the portfolio project as outlined in the current study. Some modifications could be made to the process so that students are given more guidance in creating individual entries. At the next level, students would be given broader tasks and then asked how completing these tasks showed their work toward the standards. Because they would have already been introduced to the standards at the intermediate level, students would be able to apply what they had learned by deciding which tasks and activities from their course work met each of the standards.

This study followed an implementation of a portfolio project where students were not given topics for their entries and were not guided in their reflections. It would be interesting to develop a study where students were guided in both of these areas to see their perceptions of the value of the portfolio. In addition, student perception of learning the TLC may improve if they are given topics to write about that are certainly new to them. Finally, if students are guided in their reflections, with questions and a format that needs to be followed in writing the reflections, they may have more of a sense that their learning of the target language and TLC is improving.

Through this study, the use of Web-based portfolios has been examined to give a better understanding of how their use impacts student learning of the target language and TLC.

Through using surveys, interviews, student reflective introductions to their portfolio entries, and student self-evaluations, it was determined that both the students and instructors involved in this project felt that student learning of the target language and TLC had improved through the portfolio project. The students did not always attribute their learning to the portfolio project, but especially in their reflective introductions and self-evaluations, it was possible to see that they had indeed developed a better understanding of the target language and TLC.

References

Bachman, L., & Palmer, A. (1996). *Language testing in practice*. Oxford, England: Oxford University Press.

Calvin, L. M., & Rider, N. A. (2004). Not your parents' language class: Curriculum revision to support university language requirements. *Foreign Language Annals, 37,* 11–25.

Condon, W., & Hamp-Lyons, L. (1994). Maintaining a portfolio-based writing assessment: Research that informs program development. In L. Black, D. A. Daiker, J. Sommers, & G. Stygall (Eds.), *New directions in portfolio assessment: Reflective practice, critical theory, and large-scale scoring* (pp. 277–285). Portsmouth, NH: Heinemann.

Crawford-Lange, L. M., & Lange, D. L. (1984). Doing the unthinkable in the second-language classroom: A process for the integration of language and culture. In T. V. Higgs (Ed.), *Teaching for proficiency: The organizing principle* (pp. 139–177). Lincolnwood, IL: National Textbook Company.

Delett, J. S., Barnhardt, S., & Kevorkian, J. A. (2001). A framework for portfolio assessment in the foreign language classroom. *Foreign Language Annals, 34,* 559–568.

Dugan, J. S., Nerenz, A. G., Palmer, B. W., Peden, G. M., & Vosteen, T. R. (1999). *Using the standards for foreign language learning in college-level portfolios*. In A. G. Nerenz (Ed.), Standards for a new century: Selected papers from the 1999 Central States Conference (pp. 32–41). Lincolnwood, IL: National Textbook Company.

Gatlin, L., & Jacob, S. (2002). Standards-based digital portfolios: A component of authentic assessment for preservice teachers. *Action in Teacher Education, 23*(4), 35–42.

Gomez, M. L., Graue, M. E., & Bloch, M. N. (1991). Reassessing portfolio assessment: Rhetoric and reality. *Language Arts,* 68, 620–628.

Kolb, D. A. (1984). *Experiential learning: Experience as the source of learning and development*. Upper Saddle River, NJ: Prentice Hall.

Krashen, S. D. (1981). *Second language acquisition and second language learning*. New York: Pergamon Press.

Lange, D. L. (1999). Planning for and using the new national culture standards. In J. K. Phillips & R. M. Terry (Eds.), *Foreign language standards: Linking research, theories, and practices* (pp. 57–135). Chicago: National Textbook Company.

Lee, L. (1997). Using portfolios to develop L2 cultural knowledge and awareness in students in intermediate Spanish. *Hispania,* 80, 355–367.

Moore, Z. (1996). Culture: How do teachers teach it? In Z. Moore (Ed.), *Foreign language teacher education: Multiple perspectives* (pp. 269–288). Lanham, MD: University Press of America.

Nostrand, H. L., & Grundstrom, A. W. (1996). *Acquiring cross-cultural competence: Four stages for students of French*. Chicago: National Textbook Company.

Omaggio Hadley, A. (1993). *Teaching language in context* (2nd ed.). Boston: Heinle & Heinle.

Phillips, J. K., & Terry, R. M. (1999). *Foreign language standards: Linking research, theories, and practices.* Chicago: National Textbook Company.

Portfolio assessment in the foreign language classroom. (n.d.). Retrieved March 11, 2003, from http://www.nclrc.org/portfolio/modules.html

Riggs, I., & Sandlin, R. A. (2000). Teaching portfolios for support of teachers' professional growth. *NASSP Bulletin, 84*(618), 22–27.

Storme, J., & Derakhshani, M. (2002). Defining, teaching, and evaluating cultural proficiency in the foreign language classroom. *Foreign Language Annals, 35,* 657–668.

Vygotsky, L. M. (1986). *Thought and language.* Cambridge, MA: MIT Press.

Wesche, M. B. (1983). Communicative testing in a second language. *Modern Language Journal, 67,* 41–55.

White, E. M. (1994). Portfolios as an assessment concept. In L. Black, D. A. Daiker, J. Sommers & G. Stygall (Eds.), *New directions in portfolios assessment: Reflective practice, critical theory, and large-scale learning* (pp. 25–39). Portsmouth, NH: Heinemann.

Wiedmer, T. L. (1998). Electronic portfolios: A means to bridge professional achievements and INTASC standards. *The Delta Kappa Gamma Bulletin, 64*(3), 54–61.

Wright, D. A. (2003). Fostering cross-cultural adaptability through foreign language study. *Northeast Conference on the Teaching of Foreign Languages Review, 52*(Spring), 36–40.

Awakening to the Power of Video-Based Web-Conferencing Technology to Promote Change

Paula Charbonneau-Gowdy
Canada School of Public Service

A large part of social suffering stems from the poverty of people's relationship to the educational system, which not only shapes social destinies but also the image they have of their destinies.
(Bourdieu, 1998, p. 43)

The test could not check my work here. It may test my knowledge but not my work. We are very different and maybe you can't understand me....But I will receive a rating and when I return home and my commander will see my score if it is zero, they will say during four months I did not go to class. I did not study. They will think I went to the restaurants, to the nightclubs, only had a holiday. This is a big problem. Nobody can argue that I did not work in this course. But nobody is interested what I did, only in my results....I can imagine what my commander will think!
(Sergiy, a Ukrainian participant in a 5-month ESL immersion program in Canada. Interview, May 19, 2004)

I felt pretty scared especially about my speaking. I was afraid not to make grammar mistakes, and I was rather silent and [me] being a talkative one.
(Vali, a Romanian participant in online discussions. Interview, November 24, 2004)

Bourdieu's (1998) observation that education profoundly influences learners is reflected in the comments of these two students who were participants in a study involving computer technology that took place between 2001 and 2005. Sergiy seems to be expressing his need to mediate with his interlocutor the repercussions of not succeeding on his end-of-course tests after 5 months, despite his hard work and efforts; Vali laments a missed opportunity to practice his English as a member of a UN international team in Eretria, which he attributes to his weaknesses in speaking the language. The words of both of these individuals allude strongly to the fact that what occurred in the context of language learning permeates their ways of being not only inside but also outside the four walls of those spaces in the classroom and influences their views of themselves and their possibilities for their futures.

Charbonneau-Gowdy, P. (2009). Awakening to the power of video-based Web-conferencing technology to promote change. In R. Oxford & J. Oxford, (Eds.), *Second language teaching and learning in the Net Generation* (pp. 199–216). Honolulu: University of Hawai'i, National Foreign Language Resource Center.

In working with learners from Eastern Europe in the NATO program and more recently with others in a Canadian federal public-service context, I am often struck by the passionate drive of many language learners to learn another language. In the case of learning English, this drive on a global scale is unprecedented. The debate about whether the incredible thrust to learn English, the new "global language," is a blessing or a postmodern form of colonialism has begun to abate. The controversy over the connection between learning English information and computer technology (Warschauer, 2003) and policy decisions (Nunan, 2003; Ricento, 2000) has not. Whether participating in the teaching of English equates to promoting the Western capitalist race for more markets and/or supports the spread of Western ideologies must weigh on the minds of some educators. Do educators of English, question, as I do, the role that they play in determining the future cultural practices and indeed lives of their students by their indirect or direct practices inside and outside the classroom? Do they wonder about the "social destinies" of the students that they encounter and how these social destinies are being created in the learning contexts in which they teach? Do they notice in the language-learning contexts in which they work, the human and growing technological forces such as transmission-style teaching practices and computerized standardized testing and the ideologies that these practices support? Do second-language educators see, and do they regret how such forces and their own practices constrain their students' enthusiasm to learn or lead to some learners compromising their integrity through cheating, as reports around the International English Language Testing System and Test of English as a Foreign Language are suggesting (Shepherd, 2008)?

Some second-language researchers have conceptualized language-learning motivation as a static personality trait of learners. From this perspective, educators and educational systems are relieved of the responsibility for Vali and Sergiy's dilemmas. On the other hand, other researchers, and indeed a growing number of educators, recognize the dynamic interplay of identity and social contexts as integral to learning. The dichotomous struggle between the desire to learn and the hurdles that stand in the way of learning, especially with regard to learning a second language (L2), has been a preoccupying concern of a growing number of L2 researchers. Many of these researchers (Belz, 2007; Thorne, 2000; Warschauer, 1999) have recognized that they can no longer ignore how technology fits into this struggle. From their perspective, language learning is a sociocultural process in which learning is co-constructed by learners and teachers in collaborative and empowering dialogues that are increasingly taking place online. Sociocultural theory implies that learning cannot be a neutral phenomenon (Maguire & Graves, 2001). Who will dictate the Discourses in the new "third" space (Lefebvre, 1991) online? What influence will these Discourses have on Vali and Sergiy's identities and language learning?

In this chapter, the focus is on the findings of a study I conducted (Charbonneau-Gowdy, 2005) into a multistream video-based Web-conferencing technology for the purpose of computer mediated communication (CMC). In the study, I examined the influence of the communication on the identities of two groups of military officers learning English in a 5-month immersion program and for 4 weeks online. I explored the identities of a group of officers taking part in the English immersion program in Canada and uncovered tensions, both in the classrooms and when using computer technology. To respond to those tensions, I then put in place a participatory action-research project to use video-based Web conferencing for CMC between Canada and Europe. The intention of the research was to frame the story of the experiences of the participants in the traditional and online classrooms using CMC. The aim of the work is to provide an impetus for a new second-language acquisition (SLA) theory. I argue that a new SLA theory is needed to replace the existing theories that have failed as yet to include the use of computer technology and its influence on learning, despite its burgeoning prominence everywhere, including in L2 learning sites.

Chapelle (2007) asserted that "the integration of technology, research and practice in SLA needs to be increased." This chapter is the story of a study in response to such a call and others voiced in the literature. It is also in response to a growing cry that I was beginning to witness several years ago in the L2 classrooms where I was working as well as in the research circles that I was frequenting. The chapter begins with a discussion of the theoretical assumptions on which the study was based. The discussion is followed by the story of the qualitative research process, its players, the events, and its findings. The chapter ends with words that seek to challenge all of those working in language learning—teachers, learners, and policy makers—to look "through different eyes" at how technology can redefine the somewhat ordinary act of language learning into an opportunity for positive individual and social change.

Linking language learning and identity

I begin this theoretical discussion of the role that computer technology plays in L2 education from three assumptions. The first assumption is that language learning is a social act; the second is that within all social acts there is an element of power; the third assumption is that learning is influenced by a multitude of contextual factors. Vygotsky (1962, 1978) considered individuals as inseparable from their social worlds. His work was instrumental in providing a base for further research into the role of social and individual processes (Lantolf & Appel, 1994; Lantolf & Pavlenko, 2000; Werstch, 1998) in language learning. In Vygotsky's sociocultural theory, social interaction is considered a crucial factor in understanding human behavior. From this view, social interaction not only governs the way individuals relate to one another, but also structures the intra-action, that is, the internalized acts of thinking and feeling within individual consciousness. This in turn leads to higher-order functions of thinking. Language plays an important role and serves a mediating function in this cognitive developmental process. Sociocultural theory assumes that individuals develop knowledge of the structural and functional aspects of a language by using the language socially with others. This view contrasts with a cognitive-acquisition perspective that sees language learning as a solitary cognitive act of mental processing (Donato, 2000). Thus, when a teacher and students talk together, their utterances are more than linguistic input that they need to comprehend. These intersubjective utterances result in social practices that serve to help shape, construct, and influence learning. Within a social context, learners can move from being "other-regulated" to being "self regulated." In other words, the *inter*mental activity in a social context has direct influence on the *intra*mental activity at the individual level. Indeed, Vygotsky (1989) asserted that "social interaction produces new elaborate, advanced psychological processes that are unavailable to the organism working in isolation" (p. 61).

Sociocultural theorists conceptualize language learning as a developmental process that is mediated by semiotic resources (Wertsch, 1991). Semiotic resources include discourse, the physical environment, gestures, and materials such as computers that make up learning contexts. The characteristics of these resources determine in powerful ways how learners negotiate the social interactions that constitute their language learning. Another theme in Vygotsky's sociocultural theory of learning involves the view that learners are active agents in the development of their language learning. This means that learners bring to interactions their own ways of thinking and feeling based on their historical, cultural, and personal identities that were formed through previous interactions. With these thoughts and feelings, they project their own future situations, which they apply to present situations. In their work in child development, Vygotsky & Luria (1994) have shown that through symbolic operations with signs or words, children open up a new field of action: "a field that does not lean on the existing present, but rather sketches an outline of the future situation of action and thus creates a free action, independent of the immediately effective situation" (pp. 134–135). Sociocultural theory unites the past with the present and opens up the tremendous roles that history and culture can play in shaping L2 learners' identities in the future in the context of learning language. Understanding these roles can help explain the tensions among learners, teachers, and target-language speakers whose cultures might be different. Within L2 interactions, learners are not only agents in the construction of higher-order thinking but also agents in mediating their identities. Identities are dynamic and can be *transformed* from being *conformed to* to being *opposed to*—offering empowering possibilities of social interaction in language learning.

Bakhtin's (1981, 1986) dialogic theory of language also helps to further our understanding of the importance of social interaction in empowering learners. Bakhtin used the construct of dialogism to explain the nature of social interactions to mediate meaning. From this perspective, language, in the broadest of senses (words, actions, images, spaces, etc.), always invites a response in human consciousness to the words of others. The response to a sign, whether that sign is a word, action, image, or space, is another sign. Embedded in these signs are the meanings constructed in past interactions. Therefore, each interaction, while being influenced by past interactions and present interactions, will then influence future ones. This interplay of a sign with another sign, of past, present, and future, is the basis of individual understanding and meaning. In an L2 learning context, through these interactive processes of answering one to the other, learners can create and mediate new meanings. At the same time, they can create social and ideological changes to their individual identities. In other words, in dialogic interactions there is a potential for empowering L2 learners to have voices, to invest in using their second language, and at the same time, to evolve as human beings. Thus, when L2 learners speak, they are not only using language in a particular context; they are shaping the very contexts that shape them.

Linking power and identity

A second assumption that forms the basis of this discussion of computer technology in L2 learning sites is that in any social interaction in a real or virtual setting, power relations exist. Weedon (1997) is especially helpful in conceptualizing the relationships between power, identity, and language learning. Working from a feminist poststructuralist perspective, she used her theory of subjectivity to connect language, individual experience, and social power. From this perspective, Weedon explained the nature of subjectivity, or identity, as who we are as individuals. Our identities are the combination of our innate selves and the selves that are made up of the characteristics we have acquired through our experiences of the world. Central to her concept of subjectivity is that it is a site of struggle, it can change over time, and that the nature of a subject is nonunitary and multiple (Norton, 2000). Sergiy, in his identity as a senior military officer, can expect the respect of many in his own country, but in the North American context of language learning and the testing process associated in that context, his identity suffers from a loss of prestige that even threatens to influence how he will be regarded back home. Weedon saw language as most important to this understanding of subjectivity. She explained that "language is the place where actual and possible forms of social organization and their likely social and political consequences are defined and contested. Yet it is also the place where our sense of ourselves, our subjectivity is constructed" (p. 21).

Weedon was very much influenced by how Foucault (1980, 2000) theorized power. Both have made important contributions to our understanding of the relationship between identity and power. Through language, we not only work out our identities but also set in place the power relations that determine those identities. In other words, in our social relations, we use language to establish for others and ourselves who *we are*—our beliefs, our values, our goals, and our backgrounds—based on our innate and acquired selves. At the same time, we establish who *we are in relation to others*. Human beings gravitate toward those who share similarities in beliefs, values, goals, and backgrounds. They form discourses or ways of thinking, talking, and acting as a means of communicating solidarity to each other within a particular group. Although these discursive practices serve to unite individuals, they are also responsible for marginalizing those who do not conform to the social rules and roles inherent in particular discourses. For example, many of the participants who took part in the study from Central or Eastern Europe took up a disadvantaged position in the presence of a North American teacher both in the immersion program in Canada and in the online sessions. Language and identity in the guise of discourse is about solidarity, status, and power.

Languages, identities, and discourses are constantly changing because power relations can serve to coerce or collaborate. In coercive relations, dominant groups, such as educational institutions or individual teachers, can try to protect the status quo in which the access to symbolic (e.g., knowledge) and material resources (e.g., computers, money, goods) is limited to certain groups. On the other hand, collaborative power relations can serve to empower and change inequitable relations. With regard to computer technology, Warschauer (2000, 2003) has shown that in many L2 learning sites, including the one where this inquiry was conducted, teachers and institutions are continuing to choose to use computers for drill-and-practice work, information processing, and electronic communication (communicating with machines), despite the advent of Web 2.0 technologies. This use of computers serves to prepare students for work in their second language in service industries where basic functional skills are needed. On the other hand, using computers, or more specifically, the Internet, to help students develop communication, collaborative, and critical skills may insure that the L2 learners have the more sophisticated skills required for the better jobs in society. Acquiring these skills can not only lead to having the financial stability that comes with better employment but also the potential of having a voice and agency in constructing new possibilities for the future.

Beyond the walls of formal language-learning contexts, individuals and L2 learners are increasingly using computers and the Internet as a resource for interacting in their second language through electronic communities such as chatting, blogs, e-bulletin boards, wikis, and Web conferencing. Weedon's (1997) subjectivity theory and Foucault's (2000) theory on power help us to begin to frame these interactions and to understand them in more critical terms. For example, when L2 learners use computers to learn languages, how are their identities being mediated? How are the power relations inherent to these interactions being determined? Are these relations of power serving to enable or limit the range of identities that language learners can negotiate? Are the social identities that are formed in a virtual environment different from those in more traditional communication environments?

Linking computer technology and identity

A third assumption that I make in discussing the use of computers for L2 learning is that learners bring to the learning site a set of "nested contexts." Included in these contexts are "the shifting social, cultural, economic and political boundaries that intersect, overlap and collide in complex ways" (Maguire, 2003, p. 220). These contexts represent the multiple layers of influence in learners' constructions of identities. To understand and begin to work out a new theory of how human beings with their complex identities intersect with computer technologies requires viewing learning in the online context from a sociocultural perspective. Although recent studies are beginning to reflect the sociocultural perspective with regard to language learning using computer technology (Black, 2006; O'Dowd, 2006; Thorne, 2003; Warschauer and De Florio-Hansen, 2003), too many institutions of learning and researchers intent on putting the emphasis on cognitive processes of individuals appear slow to pick up the message.

Change is destabilizing. It is also the catalyst for and sign of learning. What can we learn from our present uses of computer technology in our L2 learning sites? How can we broaden our understanding of the intersection of language and computer technology in relation to language-learning contexts? One suggestion is that "we should continue to take risks in connection with the new technologies even when those risks produce results that are unsatisfactory" (Hawisher & Selfe, 1991, p. 4). In our L2 teaching, taking risks could mean challenging the discourses that control our practices and exploring new ways of using computer technology for learning with our students. "New ways" is intended to mean finding alternatives to the dated transmission methodologies that are still too often being used in traditional classrooms; that have been simply revamped in digital, albeit attractive format through multimedia technology; and that will continue to marginalize L2 learners by denying them a voice and agency in their learning.

Kress (1998, 2003) offered a further suggestion to the dilemma of how we might meet the challenge of understanding technology as it interacts with identities. He suggested that we are the makers of meaning, and therefore, it will be up to us, as educators, "to put us [our identities] and our sign making [social interaction through language] at the centre" (2001, p. 176), not in such a way that we do as we wish, but not by allowing ourselves to be victims of control, either. Taking control of the technologies that we use will require us to take a harder and broader look at how the multiple-layered identities of our students are influenced by the present technologies in L2 education. Taking control will demand that we examine the Discourses (Gee, 1996, 1997) in our L2 learning sites as we use computer technology. Taking control will also mean that we explore how computers and the Internet can serve to mediate and expand the choices that language learners have for creating new identities. Taking control suggests that we need to use our critical studies of computer technology and language learning, as Feenberg (1991, 2003) suggested, to capitalize on the potential of this technology to influence changes not only on the level of individual identities but within societies as a whole. For L2 educators whose main aim is to help learners reach their potentials and at the same time claim a voice in the global community, this perspective of language learning and technology offers new hope and incentive.

Stage one: From theory to practice

> Analysis [from a sociocultural perspective] appears to be inherently relevant for the assessment of the future agenda. Questions for quality of cross-cultural experiences should be expanded in order to provide a more comprehensive framework for the development of a valid research agenda. (Salaberry, 2000, p. 104)

Salaberry's (2000) call for cross-cultural research in computer technology is seen as one way of moving the view of computers from more than mere tools to, as Selfe (1999) explained, "complex technological artifacts that embody and shape—and are shaped by the ideological assumptions of an entire culture" (p. 2). For researchers who have responded to Salaberry in the last several years, viewing computer use as an asocial process of skill practice and information transfer and comparing face-to-face with electronic communication are becoming less important issues. Instead, their interest lies in human/human interaction as opposed to human/machine interaction and the potential for that interaction to move learners from other-regulated to self-regulated learners.

This is the story of research that was conducted between 2001 and 2005 that responded to Salaberry's (2000) call. It began as a study of the learning experiences of a group of military officers from Eastern and Central Europe taking part in a 5-month immersion program in English as a second language sponsored by NATO at a military base in Canada. The course was designed to help these officers and, by extension, their militaries become interoperable in terms of language in multinational military activities and joint organizational institutions. The course had a goal of exposing the officers from former Warsaw pact countries to democratic life and principles in the Canadian context. In earlier stages of the study of a single group of Ukrainian military officers, findings revealed that although many of these officers came to the immersion program with all the motivation, intellectual ability, and discipline to work and succeed at their language learning, several of the older officers like Sergiy felt marginalized by their socioeconomic status and their lack of agency in the product-based North American teaching and testing practices they met there. The years of living under the former regime where many decisions were made for them left the senior officers in the group especially vulnerable to submitting to their position in the program as "outsiders" and powerless in their efforts to enter the discourses of the North American context. Most avoided social interactions, and in the end, left the program feeling like Sergiy, very disappointed with their progress in learning English. In other words, their lack of agency and lack of power had a detrimental effect on their social investment in learning and their control in changing to their benefit the situation and their identities.

Some younger officers in this group, however, were able to adapt their identities to the new cultural and learning context. Initially, when they arrived, some of these younger officers reacted with anger, apathy, shyness, and lack of confidence when they were restricted and silenced by their socioeconomic status and personal and cultural identities. However, with determination and struggle, a few of these younger officers were eventually able to gain access to Anglophone social networks through their efforts in connecting with native speakers and by showing the individual symbolic resources they had, for example, expertise in playing pool or basketball. Changes to their identities were evident in the more Westernized behavior that they assumed or displayed, for example, in more relaxed dress, chewing gum, and laughing loudly—behaviors frowned upon in their own culture and country. Some became more proactive in speaking out about weaknesses in the course or teaching practices that marginalized them. In other words, using their second language led to more changes to their identities and more opportunities to speak and be listened to.

Follow-up with some of the officers once they returned to their home countries revealed that the investment in learning and changes in ways of thinking and seeing themselves in relation to others was carried into their personal and working lives in Ukraine. Lantolf and Pavlenko (2000) observed as follows:

> More than anything else, late or adult bilingualism requires agency and intentionality (similar to crossing class lines): it is through intentional social interactions with members of the other culture, through continuous attempts to construct new meanings,

> through new discourses, that one becomes an equal participant in new discursive spaces, but apparently not without a cost. (p. 174)

The cost of moving individuals to a place where they are more empowered, not only at the microlevel of their learning a language but at the macrolevel of their social interactions beyond the classrooms, has serious implications for educators. It led me as a researcher and educator to consider ways of resolving some of the tensions that were seen in this particular group of Ukrainians for other future groups of learners. I considered technology a likely place where these tensions could be resolved in a new and different way. I felt that in this new virtual space, or what Lefebvre (1991) refers to as the "third space," new ways of acting and being, new Discourses could be possible. I also felt that because language served as a means of calling attention to the tensions in the lives of these Ukrainian newcomers learning English, perhaps technology would provide opportunities for language to resolve some of these tensions. As an education researcher concerned about learners meeting their potential, I believe that observing, noting, and walking away is never an option. Action is the only recourse.

The next stage of the study involved observing, interviewing, and recording new groups of learners in the immersion program who were using various kinds of technology programs. An important factor in the study was taking into account the multiple nested contexts (Maguire, 1994)—historical, cultural, socioeconomic, sociolinguistic, educational, political, personal, and computer technological—that played a role in the experiences of the learners as they negotiated their learning in certain technological spaces. The question at the basis of this stage of the study was, what role could technology play in identity construction and language learning? In most of the former political contexts in which these learners had lived, the state interfered with or more often silenced the conversations that took place there. An important theme that emerged in working with the learners in all stages of the action-research study was their need to "practice speaking," that is, to engage in authentic and meaningful conversations and dialogues to improve their L2 proficiency. However, certain factors in their language-learning contexts prevented them from having that opportunity. Although they were fully aware that they needed to speak English to improve, they could interact with few speakers of the English language in their own countries or in the Canadian formal learning context. One of the participants, Kahlil, expressed the dilemma of so many learners this way: "English is like an ocean—[It is] is too difficult to swim in the whole ocean.... The main problem is we don't speak good because we only have a short time to talk to teacher. We, some people need to speak to other people" (interview, March 23, 2004). As Tarule (1996) holds: "Learning is in the conversation" (p. 282). Could technology offer opportunities for those conversations to take place, and what would be the influence of the use of technology to support such conversations on the identities and language learning of those who participated?

Stage two: Language learning using writing-based technologies

At this stage, extensive and rich qualitative data were collected from the participants using computer technology in three ways: using the Internet, working alone with a multimedia in-house military-based language-learning program, and communicating asynchronously and synchronously using a writing-based tool (Daedalus). In these essentially writing-based contexts, the findings indicated that the learning experiences of the participants varied. When the students first arrived in the immersion program, accessibility to the Internet was an issue. Military institutional control factors or a lack of technical know-how on the part of certain delegations of officers were at the root of these barriers to the Internet. In either case, the loss of control that the officers reported feeling by being excluded from using the Internet equated to their being denied access to opportunities to use the second language and led to feelings of being marginalized. Without these opportunities, many felt that their linguistic progress was jeopardized and that they were powerless in entering the dialogues that took place there, dialogues that could enable them to be a part of the North American Discourse. In the case of the Afghans, however, some of the younger officers managed to develop the skills necessary to access the Internet. The impact on their ways of acting and being were obvious in the Western ways and cultural know-how that they assumed. Armed with this cultural know-how, many of these younger officers reported that they felt a greater affiliation with the North American milieu and that they developed more empowered subjectivities when entering into native-speaker conversations. Their time on the Internet, however, revealed a less marked influence on their actual linguistic knowledge.

When the learners were first exposed to the slick, visually appealing, and supposedly interactive multimedia in-house program, most were very enthused. This enthusiasm soon waned, and teachers reported great difficulty in encouraging their students to use the software. This particular program, like many similar software programs, claim features such as interactivity, the fact that learners are able to work alone at their own paces, and accessibility at any hour to language training as powerful advantages of computers in relation to classroom language learning. Much of the hype that has surrounded this use of computers in language-learning sites has failed to consider the actual practices of the learners they purport to address. Although well-intentioned technical expertise in instructional design has been valuable in providing attractive, learner-centered material for learners to manipulate, the lack of experience of these experts with the contexts of learning a second language has resulted, as in the case of this study, in short-lived enthusiasm for working with such software. As Hodas (1993) pointed out, "teachers...are witness and partner to human development in a richer and more complex sense than educational technologists will ever be" (p. 15). Presenting a uniform product to single learners working alone ignores the fact that L2 learners have limitless interests and a need to interact through dialoguing with others in a Bakhtinian sense to learn a second language. Failure to understand the importance of human interaction to L2 learning, or any learning for that matter, on the part of computer-technology design experts makes much of this software material attractive to some in theory but counterproductive in practice.

The evolution in the computer industry to Web 2.0 technologies has positive implications for communication among language learners. Unfortunately, in formal learning institutions, such as at the sites where the study took place, the message is apparently not yet being heard. In this context, computers were being used to provide "solitary" busy work and at the same time, to deprive the officers of something that they had all professed as their singular most important reason for coming to Canada—a chance to communicate in English with other speakers of the language. Furthermore, their results could then be tabulated for those in control, for example, the teacher, to evaluate.

Pavlenko and Lantolf (2000) argued that loss of agency, in this case, while using computers in this way, is not only about "severing one's union with the world inhabited by others, it is, and perhaps more profoundly so, about losing connection to one's own inner world" (p. 165). Although Pavlenko and Lantolf were basing their comments on the narratives of immigrants to a new culture and language, their words are especially relevant in this case as well. The loss of agency that the learners voiced as they worked with the multimedia technology involved a severance from their own Polish, Hungarian, Czech, Russian, and Ukrainian worlds and from the inner speech that would allow them to negotiate with the world that was being presented on screen. Instead, they were being manipulated to think only in terms of how the technical designers thought, the sentences they chose to display on the screen, the possible answers that could be used as responses, the sequence of ideas that followed one after another, and the vocabulary that was available to them.

Both Bakhtin (1986) and Vygotsky (1962) considered inner speech a central human mental function that allows individuals to make sense of their experiences of the world. Without inner speech, then, there are no experiences, and for these learners, that means that their sociohistorical perspectives are suppressed. Bakhtin and Vygotsky also agreed that through inner speech, we organize and integrate the events that take place in our lives. Without this inner speech, the participants were unable to organize or integrate into the English-speaking world—a prerequisite for learning and developing in a second language.

In this stage of the study, in the immersion program, groups of participants used a computer software program called Daedalus to write synchronously in chat sessions and asynchronously in a forum-type activity. In these spaces, the findings indicated that for some learners who felt marginalized in the classroom, either for socioeconomic, linguistic, or cultural reasons, the use of this particular technology offered an alternative scenario. Daedalus differed considerably from other commercial software that the students had used prior to coming to Canada and indeed while in the immersion program with the multimedia program that had been developed in-house. Although the latter emphasized decontextualized practice of words and functions as a means to becoming proficient in the language, the former is based on the concept that language learning is a dialogic constructive process in the act of communicating. Although the latter group of software puts control of the material that is used and the evaluation of learners in the hands of the developer and the teacher, the former puts control of the content of the message in the hands of the learners themselves and makes evaluation a shared group activity. Although the latter treats the learner as stable and unified, the former allows for learners to change and develop, to take on new identities. Ferenc, for example, was able to overcome his usual shyness about his linguistic capabilities in speaking in the classroom by drawing on his resources as a writer and to take part in social interaction much more actively during both the synchronous and asynchronous group discussions. These activities were very liberating for Ferenc. In subsequent classes, he reported that he was continuing to be a much more active player in oral discussions. After these online discussions, he tried very hard to speak in class and even to strangers at the military base where the immersion program took place. Noteworthy is the fact that Ferenc was very pleased with his results at the end of the course, especially in speaking, despite his initial struggles.

However, this rosy picture was not uniform to all those who participated in the writing-based communication sessions. Some were unable to shed their subordinate positions in relation to other officers. Others who were very active in oral discussions in class became silenced by their lack of control over their writing abilities and reported that they felt marginalized by this weakness. Lazlo, an outgoing participative learner in the classroom, reported such feelings. He commented after one of these sessions: "For me the problem is [writing] the words. My brain works differently than others" (interview, March 29, 2004). Note that learners who experienced difficulties in this writing-based site preferred the synchronous "chat" sessions to the asynchronous e-mail ones for practicing their second language. It appears that they, too, chose the session that was more like talking and where attention to the rules of the language was less of an issue. In this writing/talking context, they were able to transfer their more outgoing L2 "speaking" identities into the chat sessions. This is not surprising, perhaps, given the impact that the enormous popularity of commercial Internet chat networks has had on literacy. In this medium, literacy is taking on new meaning, and traditional rules of the language are being challenged or ignored. With the emphasis on dialogue within digital communications, focus on form is losing ground even in first-language interactions (Baron, 2008). This point became particularly relevant to the inquiry where the aim was not only to understand identity construction using computer technology but also to respond to the participants like Lazlo and others who expressed that they felt "marginalized" and silenced in a more traditional written communication medium and yet who desperately wanted to have opportunities to "speak" their other language.

Stage three: Talking online between Europe and North America

October 19, 2004 was a memorable day for language learning for 19 participants in the study who took part in online communications between Europe and North America. This was the first day of a transatlantic connection from North America via Internet to military individuals in the Czech Republic and Romania. It was the first day that these learners could forget the barriers in their own countries that prevented them from having occasions to discuss issues that concerned them in English with a speaker of English—an opportunity that their own institutions could not provide. It was the first day that a new low-cost technology (ICI *Wave*, subsequently called *Waveasy*) allowed learners in multiple sites and in institutions with very limited budgets to synchronously converse in real time with all the added advantages that the combination of audio and visual stimuli adds to communications (see Figure 1). It was the first day that the participants at this stage of the study experienced, as they reported later, that their lives and their interests were at the heart of the learning, that their agency in their learning mattered, and that the learning made a difference. It was the first time for all of these participants to enter into a dialogue in their second language that would have an influence on their identities, their ways of viewing technology, their future language learning, and ultimately, their lives.

Figure 1: Meeting online with students in the Czech Republic, November 2004.

Despite the significance of this day, many of the learners came somewhat reluctantly to the online site because of fear of wasting precious learning time from more formalized form-focused learning, fear of not being able to perform in a second language with a speaker of the language from North America (for many of the learners, this was their first encounter with a North American), and fear of the technology. The stories of the changes that took place in virtually all of the individuals who participated in the online discussions are testimonials to the role technology, if used wisely, can play at the microlevel of the classroom and at the macrolevel of society. The stories are reflected in the words of the participants.

There is the story, for example, of Mignona, who at the outset spoke disparagingly of her abilities in speaking English, despite the fact that she did translation, of her earlier educational experiences, of her personal and cultural identity as a woman, as a Romanian, and as a member of the military. Her remarks made in the discussions and in follow-up e-mails early on in the sessions reflect these sentiments: "I am self-taught. That's why I don't speak so well," adding, in an attempt to include others in her observation, "We are like intelligent dogs. We know our limitations. It's a [national Romanian] complex" (Mignona, field notes, October 20, 2004) and "I am a civilian, a woman and a blonde in a military system? Who would pay attention to what I have to say?" As the discussions evolved, Mignona observed, "I realize that my mistakes [in English] reduce day by day. I think it is a good thing" (online notes, November 2, 2004). Mignona was not only making progress linguistically through the online discussions, but at the end of these online sessions, I noted a considerable change in her identity as well. Her comments as she reflected on her future attest to this change: "The final step will to be to apply to a UN job....So I'm getting busier and busier (and, of course more and more daring) every day. That is why, by the end of 2009 (if I live that long and I'm a little bit lucky) you will be talking to a UN employee working all over the world. No matter what, I'll struggle. Life is a continuous fight, isn't it?" (e-mail, November 10, 2004). The strength and determination that Mignona displays in this excerpt contrasts sharply with the self-effacing and self-doubting person her previous e-mails had shown. Whether this change came as a result of the discussions we had in English, one cannot be certain. However, having a forum via CALL to discuss and question the various power structures—political, historical, and military—that controlled her life from her perception is noteworthy.

Opportunities previous to the online sessions to speak English in international exercises had left George, a Czech, silenced by fear that he would make mistakes: "I could spoke to them many times but I had a fear. I was shy to speak to someone. I made many mistakes, so I was a silent boy" (interview, November 23, 2004). As the online sessions continued, he began to look critically at the political, cultural, and pedagogical contexts in his life that had resulted in his fear to speak: "Now we have a chance to speak, before we didn't" (field notes, November 2, 2004). In the end, he reported: "Yes it was a big difference two months ago and today.... I have no fear to speak. It's excellent" (interview, November 23, 2004). He further noted,

> I saw many people and many groups. I was mostly in all discussions and I can see that people in second and third time discussions were not so much scared as before. I think this discussion is the best maybe not just for learn more words but break the scared for speak, you know what I mean. I think it is the most for me it's the most important thing (group interview, November 22, 2004).

I understood George's comments of "breaking the scared to speak" to mean much more than a simple change in linguistic confidence. The impact of being silenced by the historical, cultural, and political realities on many of the participants in the study was hard to shed even after a decade of transition to democracy. Finding his voice and witnessing others doing the same in the context of learning another language, for George, *that* indeed was "the most important thing." Mignona, the Romanian, observed the impact of the past political situation on her life and those of others who lived during the communist time: "We look into the future but sometimes forget that many things from the past (which we sometimes consider them as unimportant details) influenced and still influence our life" (online and e-mail, November 12, 2004).

Leo, a quiet, highly academic Romanian officer, attributed his feelings of being marginalized in the language classroom to early experiences in a formal language-learning context. These experiences, he felt, had marked him for life. To him, apparently, any classroom context was counterproductive to learning a language. He explained: "All the time school is for me very difficult for me to make connection [to life]" (interview notes, November 25, 2004). However, he, too, changed in the course of the online discussions and attributed these changes to the agency he felt in his learning. In an interview with Leo at the end of the course, he was very explicit about how the changes in his fluency had taken place:

> The online course [discussion sessions] is for me very helpful because you treat me like an equal.... I say a word if I can, you put me another question. I understand that question, not very difficult for me. You find the correct words for me. I lose shy, I lose fear and slow day by day I improve my explanation, my discourse. I remember last day, I speak many sentences, not stopping—fluently. That not happen in the first day. The first day I say very short sentences, very difficult for me. (interview, November 26, 2004)

In the intricate and complex way that individuals communicate, Leo saw our dialogic interaction as a mediating process through which he was able to construct linguistic knowledge or competence and at the same time (re)construct a more powerful position in the group of learners than he had had in the beginning. "I lose shy. I lose fear," he observed. From this more powerful position, he was able to claim his voice in a group where, as a latecomer, he was initially silenced by his lack of linguistic skills compared to the others. In using his second language to construct new meanings, he began to improve in it.

However, Leo's recognition that he had improved in English brought more than the satisfaction that comes with learning a second language. Later, in a face-to-face interview, he indicated that what he felt was the real significance of the improvement he had made in English during the online oral sessions. In the Czech Republic, George had suggested a similar idea when he expressed how improving in his language online "opened new doors" for him. In the following excerpt, Leo was able to verbalize the significance to him of those "new doors" being opened:

> For me it is interesting how experienced lived people in that place and for me it is a comparison. I live in Romania. I live in the 21st century. I had a grandfather. He is killed in the Russian fields in the war. You, what [who was] your grandfather? What kind of job you have? What kind of people? What kind of children? How your children understand you? It [Being able to communicate in English with others] is for me another experience. I put that experience in addition. It is for me like a book, like an open book. One chapter is good; one sheet [page] is good. It is for me an addition to my chapter and I improve my experience, my human experience. It is good for me, good for my children to explain in another way some kind of situation, because I know what's happened here what's happened there. It is many points of view. It is a point of view of mine It's a point of view of an American. It's a point of view of a Czech. It's a collection of a point of views. It is better for me in my way to choose the way for me is correct. (interview, November 26, 2004)

Leo's change in identity and language learning was valuable to him because it allowed him a key to interacting with others who were different than him and to compare his life with theirs. For Freire, "the foundation stone of the whole [educational] process is human curiosity. This is what makes me question, act, ask again, recognize" (1998, p. 189). Each interaction is a new story, a new page to add to Leo's book of life and act of being. Using English to interact with others is more important than merely sharing knowledge. It allows him to see from many perspectives, to question, to try to understand many realities, and to create, of his own choosing, new possibilities for himself and his children. Norton (2005) remarked that the desire for English, like literacy, is based on a desire on the part of many in evolving nations "to engage with the international community from a position of strength rather than weakness" (p. 237).

Summary

The role of computer technology needs to be (re)examined to determine its influence on identity construction and investment in learning in L2 learning settings. The stories related here and the many others that have had to be left untold have demonstrated that for the learners in this study, computers sometimes acted as a means to marginalize and objectify them, depriving them of agency and convincing them of their "intrinsic inferiority," and at other times, computers served as an interface for empowering conversations between learners of English and speakers of English. When computers were used for transmitting facts about the language, for manipulating words and structures in drill exercises, or for supporting testing, this particular group of participants expressed the feeling that that their symbolic capital (Bourdieu, 1998)—their social, intellectual and cultural funds of knowledge (Moll & Dworin, 1996)—seemed of little value. They claimed that they quickly forgot or felt they could not use the knowledge that was presented. However, when computers were used specifically for communication and the exchange of ideas or the acting out of "different types of selves" (Gee, 1996), evidence showed that that had implications on both micro- and macrolevels. On the microlevel, the conversations offered several of the participants opportunities for constructing more empowered identities and greater investment in language learning. The way computers were used in this scenario enabled communication through not only written but also audio/video data transmission. The topics of the discussions were related to the lived experiences of the learners. On the macrolevel, computers allowed some participants to use these conversations to read their lives in a critical way. They looked critically at the way that they had been historically governed, the system of education that had deprived them of the opportunities they desired, and the military jobs that ignored their intellectual capital. Using the conversations to dialogically (re)construct their lives, some of the participants were able to envision new possibilities and to connect their lives beyond their national borders to the global community. I make the case that when computers are used to support the kinds of conversations in which this particular group of learners participated, new understandings can be generated and new possibilities can be provided for global communities of learning in a second language.

Evolving stories

The study reported here is evolving, and so are the stories. The international discussions with central Europe are sustained, but now, Canadian regional and interregional contexts have been added. The vast expanses of Canada with a public service mandated to offer bilingual services, in a context that is increasingly multicultural, and that spreads from small coastal fishing towns to northern outposts to forested mountain park reserves offers new challenges for the questions that underline the original study: What are the tensions when learners in this site learn the other official language? What influence does and can computer technology have on the identities and learning experiences of this latest group as they negotiate their language learning?

Figure 2: Discussions online with Canadian civil servants, March 2008.

Figure 3: Discussions online with Czech military participants, February 2008.

The faces have changed (see Figure 2); the stories are naturally different. These stories reflect the myriad identities and life experiences of the individuals that they represent. Yet, many of the themes that surface in these latter stories are familiar, with many parallels. I see a parallel, for example, between Sergiy, with his need to understand the disjuncture between his efforts and motivation to learn English and his disappointing final test results, and emotionally distraught civil servants who appeared in my office looking for answers to why their hard work and drive to learn the other language had resulted in failure on the official government tests. I see parallels between the Eastern and Central European military officers, with limited access to practicing the language displaying disadvantaged positions and a reluctance to engage in opportunities to use English, and Canadian civil servants living outside major centers in Canada who lack access to quality language courses, who express frustration at their powerlessness in being denied opportunities for advancement, and who express uneasiness in speaking to clients in the other language. I see parallels, for example, between Vali, unwilling to speak for fear of making errors, attributable, some would argue, to the form-focused nature of his former language-learning experiences with technology software, and the young Canadians seeking employment in the government yet lacking language required in the government despite years of formal form-focused language training supported by information technology.

Can the video-based Web-conferencing technology used in this study and the kinds of discussion-based CMC approaches to learning that this particular Web 2.0 supports influence the identities and learning of these new groups of participants? Can such discussions online empower these learners in similar ways? These questions are beginning to be answered in encouraging ways. I believe that it will take not only the stories related here but the evolving stories of the current participants and the many more stories yet to be told before educators, researchers, and policy makers awaken to the power that computer technology has to influence the identities, learning, and global community-building of present and future generations of language learners.

References

Bakhtin, M. M. (1981). *The dialogic imagination*. Austin: University of Texas Press.

Bakhtin, M. M. (1986). *Speech genres and other late essays*. Austin: University of Texas Press.

Baron, N. S. (2008). *Always on: Language in an online mobile world*. New York: Oxford University Press.

Belz, J. A. (2007). The role of computer mediation in the instruction and development of L2 pragmatic competence. *Annual Review of Applied Linguistics, 27*, 45–75.

Black, R. W. (2006). Language, culture and identity in online fanfiction. *E-learning, 3*(2), 170–184.

Bourdieu, P. (1998). *Acts of resistance: Against the new myths of our time*. Cambridge, England: Polity Press.

Chapelle, C. A. (2007). Technology and second language acquisition. *Annual Review of Applied Linguistics, 27*, 98–114.

Charbonneau-Gowdy, P. (2005). *Forbidden fruit: Identity, power and investment issues in learning a second language through computer-mediated communication*. Unpublished doctoral dissertation, McGill University, Montreal, Quebec, Canada.

Daedalus Integrated Writing Environment [computer software]. (1997). Available from The Daedalus Group: http://www.daedalus.com

Donato, R. (2000). Sociocultural contributions to understanding the foreign and second language classroom. In J. P. Lantolf (Ed.), *Sociocultural theory and second language learning* (pp. 27–50). Oxford, England: Oxford University Press.

Feenberg, A. (1991). *Critical theory of technology*. New York: Oxford University Press.

Feenberg, A. (2003). *Modernity and technology*. New York: Oxford University Press.

Foucault, M. (1980). *Power/knowledge: Selected interviews and other writings, 1972–1977*. (C. Gordon, Ed.; C. Gordon, L. Marshall, J. Mephan, & M. Soper, Trans.). New York: Pantheon Books.

Foucault, M. (2000). *Power/Michel Foucault*. (J. D. Faubion, Ed.). New York: New Press.

Freire, P. (1998). *Pedagogy of freedom*. New York: Rowman & Littlefield Publishers.

Gee, J. (1996). *Social linguistics and literacies: Ideology in discourses*. Bristol, PA: Taylor & Francis.

Gee, J. (1997). Thinking, learning and reading. In D. Kirshner & J. A. Whitson (Eds.), *Situated cognition: Social, semiotic, and psychological perspectives* (pp. 235–260). Mahwah, NJ: Erlbaum.

Hawisher, G., & Selfe, C. L. (Eds.). (1991). *Evolving perspectives on computers and composition studies*. Urbana, IL: National Council of Teachers of English.

Hodas, S. (1993). Technology refusal and the organizational culture of schools. *Education Policy Analysis Archives, 1*(10), 1–19.

Kress, G. R. (1998). Languages as social practice. In G. R. Kress (Ed.), *Communication and culture* (pp. 82–104). Kensington, Australia: University of New South Wales Press.

Kress, G. R. (2003, 2004). *Literacy in the new media age* (1st & 2nd eds.). New York: Routledge.

Kress, G. R., & Van Leeuwen, T. (2001). *Multimodal discourse: The modes and media of contemporary communication*. London: Edward Arnold.

Lantolf, J. P., & Appel, G. (Eds.). (1994). *Vygotskian approaches to second language research*. Norwood, NJ: Ablex Press.

Lantolf, J. P. & Pavlenko, A. (2000). Second language learning as participation and the (re) construction of selves. In J. P. Lantolf (Ed.), *Sociocultural theory and second language learning* (pp. 155–178). Oxford, England: Oxford University Press.

Lefebvre, H. (1991). *The production of space* (D. Nicholson-Smith, Trans.). Cambridge, England: Blackwell.

Maguire, M. H. (1994). Getting beyond programs and instructional time in second language teaching and learning: Who is mediating what? For whom? In what context? *Journal of the CAAL, 16*(1), 105–123.

Maguire, M. H. (1997). Shared and negotiated territories: The socio-cultural embeddedness of children's acts of meaning. In A. Pollard, D. Thiessen, & A. Filer (Eds.), *Children and their curriculum: The perspectives of primary and elementary children* (pp. 51–80). London: Falmer Press.

Maguire, M. H., & Graves, B. (2001). Speaking personalities in primary school children's L2 writing. *TESOL Quarterly, 35*, 561–593.

Moll, L. C., & Dworin, J. (1996). Biliteracy development in classrooms: Social dynamics and cultural possibilities. In D. Hicks (Ed.), *Discourse, learning and schooling* (pp. 221–245). Cambridge, England: Cambridge University Press.

Norton, B. (2000). *Identity and language learning: Gender, ethnicity and educational change*. London: Longman/Pearson Education Press.

Norton, B. (2005). A portrait of literacy from the youth millennium project. In J. Anderson, M. Kendrick, T. Rogers, & S. Smythe (Eds.), *Portraits of literacy across families, communities and schools* (pp. 225–239). Mahwah, NJ: Lawrence Erlbaum Associates Publishers.

Nunan, D. (2003). The impact of English as a global language on educational policies and practices in the Asia-Pacific region. *TESOL Quarterly, 37*, 589–613.

O'Dowd, R. (2006). The use of videoconferencing and e-mail as mediators of intercultural student ethnography. In J. Beltz & S. L. Thorne (Eds.), *Internet-mediated intercultural foreign language education* (pp. 86–119). Boston: Thomson Heinle Publishers.

Pavlenko, A., & Lantolf, J. (2000). Second language learning as participation and the (re) construction of selves. In J. P. Lantolf (Ed.), *Sociocultural theory and second language learning* (pp. 155–178). Oxford, England: Oxford University Press.

Ricento, T. (Ed.). (2000). *Ideology, politics and language policies: Focus on English*. Philadelphia: John Benjamins Publishers.

Salaberry, M. R. (2000). Pedagogical design of computer-mediated communication tasks: Learning objectives and technological capabilities. *Modern Language Journal, 84*, 28–37.

Selfe, C. L. (1999). Lest we think the revolution is a revolution: Images of technology and the nature of change. In G. Hawisher & C. L. Selfe (Eds.), *Passions, pedagogies, and 21st century technologies* (pp. 292–322). Logan: Utah State University Press.

Shepherd, J. (2008). Cheating gets closer examination. *Guardian Weekly, 179*(1), 1–2.

Tarule, J. M. (1996). Voices in dialogue: Collaborative ways of knowing. In N. Goldberger, J. Tarule, B. Clinchy, & M. Belenky (Eds.), *Knowledge, difference and power: Women's ways of knowing* (pp. 274–304). New York: Basic Books.

Thorne, S. (2000). Language acquisition theory and the truth(s) about relativity. In J. Lantolf (Ed.), *Sociocultural theory and second language learning* (pp. 219–244). Oxford, England: Oxford University Press.

Thorne, S. L. (2003). Artifacts and cultures-of-use in intercultural communication. *Language Learning and Technology, 7*(2), 38–67.

Vygotsky, L. S. (1962). *Thought and language*. Cambridge, MA: Harvard University Press.

Vygotsky, L. S. (1978). *Mind in society: The development of higher psychological processes*. (M. Cole, V. John-Steiner, S. Scribner, & E. Souberman, Eds.). Cambridge, MA: Harvard University Press.

Vygotsky, L. S. (1989). Concrete human psychology. *Soviet Psychology, 27*(2), 53–77.

Vygotsky, L. S., & Luria, A. (1994). Tool and symbol in child development. In R. van de Veer & J. Valsiner (Eds.), *The Vygotsky reader* (pp. 99–174). Cambridge, MA: Blackwell.

Warschauer, M. (1999). *Electronic literacies: Language, culture, and power in online education*. Mahwah, NJ: Erlbaum.

Warschauer, M. (2000). The changing global economy and the future of English teaching. *TESOL Quarterly, 34*, 511–535.

Warschauer, M. (2003). *Technology and social inclusion: Rethinking the digital divide*. Cambridge, MA: The MIT Press.

Warschauer, M., & De Florio-Hansen, I. (2003). Multilingualism, identity and the Internet. In A. Hu & I. De Florio-Hansen (Eds.), *Multiple identity and multilingualism* (pp. 155–179). Tubengin, Denmark: Stauffenburg.

Waveasy [Computer software]. (2007). Available from ICI *Wave* Telecommunications: http://www.waveasy.com/

Weedon, C. (1997). *Feminist practice and poststructuralist theory*. London: Blackwell.

Wertsch, J. (1991). *Voices of the mind: A sociocultural approach to mediated action*. Cambridge, MA: Harvard University Press.

Wertsch, J. (1998). *Mind as action*. New York: Oxford University Press.

About the Contributors

Editors

Raquel Oxford teaches courses in second language education at the University of Wisconsin–Milwaukee, where she is an assistant professor of curriculum and instruction. She is also director of the world language teacher certification program and an associate editor for *Hispania*, the official journal of the American Association of Teachers of Spanish and Portuguese (AATSP). She received her PhD from the University of North Texas in curriculum and instruction/computer education. Her research interests include second language teacher preparation and mentoring, technology integration in second language instruction, multicultural education, and schooling for language minority students.

Jeffrey Oxford is a professor of Spanish and chair of the Department of Spanish and Portuguese at the University of Wisconsin–Milwaukee. He has long been a proponent of technology in the classroom, has taught several blended (hybrid) courses, and more recently led his department in developing blended courses as a part of the normal first-year language course offerings. He has published numerous articles, books, and edited volumes, including a conversational Spanish textbook, *Conversar para aprender.* He received his PhD from Texas Tech University, and his current research interests include nineteenth century naturalism, social justice, and Mexico/Texas border issues.

Authors

Nancy Bird-Soto is an assistant professor of Spanish at the University of Wisconsin–Milwaukee, where she teaches Latin American and U.S. Latino/a literature. In 2006, she collaborated on the "Personalidades de la cultura hispánica" podcasting project at the University of Wisconsin–Madison. She has published articles on Puerto Rican writer-activist Luisa Capetillo and Chicana playwright Josefina López. In early 2009, her book *Sara la obrera y otros cuentos: El repertorio femenino de Ana Roqué* was published by The Edwin Mellen Press. She is currently part of a research cluster on Arabic for French and Spanish speakers.

Paula Charbonneau-Gowdy is a senior advisor to the Canada School of Public Service, a department of the government of Canada, on matters related to learning development and technology. Her 30 years of experience span many levels from early childhood to adolescents and adults in university, government, and the private sector. For the last seven years, she has concentrated her efforts on researching the influence of technology on learner identity and investment in language learning. She has published a book on using video-based web conferencing. She received her PhD from McGill University.

Gloria Jeanne Bodtorf Clark is currently an associate professor of humanities and Spanish at Penn State University, Harrisburg campus, teaching Spanish language and humanities courses. She is also a member of the graduate humanities faculty, with a specialty in Latin American literature and culture. Her latest book is an edited version of *La verdad sospechosa* by Juan Ruíz de Alarcón, published in 2002 by Juan de la Cuesta Press. With Brett Bixler, also of Penn State, she established the Hacienda in Second Life for Penn State Harrisburg and currently teaches and researches pedagogical applications of Second Life for foreign language teaching.

Jessamine Cooke-Plagwitz is an associate professor in the Department of Foreign Languages and Literatures at Northern Illinois University, where she directs the department's graduate certificate program in foreign language instructional technology. She teaches courses in technology-enhanced foreign language instruction and German language and culture. Her research interests include online L2 instruction in virtual environments, authentic assessment models, and technology-enhanced constructivist learning models. She has also published and presented widely on these topics. She is the co-editor of Heinle's *Teaching with Technology* volume in their Professional Series in Language Instruction. She earned her PhD from Queen's University in Kingston, Ontario.

Lara Ducate received her PhD in Germanic studies with a focus on foreign language pedagogy from the University of Texas at Austin. She is currently an assistant professor of German at the University of South Carolina where she teaches courses on German language and culture as well as teaching methods. Her research interests and publications are in the area of computer-mediated communication—including blogs, podcasts, and wikis—and teacher training, and she has co-edited a volume on computer assisted language learning entitled *Calling on CALL: From Theory and Research to New Directions in Foreign Language Teaching.*

Clara Inés Lozano Espejo received her MA in Spanish linguistics from Instituto Caro y Cuervo in Bogotá, and is currently teaching English and applied linguistics in the English program of the education department at Universidad La Gran Colombia. She also teaches English as a foreign language at a Costa Rica public school, and has presented workshops for teachers in the "Maestros que Aprenden de Maestros" (Teachers Learning From Teachers) program including demonstrating the use of blogs in teaching and learning. Her current research interest is in the development of projects that involve the exchange of cultural and social information through the use of technology.

Carolin Fuchs, PhD, is a lecturer in the TESOL program in the Department of Arts & Humanities at Teachers College, Columbia University. Her research has primarily focused on technology-enhanced language teaching and learning, electronic literacy skills, task-based language teaching, and language play. She has conducted a number of international computer-mediated communication projects with various institutions in countries such as the U.S., the U.K., Poland, and Germany in order to connect students for the purpose of language study and to form online communities of practice among student teachers, teachers, and researchers.

Senta Goertler (PhD, University of Arizona) is an assistant professor of second language studies and German at Michigan State University (MSU). Currently she serves on the executive board of the Computer-Assisted Language Instruction Consortium (CALICO) and is the co-chair of its computer-mediated communication (CMC) special interest group. Together with Paula Winke, she edited the 2008 CALICO monograph entitled *Opening doors through distance language education: Principles, perspectives, and practices*. Her research interest is computer-mediated language learning, particularly the role of CMC for language development. At MSU, she teaches language courses, as well as courses on SLA theory, pedagogy, and technology-enhanced language learning. She is also the German faculty liaison for MSU's Community Language School.

Vanessa Lazo-Wilson is a former faculty member of Spanish and foreign language teaching methodology at Eastern Washington University and is currently an independent scholar. She received her PhD in foreign language education under the umbrella of curriculum and instruction in May of 2007 from the University of Texas at Austin. Her research interests encompass innovations and best practices in modern language teaching, K–12 teacher education, and technology integration in and across the curriculum. Dr. Lazo-Wilson currently resides in San Antonio, Texas with her husband and two daughters.

Lara Lomicka is an associate professor of French and linguistics at the University of South Carolina. Her publications appear in the *Calico Journal*, *Language Learning & Technology*, *Foreign Language Annals*, and *System*, among others. She has edited two volumes on technology: *Teaching with Technology* (Heinle/Cengage) and *The Next Generation: Social Networking and Online Collaboration in Foreign Language Learning* (CALICO Monograph Series). She was awarded the 2008 ACTFL/Cengage Learning Award for Excellence in Foreign Language Instruction Using Technology. Her research interests include technology, intercultural communication, and foreign language education.

Claire McCourt is a recent graduate of the University of North Texas, where she received an MA in French and completed her thesis on "Learner use of French second-person pronouns in synchronous electronic communication." She currently is an instructor of French at the Pennsylvania State University at Altoona. Her research and teaching interests include the use of technology as a tool for communication and evaluation in second language learning environments.

Ana Niño is currently a senior language tutor in Spanish as a foreign language at the Language Centre of The University of Manchester. She coordinates and teaches general and specialized (business and medical) Spanish courses and has also been developing e-learning resources to enhance the students' language learning experience. She has published a book on grammar and communicative resources for learners of Spanish and several articles on applied linguistics (translation, computers and language teaching and e-learning). She received her PhD from The University of Manchester. Her current research interests include the use of virtual learning environments for language teaching and learning purposes.

Patricia Rengel is a dissertator teaching Spanish at the University of Wisconsin–Madison. She developed a web page, "Personalidades de la cultura hispánica," of audio and video podcasts with interviews ranging from artists (musicians, sculptors, writers) to victims of state terrorism in Latin America and as a result won a campus-wide teaching award, "Innovation in Teaching." She also worked on a technology project (T4 FLP) that developed an interactive, listening, and viewing comprehension program for teaching Spanish using video and audio.

Lauren Rosen is currently the director of the University of Wisconsin System Collaborative Language Program. For the past twenty years, she has been integrating technology into her language courses. In addition, she works closely with language educators in developing engaging collaborative approaches to technology integration into a variety of language learning environments including both traditional and distance courses. She has published numerous articles on the integration of Internet technology for learning world languages. She received her MEd from the University of Minnesota. Her current research focus is on the impact of Web 2.0 technologies in language learning.

Rémi A. van Compernolle is a PhD student in applied linguistics and a research assistant for the Center for Language Acquisition at the Pennsylvania State University. His current research interests include integrating the use of Internet technologies in the second language classroom as one of many types of tools for assessing, evaluating, and teaching for sociolinguistic and pragmatic development. In addition, he has published a number of articles on native speaker sociolinguistic and pragmatic variation in a wide range of computer-mediated communication contexts, focusing primarily on pronominal, morphosyntactic, and orthographic variation.

Jane Blyth Warren's current research involves using online digital portfolios and podcasts to improve oral English skills in Japanese university students. During the 2008–2009 academic year, she was a visiting researcher in the department of culture and information science at Doshisha University in Kyoto, Japan. Warren has taught both Japanese and English as a second language at Kalamazoo College and Indiana State University, as well as Japanese at Moorhead State University and Valley City State University. She received her PhD from Indiana State University in curriculum and instruction with a focus on language education.

Lawrence Williams is an associate professor of foreign languages and literatures (French) and director of curriculum and assessment in the Department of Foreign Languages and Literatures at the University of North Texas, where he teaches, among other things, discourse analysis, French linguistics, and foreign language teaching methods. His research focuses on the use of new technologies as tools for communication and foreign language education as well as sociolinguistic and pragmatic features of French discourse in both educational and non-educational contexts.

Pragmatics & Interaction

Gabriele Kasper, series editor

Pragmatics & Interaction ("P&I"), a refereed series sponsored by the University of Hawai'i National Foreign Language Resource Center, publishes research on topics in pragmatics and discourse as social interaction from a wide variety of theoretical and methodological perspectives. P&I welcomes particularly studies on languages spoken in the Asian-Pacific region.

TALK-IN-INTERACTION: MULTILINGUAL PERSPECTIVES

KATHLEEN BARDOVI-HARLIG, CÉSAR FÉLIX-BRASDEFER, & ALWIYA S. OMAR (EDITORS), 2006

This volume offers original studies of interaction in a range of languages and language varieties, including Chinese, English, Japanese, Korean, Spanish, Swahili, Thai, and Vietnamese; monolingual and bilingual interactions, and activities designed for second or foreign language learning. Conducted from the perspectives of conversation analysis and membership categorization analysis, the chapters examine ordinary conversation and institutional activities in face-to-face, telephone, and computer-mediated environments..

430 pp., ISBN(10): 0–8248–3137–3, ISBN(13): 978–0–8248–3137–0 $30.

Pragmatics & Language Learning

Gabriele Kasper, series editor

Pragmatics & Language Learning ("PLL"), a refereed series sponsored by the National Foreign Language Resource Center, publishes selected papers from the biannual International Pragmatics & Language Learning conference under the editorship of the conference hosts and the series editor. Check the NFLRC website for upcoming PLL conferences and PLL volumes.

PRAGMATICS AND LANGUAGE LEARNING VOLUME 11

KATHLEEN BARDOVI-HARLIG, CÉSAR FÉLIX-BRASDEFER, & ALWIYA S. OMAR (EDITORS), 2006

This volume features cutting-edge theoretical and empirical research on pragmatics and language learning among a wide-variety of learners in diverse learning contexts from a variety of language backgrounds (English, German, Japanese, Persian, and Spanish) and target languages (English, German, Japanese, Kiswahili, and Spanish). This collection of papers from researchers around the world includes critical appraisals on the role of formulas in interlanguage pragmatics and speech-act research from a conversation-analytic perspective. Empirical studies examine learner data using innovative methods of analysis and investigate issues in pragmatic development and the instruction of pragmatics.

430 pp., ISBN(10): 0–8248–3137–3, ISBN(13): 978–0–8248–3137–0 $30.

NFLRC Monographs

Richard Schmidt, series editor

Monographs of the National Foreign Language Resource Center present the findings of recent work in applied linguistics that is of relevance to language teaching and learning (with a focus on the less commonly-taught languages of Asia and the Pacific) and are of particular interest to foreign language educators, applied linguists, and researchers. Prior to 2006, these monographs were published as "SLTCC Technical Reports."

CASE STUDIES IN FOREIGN LANGUAGE PLACEMENT: PRACTICES AND POSSIBILITIES

Thom Hudson & Martyn Clark (Editors), 2008

Although most language programs make placement decisions on the basis of placement tests, there is surprisingly little published about different contexts and systems of placement testing. The present volume contains case studies of placement programs in foreign language programs at the tertiary level across the United States. The different programs span the spectrum from large programs servicing hundreds of students annually to small language programs with very few students. The contributions to this volume address such issues as how the size of the program, presence or absence of heritage learners, and population changes affect language placement decisions.

201pp., ISBN 0–9800459–0–8 $40.

CHINESE AS A HERITAGE LANGUAGE: FOSTERING ROOTED WORLD CITIZENRY

Agnes Weiyun He & Yun Xiao (Editors), 2008

Thirty-two scholars examine the socio-cultural, cognitive-linguistic, and educational-institutional trajectories along which Chinese as a Heritage Language may be acquired, maintained and developed. They draw upon developmental psychology, functional linguistics, linguistic and cultural anthropology, discourse analysis, orthography analysis, reading research, second language acquisition, and bilingualism. This volume aims to lay a foundation for theories, models, and master scripts to be discussed, debated, and developed, and to stimulate research and enhance teaching both within and beyond Chinese language education.

280pp., ISBN 978–0–8248–3286–5 $40.

PERSPECTIVES ON TEACHING CONNECTED SPEECH TO SECOND LANGUAGE SPEAKERS

James Dean Brown & Kimi Kondo-Brown (Editors), 2006

This book is a collection of fourteen articles on connected speech of interest to teachers, researchers, and materials developers in both ESL/EFL (ten chapters focus on connected speech in English) and Japanese (four chapters focus on Japanese connected speech). The fourteen chapters are divided up into five sections:

- What do we know so far about teaching connected speech?
- Does connected speech instruction work?
- How should connected speech be taught in English?
- How should connected speech be taught in Japanese?
- How should connected speech be tested?

290 pp., ISBN(10) 0–8248–3136–5, ISBN(13) 978–0–8248–3136–3 $38.

CORPUS LINGUISTICS FOR KOREAN LANGUAGE LEARNING AND TEACHING

ROBERT BLEY-VROMAN & HYUNSOOK KO (EDITORS), 2006

Dramatic advances in personal-computer technology have given language teachers access to vast quantities of machine-readable text, which can be analyzed with a view toward improving the basis of language instruction. Corpus linguistics provides analytic techniques and practical tools for studying language in use. This volume provides both an introductory framework for the use of corpus linguistics for language teaching and examples of its application for Korean teaching and learning. The collected papers cover topics in Korean syntax, lexicon, and discourse, and second language acquisition research, always with a focus on application in the classroom. An overview of Korean corpus linguistics tools and available Korean corpora are also included.

265 pp., ISBN 0–8248–3062–8 $25.

NEW TECHNOLOGIES AND LANGUAGE LEARNING: CASES IN THE LESS COMMONLY TAUGHT LANGUAGES

CAROL ANNE SPREEN (EDITOR), 2002

In recent years, the National Security Education Program (NSEP) has supported an increasing number of programs for teaching languages using different technological media. This compilation of case study initiatives funded through the NSEP Institutional Grants Program presents a range of technology-based options for language programming that will help universities make more informed decisions about teaching less commonly taught languages. The eight chapters describe how different types of technologies are used to support language programs (i.e., Web, ITV, and audio- or video-based materials), discuss identifiable trends in elanguage learning, and explore how technology addresses issues of equity, diversity, and opportunity. This book offers many lessons learned and decisions made as technology changes and learning needs become more complex.

188 pp., ISBN 0–8248–2634–5 $25.

AN INVESTIGATION OF SECOND LANGUAGE TASK-BASED PERFORMANCE ASSESSMENTS

JAMES DEAN BROWN, THOM HUDSON, JOHN M. NORRIS, & WILLIAM BONK, 2002

This volume describes the creation of performance assessment instruments and their validation (based on work started in a previous monograph). It begins by explaining the test and rating scale development processes and the administration of the resulting three seven-task tests to 90 university level EFL and ESL students. The results are examined in terms of (a) the effects of test revision; (b) comparisons among the task-dependent, task-independent, and self-rating scales; and (c) reliability and validity issues.

240 pp., ISBN 0–8248–2633–7 $25.

MOTIVATION AND SECOND LANGUAGE ACQUISITION

ZOLTÁN DÖRNYEI & RICHARD SCHMIDT (EDITORS), 2001

This volume—the second in this series concerned with motivation and foreign language learning—includes papers presented in a state-of-the-art colloquium on L2 motivation at the

American Association for Applied Linguistics (Vancouver, 2000) and a number of specially commissioned studies. The 20 chapters, written by some of the best known researchers in the field, cover a wide range of theoretical and research methodological issues, and also offer empirical results (both qualitative and quantitative) concerning the learning of many different languages (Arabic, Chinese, English, Filipino, French, German, Hindi, Italian, Japanese, Russian, and Spanish) in a broad range of learning contexts (Bahrain, Brazil, Canada, Egypt, Finland, Hungary, Ireland, Israel, Japan, Spain, and the US).

520 pp., ISBN 0–8248–2458–X $25.

A FOCUS ON LANGUAGE TEST DEVELOPMENT: EXPANDING THE LANGUAGE PROFICIENCY CONSTRUCT ACROSS A VARIETY OF TESTS

Thom Hudson & James Dean Brown (Editors), 2001

This volume presents eight research studies that introduce a variety of novel, non-traditional forms of second and foreign language assessment. To the extent possible, the studies also show the entire test development process, warts and all. These language testing projects not only demonstrate many of the types of problems that test developers run into in the real world but also afford the reader unique insights into the language test development process.

230 pp., ISBN 0–8248–2351–6 $20.

STUDIES ON KOREAN IN COMMUNITY SCHOOLS

Dong-Jae Lee, Sookeun Cho, Miseon Lee, Minsun Song, & William O'Grady (Editors), 2000

The papers in this volume focus on language teaching and learning in Korean community schools. Drawing on innovative experimental work and research in linguistics, education, and psychology, the contributors address issues of importance to teachers, administrators, and parents. Topics covered include childhood bilingualism, Korean grammar, language acquisition, children's literature, and language teaching methodology. [in Korean]

256 pp., ISBN 0–8248–2352–4 $20.

A COMMUNICATIVE FRAMEWORK FOR INTRODUCTORY JAPANESE LANGUAGE CURRICULA

Washington State Japanese Language Curriculum Guidelines Committee, 2000

In recent years the number of schools offering Japanese nationwide has increased dramatically. Because of the tremendous popularity of the Japanese language and the shortage of teachers, quite a few untrained, non-native and native teachers are in the classrooms and are expected to teach several levels of Japanese. These guidelines are intended to assist individual teachers and professional associations throughout the United States in designing Japanese language curricula. They are meant to serve as a framework from which language teaching can be expanded and are intended to allow teachers to enhance and strengthen the quality of Japanese language instruction.

168 pp., ISBN 0–8248–2350–8 $20.

FOREIGN LANGUAGE TEACHING AND MINORITY LANGUAGE EDUCATION

Kathryn A. Davis (Editor), 1999

This volume seeks to examine the potential for building relationships among foreign language, bilingual, and ESL programs towards fostering bilingualism. Part I of the volume examines the sociopolitical contexts for language partnerships, including:

- obstacles to developing bilingualism
- implications of acculturation, identity, and language issues for linguistic minorities.
- the potential for developing partnerships across primary, secondary, and tertiary institutions

Part II of the volume provides research findings on the Foreign language partnership project designed to capitalize on the resources of immigrant students to enhance foreign language learning.

152 pp., ISBN 0–8248–2067–3 $20.

DESIGNING SECOND LANGUAGE PERFORMANCE ASSESSMENTS

JOHN M. NORRIS, JAMES DEAN BROWN, THOM HUDSON, & JIM YOSHIOKA, 1998, 2000

This technical report focuses on the decision-making potential provided by second language performance assessments. The authors first situate performance assessment within a broader discussion of alternatives in language assessment and in educational assessment in general. They then discuss issues in performance assessment design, implementation, reliability, and validity. Finally, they present a prototype framework for second language performance assessment based on the integration of theoretical underpinnings and research findings from the task-based language teaching literature, the language testing literature, and the educational measurement literature. The authors outline test and item specifications, and they present numerous examples of prototypical language tasks. They also propose a research agenda focusing on the operationalization of second language performance assessments.

248 pp., ISBN 0–8248–2109–2 $20.

SECOND LANGUAGE DEVELOPMENT IN WRITING: MEASURES OF FLUENCY, ACCURACY, AND COMPLEXITY

KATE WOLFE-QUINTERO, SHUNJI INAGAKI, & HAE-YOUNG KIM, 1998, 2002

In this book, the authors analyze and compare the ways that fluency, accuracy, grammatical complexity, and lexical complexity have been measured in studies of language development in second language writing. More than 100 developmental measures are examined, with detailed comparisons of the results across the studies that have used each measure. The authors discuss the theoretical foundations for each type of developmental measure, and they consider the relationship between developmental measures and various types of proficiency measures. They also examine criteria for determining which developmental measures are the most successful and suggest which measures are the most promising for continuing work on language development.

208 pp., ISBN 0–8248–2069–X $20.

THE DEVELOPMENT OF A LEXICAL TONE PHONOLOGY IN AMERICAN ADULT LEARNERS OF STANDARD MANDARIN CHINESE

SYLVIA HENEL SUN, 1998

The study reported is based on an assessment of three decades of research on the SLA of Mandarin tone. It investigates whether differences in learners' tone perception and production are related to differences in the effects of certain linguistic, task, and learner factors. The learners of focus are American students of Mandarin in Beijing, China. Their performances on two perception and three production tasks are analyzed through a host of variables and methods of quantification.

328 pp., ISBN 0–8248–2068–1 $20.

NEW TRENDS AND ISSUES IN TEACHING JAPANESE LANGUAGE AND CULTURE

HARUKO M. COOK, KYOKO HIJIRIDA, & MILDRED TAHARA (EDITORS), 1997

In recent years, Japanese has become the fourth most commonly taught foreign language at the college level in the United States. As the number of students who study Japanese has increased, the teaching of Japanese as a foreign language has been established as an important academic field of study. This technical report includes nine contributions to the advancement of this field, encompassing the following five important issues:

- Literature and literature teaching
- Technology in the language classroom
- Orthography
- Testing
- Grammatical versus pragmatic approaches to language teaching

164 pp., ISBN 0–8248–2067–3 $20.

SIX MEASURES OF JSL PRAGMATICS

Sayoko Okada Yamashita, 1996

This book investigates differences among tests that can be used to measure the cross-cultural pragmatic ability of English-speaking learners of Japanese. Building on the work of Hudson, Detmer, and Brown (Technical Reports #2 and #7 in this series), the author modified six test types that she used to gather data from North American learners of Japanese. She found numerous problems with the multiple-choice discourse completion test but reported that the other five tests all proved highly reliable and reasonably valid. Practical issues involved in creating and using such language tests are discussed from a variety of perspectives.

213 pp., ISBN 0–8248–1914–4 $15.

LANGUAGE LEARNING STRATEGIES AROUND THE WORLD: CROSS-CULTURAL PERSPECTIVES

Rebecca L. Oxford (Editor), 1996, 1997, 2002

Language learning strategies are the specific steps students take to improve their progress in learning a second or foreign language. Optimizing learning strategies improves language performance. This groundbreaking book presents new information about cultural influences on the use of language learning strategies. It also shows innovative ways to assess students' strategy use and remarkable techniques for helping students improve their choice of strategies, with the goal of peak language learning.

166 pp., ISBN 0–8248–1910–1 $20.

TELECOLLABORATION IN FOREIGN LANGUAGE LEARNING: PROCEEDINGS OF THE HAWAI'I SYMPOSIUM

Mark Warschauer (Editor), 1996

The Symposium on Local & Global Electronic Networking in Foreign Language Learning & Research, part of the National Foreign Language Resource Center's 1995 Summer Institute on Technology & the Human Factor in Foreign Language Education, included presentations of papers and hands-on workshops conducted by Symposium participants to facilitate the sharing of resources, ideas, and information about all aspects of electronic networking for foreign language teaching and research, including electronic discussion and conferencing, international cultural exchanges, real-time communication and simulations, research and resource retrieval via the Internet, and research using networks. This collection presents a sampling of those presentations.

252 pp., ISBN 0–8248–1867–9 $20.

LANGUAGE LEARNING MOTIVATION: PATHWAYS TO THE NEW CENTURY

Rebecca L. Oxford (Editor), 1996

This volume chronicles a revolution in our thinking about what makes students want to learn languages and what causes them to persist in that difficult and rewarding adventure. Topics in this book include the internal structures of and external connections with foreign language motivation; exploring adult language learning motivation, self-efficacy, and anxiety; comparing the motivations and learning strategies of students of Japanese and Spanish; and enhancing the theory of language learning motivation from many psychological and social perspectives.

218 pp., ISBN 0–8248–1849–0 $20.

LINGUISTICS & LANGUAGE TEACHING: PROCEEDINGS OF THE SIXTH JOINT LSH-HATESL CONFERENCE

CYNTHIA REVES, CAROLINE STEELE, & CATHY S. P. WONG (EDITORS), 1996

Technical Report #10 contains 18 articles revolving around the following three topics:

- Linguistic issues—These six papers discuss various linguistic issues: ideophones, syllabic nasals, linguistic areas, computation, tonal melody classification, and wh-words.
- Sociolinguistics—Sociolinguistic phenomena in Swahili, signing, Hawaiian, and Japanese are discussed in four of the papers.
- Language teaching and learning—These eight papers cover prosodic modification, note taking, planning in oral production, oral testing, language policy, L2 essay organization, access to dative alternation rules, and child noun phrase structure development.

364 pp., ISBN 0–8248–1851–2 $20.

ATTENTION & AWARENESS IN FOREIGN LANGUAGE LEARNING

RICHARD SCHMIDT (EDITOR), 1996

Issues related to the role of attention and awareness in learning lie at the heart of many theoretical and practical controversies in the foreign language field. This collection of papers presents research into the learning of Spanish, Japanese, Finnish, Hawaiian, and English as a second language (with additional comments and examples from French, German, and miniature artificial languages) that bear on these crucial questions for foreign language pedagogy.

394 pp., ISBN 0–8248–1794–X $20.

VIRTUAL CONNECTIONS: ONLINE ACTIVITIES AND PROJECTS FOR NETWORKING LANGUAGE LEARNERS

MARK WARSCHAUER (EDITOR), 1995, 1996

Computer networking has created dramatic new possibilities for connecting language learners in a single classroom or across the globe. This collection of activities and projects makes use of email, the internet, computer conferencing, and other forms of computer-mediated communication for the foreign and second language classroom at any level of instruction. Teachers from around the world submitted the activities compiled in this volume—activities that they have used successfully in their own classrooms.

417 pp., ISBN 0–8248–1793–1 $30.

DEVELOPING PROTOTYPIC MEASURES OF CROSS-CULTURAL PRAGMATICS

THOM HUDSON, EMILY DETMER, & J. D. BROWN, 1995

Although the study of cross-cultural pragmatics has gained importance in applied linguistics, there are no standard forms of assessment that might make research comparable across studies and languages. The present volume describes the process through which six forms of cross-cultural assessment were developed for second language learners of English. The models may be used for second language learners of other languages. The six forms of assessment involve two forms each of indirect discourse completion tests, oral language production, and self-assessment. The procedures involve the assessment of requests, apologies, and refusals.

198 pp., ISBN 0–8248–1763–X $15.

THE ROLE OF PHONOLOGICAL CODING IN READING KANJI

SACHIKO MATSUNAGA, 1995

In this technical report, the author reports the results of a study that she conducted on phonological coding in reading kanji using an eye-movement monitor and draws some pedagogical implications. In addition, she reviews current literature on the different schools of thought regarding instruction in reading kanji and its role in the teaching of non-alphabetic written languages like Japanese.

64 pp., ISBN 0–8248–1734–6 $10.

PRAGMATICS OF CHINESE AS NATIVE AND TARGET LANGUAGE

GABRIELE KASPER (EDITOR), 1995

This technical report includes six contributions to the study of the pragmatics of Mandarin Chinese:

- A report of an interview study conducted with nonnative speakers of Chinese; and
- Five data-based studies on the performance of different speech acts by native speakers of Mandarin—requesting, refusing, complaining, giving bad news, disagreeing, and complimenting.

312 pp., ISBN 0–8248–1733–8 $15.

A BIBLIOGRAPHY OF PEDAGOGY AND RESEARCH IN INTERPRETATION AND TRANSLATION

ETILVIA ARJONA, 1993

This technical report includes four types of bibliographic information on translation and interpretation studies:

- Research efforts across disciplinary boundaries—cognitive psychology, neurolinguistics, psycholinguistics, sociolinguistics, computational linguistics, measurement, aptitude testing, language policy, decision-making, theses, dissertations;
- Training information covering program design, curriculum studies, instruction, school administration;
- Instruction information detailing course syllabi, methodology, models, available textbooks; and
- Testing information about aptitude, selection, diagnostic tests.

115 pp., ISBN 0–8248–1572–6 $10.

PRAGMATICS OF JAPANESE AS NATIVE AND TARGET LANGUAGE

GABRIELE KASPER (EDITOR), 1992, 1996

This technical report includes three contributions to the study of the pragmatics of Japanese:

- A bibliography on speech act performance, discourse management, and other pragmatic and sociolinguistic features of Japanese;
- A study on introspective methods in examining Japanese learners' performance of refusals; and
- A longitudinal investigation of the acquisition of the particle ne by nonnative speakers of Japanese.

125 pp., ISBN 0–8248–1462–2 $10.

A FRAMEWORK FOR TESTING CROSS-CULTURAL PRAGMATICS

THOM HUDSON, EMILY DETMER, & J. D. BROWN, 1992

This technical report presents a framework for developing methods that assess cross-cultural pragmatic ability. Although the framework has been designed for Japanese and American cross-cultural contrasts, it can serve as a generic approach that can be applied to other language contrasts. The focus is on the variables of social distance, relative power, and the degree of imposition within the speech acts of requests, refusals, and apologies. Evaluation of performance is based on recognition of the speech act, amount of speech, forms or formulæ used, directness, formality, and politeness.

51 pp., ISBN 0–8248–1463–0 $10.

RESEARCH METHODS IN INTERLANGUAGE PRAGMATICS

GABRIELE KASPER & MERETE DAHL, 1991

This technical report reviews the methods of data collection employed in 39 studies of interlanguage pragmatics, defined narrowly as the investigation of nonnative speakers' comprehension and production of speech acts, and the acquisition of L2-related speech act knowledge. Data collection instruments are distinguished according to the degree to which they constrain informants' responses, and whether they tap speech act perception/comprehension or production. A main focus of discussion is the validity of different types of data, in particular their adequacy to approximate authentic performance of linguistic action.

51 pp., ISBN 0–8248–1419–3 $10.

Printed in the United States
149331LV00002B/2/P

9 780980 045925